The Human Semantic Potential

Neural Network Modeling and Connectionism
Jeffrey L. Elman, editor

The Human Semantic Potential

Spatial Language and Constrained Connectionism

Terry Regier

A Bradford Book
The MIT Press
Cambridge, Massachusetts
London, England

This book was set in Palatino by Publication Services
Printed on recycled paper and bound in the United States of America

Library of Congress Cataloging-in-Publication Data

Regier, Terry
  The human semantic potential : spatial language and constrained
  connectionism / Terry Regier.
      p.   cm. — (Neural network modeling and connectionism)
  "Bradford book."
  Includes bibliographical references and index.
  ISBN 0-262-18173-8
  1. Space and time in language. 2. Semantics—Psychological
aspects. 3. Connectionism. 4. Cognitive grammar. 5. Linguistic
models. I. Title. II. Series.
P37.5.S67R44   1996
401'.43—dc20   95-26555
                                                                                        CIP

To my parents, Frank and Mary Regier

Contents

Series Foreword

The goal of this series, Neural Network Modeling and Connectionism, is to identify and bring to the public the best work in the exciting field of neural network and connectionist modeling. The series includes monographs based on dissertations, extended reports of work by leaders in the field, edited volumes and collections on topics of special interest, major reference works, and undergraduate and graduate-level texts. The field is highly interdisciplinary, and works published in the series will touch on a wide variety of topics ranging from low-level vision to the philosophical foundations of theories of representation.

Jeffrey L. Elman, editor

Associate editors:

James Anderson, Brown University
Andrew Barto, University of Massachusetts, Amherst
Gary Dell, University of Illinois
Jerome Feldman, University of California, Berkeley
Stephen Grossberg, Boston University
Stephen Hanson, Princeton University
Geoffrey Hinton, University of Toronto
Michael Jordan, Massachusetts Institute of Technology
James McClelland, Carnegie-Mellon University
Domenico Parisi, Instituto di Psicologia del CNR
David Rumelhart, Stanford University
Terrence Sejnowski, The Salk Institute
Paul Smolensky, University of Colorado
Stephen P. Stich, Rutgers University
David Touretzky, Carnegie-Mellon University
David Zipser, University of California, San Diego

Foreword

This book fundamentally reorients the study of natural language semantics and of human conceptual systems. Philosophically, it is a major step in the rethinking of the nature of concepts. Psychologically, it is a major advance in understanding how learning can take place without negative examples. And linguistically, it provides the first glimmerings of an explanation for the shape of a central part of human semantic systems—the semantics of spatial relations. More importantly, it moves linguistics out of its straitjacket of studying language independently of perception and learning mechanisms. What Regier has demonstrated is that the human semantic potential—the ability to learn and reason with human conceptual systems—has everything to do with the nature of perception and learning as well as with the kinds of detailed structures our brains have at birth.

The task undertaken by Regier is easy enough to describe. Give a connectionist network the following input: (1) Project on a screen a set of "movies" consisting of a sequence of pictures of a geometrical figure either stationary or moving relative to others. (2) Pair each movie with a spatial relation term in some natural language that correctly characterizes the spatial relation depicted on the input screen. Given such pairs of movies and terms, have the network learn, with no negative examples, what the spatial relations concepts of the language are and how they are named. Test the result by having the network name new examples of spatial relations depicted in new movies.

The significance of this task is that it requires that the network acquire a way to perceive and categorize visual scenes in terms of human spatial relations. Moreover, it must be able to learn spatial relations for any arbitrarily chosen natural language. The network thus provides us with a model of the universal human potential for spatial categorization.

The model combines a traditional connectionist learning architecture with built-in constraints of the sort that Jerome Feldman has pioneered in the study of "structured connectionism." The resulting model is of a form that Regier refers to as "constrained connectionism."

The first thing that is interesting about Regier's model is the set of constraints that were used. To arrive at such constraints, Regier used the results of cognitive semantics, primarily the work of Len Talmy, Claudia Brugman, and Ron Langacker, plus the results of Steven Levinson's Cognitive Anthropology Research Group at the Max-Planck Institute for Psycholinguistics at Nijmegen. These scholars and their coworkers have made great progress in describing the systems of spatial relations concepts in the world's languages. In part, their results show that certain semantic primitives form the foundation of the vast variety of spatial relations systems. Regier was determined to make use of those primitives.

But how? Regier's approach was to build constrained networks that either could compute, or could learn to compute, those primitives and then link those constrained subnetworks within a parallel distributed processing (PDP) architecture that could learn how the primitives are combined in different spatial relations systems.

To motivate the computation of these spatial relations primitives, Regier turned to results in cognitive neuroscience and visual psychophysics. He incorporated topographic maps of the visual field, orientation-sensitive cells, and cells with center-surround receptive fields. He also incorporated a structure motivated by the phenomenon of apparent motion, and one that employs a visual routine of filling-in, shown to exist in the human visual system. By including these independently motivated mechanisms, Regier was able to devise a computational system that could compute primitive spatial relations, combine them to form complex spatial relations concepts and systems of concepts, and associate language with those concepts.

What results is a model that learns a significant range of spatial relations terms. In addition, the model takes important steps toward explaining why the spatial relations systems in the world's languages look the way they do. The explanation is not language-internal. Instead, it is based on the nature of the human visual system and the mechanisms of visual perception. In short, the human semantic potential arises, in the case of spatial relations concepts, from the details of the mechanisms of visual perception.

In addition, Regier has taken a step toward cracking a major problem of human language learning: how is it possible to learn without negative examples? In general, when children learn language, they hear mostly correct examples, and they are not corrected all that often for making mistakes. Regier's solution to the problem of learning without negative examples builds on a suggestion made in the child language literature, namely, that the child may initially assume that words are mutually exclusive. For example, if a given spatial configuration is referred to as *above*, the child may take that configuration as a negative example of other spatial terms, such as *below, in,* and *outside*. This simple heuristic breaks down in the case of overlapping concepts: for instance, the inference that a positive example of *above* is a negative example of *outside* is not a valid one. However, in Regier's version of this learning heuristic, implicit negative instances are given less weight than are explicit positive instances. This approach supports successful learning even in the case of overlapping concepts.

What makes Regier's work important is not just that it succeeded, but how it succeeded. It succeeded because Regier made use of the relevant cognitive science: the relevant linguistics, visual science, and neurophysiology. It succeeded because Regier was able to combine what was important about two strands of connectionist research—PDP learning models and Feldman's structured connectionism—to yield a constrained connectionism, a form of connectionism that admits adaptation, but only within clearly specifiable and motivated limits. And it succeeded because he was able to crack a crucial part of the problem of learning without negative examples.

At this point, a caveat is warranted. Any computer model is bound to contain a number of elements that are not theory-relevant, but that are there just to get the model to work given the pragmatic constraints of limited time and resources. This model, like any other, has such elements. What I find wonderful about this book is that Regier clearly states what parts of the model are to be taken seriously and why. I appreciate this. It is an ethic that I wish were followed scrupulously throughout the field of computational modeling.

But before you jump in, it is worth considering the philosophical importance of this work. There was a time when natural language semantics was taken to be the study of the relationship between symbols and things in the world. In the fields of philosophical logic and formal semantics, it still is. In those fields, the human perceptual system and its underlying neurophysiology do not count at all. They are not even part of the picture.

Since the mid-1970s it has been clear that color concepts cannot be characterized in this way. Color does not exist objectively in the world; it is a product of how our eyes and our brains work, when presented with objects with various reflectance properties under various lighting conditions. Color semantics is outside the range of logical semantics.

Regier's research suggests that spatial relations behave very much like color. They are a product not only of how things are located with respect to one another in the world, but also—and most importantly—of our neural makeup and our system of visual perception. Logic alone cannot characterize the semantics of spatial relations. The human semantic potential for spatial relations concepts is fully characterizable only in cognitive and neural terms.

This matters a great deal, for spatial relations concepts—English concepts like *in, out, from, to, on, off, front, back, above, below*—are not merely used in reasoning about space. Because we have systems of conceptual metaphor, these concepts and their associated inference patterns are reflected in abstract domains. Spatial reasoning, as projected via metaphor, is a large part of abstract reason.

If spatial relations are embodied rather than disembodied, then reason as a whole is also fundamentally embodied. Regier's work is a crucial step in showing that rationality itself arises from our bodily nature. It cannot be attributed to an abstract soul or to some transcendent structure of the universe. Reason as we know it arises from the body. It is important to bear this in mind as you read about topographic maps and orientation-sensitive cells and the visual routine of filling-in. This book is not just about a computer model for learning spatial relations terms. It is ultimately about who we are and what it means to be capable of reason.

George Lakoff

Acknowledgments

The work described here was done while I was a graduate student in computer science at the University of California at Berkeley, where Jerry Feldman was my advisor and George Lakoff was in many ways a coadvisor. It was Jerry's work in structured connectionism that got me to think in terms of building concrete hypotheses into connectionist networks. And it was George's work on the use of spatial metaphor in conceptual systems that motivated me to look into the linguistic structuring of space. Through a combination of genuine involvement in the subject matter, judicious advice, and an insistence on keeping the big picture in mind, both Jerry and George have been instrumental in the development of the ideas presented here.

Many others at Berkeley have contributed to this work, through helpful and enjoyable conversations. I would like to thank in particular David Bailey, Donald Glaser, Dan Jurafsky, Srini Narayanan, Valeriy Nenov, Stephen Palmer, Andreas Stolcke, Nigel Ward, Susan Weber, Robert Wilensky, and Jordan Zlatev. And in Chicago, thanks to Larry Barsalou, Gerd Gigerenzer, Muhammad Ali Khalidi, Frances Kuo, and Artie Shapiro for some very helpful feedback.

Thanks also to Jeff Elman, for suggesting I turn my thesis into a book; to the reviewers, whose comments were a great help; and to the folks at MIT Press who have helped make this a reality.

Many, many thanks to Chris Regier, Shillet Hasaballah, Salim Yaqub, Clay Scott, Ljuba Veselinova, Deemah Shehadeh, and the members of Nervous for Nigel, all of whom have helped grace my days while I was absorbed in this project.

And of course, my most heartfelt gratitude and love go to Mom and Dad Regier. If it weren't for them, you wouldn't be reading this.

Chapter 1

Introduction

He felt that life was large, and wide.
—G. Kanafani

$\Delta_p w_{ji} = \eta \delta_{pj} o_{pi}$
—D. Rumelhart, G. Hinton, and R. Williams

1.1 Matter and Method

This book describes a search for semantic universals, and a modeling technique that grew out of it.

On the one hand, the book is an attempt to characterize what I shall be calling the *human semantic potential*. By this, I mean that capacity for meaning shared by all human beings and molded through language learning into the semantic system of an individual speaker's language. As we shall see, languages vary substantially in their semantic structure, and this raises the issue of what limits there are, if any, to this variation. The book addresses this question from the standpoint of the *learnability* of particular linguistically expressed concepts. The idea is to show that some concepts are not learnable as the semantics for single linguistic forms; they are too complex to be expressed by a single word or morpheme. This then places constraints on the semantic scope of such forms in human language generally, and those constraints provide a characterization of the human semantic potential. This book focuses in particular on the semantics of spatial relations and events, and attempts to characterize the human semantic potential for that domain.

On the other hand, this is also a book about the use of connectionist models in cognitive theorizing. Although these models are widespread by now in the field of cognitive science, dominating much of the modeling discourse, qualms are still expressed on a fairly regular basis regarding their status as cognitive models. One point in particular that has been brought up in this regard is that connectionist models, especially trained multilayer perceptrons, are too unconstrained to have the explanatory power one should require of a model (Massaro 1988). In response, I shall be advocating a network design philosophy that I call *constrained connectionism*. This is a particular type of structured connectionism (Feldman, Fanty, and Goddard 1988) in which complex domain-specific structures are built into the network, constraining its operation in clearly understandable and analyzable ways. The hope is that this methodology will address some of the misgivings that have been expressed and will help to clarify the role that connectionist models can play in cognitive theories.

What do these two things, semantic potential and constrained connectionism, have to do with each other? Why are they treated together? There is a story in that.

Languages differ in interesting ways in their categorization of space. The Australian language Guugu Yimithirr, for example, does not use the relative orientations we are used to in English, such as *front, back, left,* and *right,* but rather uses absolute orientations such as *north, south, east,* and *west.* So rather than say, "Place the fork to the left of the plate," a speaker of Guugu Yimithirr would say, "Place the fork to the north of the plate," or south or east or west, depending on the table's overall orientation (Levinson 1992a). This is the standard means for expressing these spatial relations in Guugu Yimithirr, and as Levinson points out, this has profound cognitive consequences. Speakers of this language must actually *conceive* of space in a manner distinct from that of English speakers: they must be constantly aware of the four cardinal directions, whereas English speakers often are not.

Is crosslinguistic variation of this sort constrained in any way, or can languages vary without limit in their structurings of space? It is at least conceivable that there are no constraints whatsoever and that each language categorizes space, and indeed the rest of the world, in its own idiosyncratic manner, without bound, free from any limitations. Under this view, there are no semantic universals, since each language is free to carve up the world presented to it in any manner it chooses.

However, there is good reason to believe that this is not the case. All linguistic spatial systems are based on human experience of space, which is necessarily constrained by the nature of the human perceptual system. It is therefore extremely likely that constraints on semantic variation are imposed from that source. As we shall see, models of this sort of perceptual hemming-in of semantic diversity have already been developed in the domain of basic color terms (Kay and McDaniel 1978). It is quite reasonable to expect this sort of constraint to operate in other perceptually grounded semantic domains as well.

This book presents a connectionist model that contributes to the search for semantic universals in the spatial domain. It is a model of the acquisition of semantics for spatial terms and thus furnishes us with a computational context within which to investigate the learnability of particular semantic contents. Its design incorporates a number of structural devices motivated by neurobiological and psychophysical evidence concerning the human visual system; these provide a universal perceptual core that constrains the process of semantic acquisition. It is in this sense that the model is a constrained connectionist model. Using these structures, the system learns the perceptually grounded semantics for spatial terms from a range of languages, providing us with at least a preliminary model of the human capacity for categorizing spatial events and relations. It is a characterization of that capacity, after all, that is the primary scientific goal of the work reported here. And it is the technique of constrained connectionism that will be our vehicle. This is the link between the two themes of this book; this is why they are treated together.

These two foci of the book, semantic potential and constrained connectionism, suggest two general approaches one might take to the work described here. Under one approach, the learning task is viewed primarily *scientifically*, as an explanatory model of a cognitive faculty that we are attempting to understand, namely, the general human potential for spatial semantics. Here, what counts as a result is an explanation of some sort of the capacity under study. Science, after all, is about the construction of models for the purpose of explaining the world, models that can generate predictions about the processes they claim to explain. One can then subject models to attempts at empirical falsification. If such a model is constructed along purely conventional lines, using conventional methodology, that is immaterial to the scientist; the central criterion for evaluation is simply that the model must shed some sort of explanatory light.

The other approach views the work not so much as a scientific model of interest in its own right, but rather *methodologically*, as one of many possible models whose design follows a particular modeling technique—in this case, the technique of constrained connectionism. Here, the primary interest is not the process or capacity being explained by the model, but rather the model's general character. In this case, if the model were built along purely conventional lines, the work would lose its interest, regardless of its explanatory power. Thus, the work would be evaluated primarily in terms of any methodological contributions it may make to the field of connectionist modeling. Under this view, valid contributions might be such things as novel design strategies, the use of architectural structures that can be seen to be of general value, and the like. In sum, the emphasis here would be on whatever widely applicable tools the work presented adds to the connectionist toolbox.

In this book I adopt both of these viewpoints, as twin frameworks within which to situate the work presented. The two are by no means independent of one another, however: as we shall see, each drives the other. The modeling effort undertaken here—that is, the scientific task of characterizing the human semantic potential—has necessitated the adoption of the methodology of constrained connectionism. Similarly, the explanation and predictions that follow from the model, concerning the acquisition of semantics—that is, the scientific results of the effort as a whole—are critically dependent on the particular modeling methodology used.

The interplay between these two frameworks will appear throughout this book. In fact, it is a central function of the book as a whole to highlight both the utility of constrained modeling methodologies for the purposes of semantic inquiry and the fact that such a semantic modeling effort may result in methods and techniques that will find applicability outside the particular domain for which they were originally conceived.

1.2   Space and Semantic Potential

The linguistic categorization of space is a topic that has captured the attention of linguists and other cognitive scientists for a number of years. There are good reasons for this, which I shall review in detail in chapter 2. For the time being, a somewhat briefer overview of these reasons will serve to motivate the modeling work that is the central focus of this book, and to explicitly situate it in the intellectual context that gave rise to it.

The semantics of spatial location, a seemingly obscure corner of linguistic inquiry, has in fact commanded considerable fascination largely because space has a privileged position as a foundational ontological category in language, a position that most other domains do not share. Spatial location is often expressed by *closed-class* forms, which have "the fundamental role of acting as an organizing structure for further conceptual material" (Talmy 1983, 4). Closed-class sets of linguistic elements contain relatively few items and only rarely admit new members. Thus, prepositions and verbal prefixes are examples of closed-class sets. In contrast, open-class sets such as nouns or verbs contain comparatively many items and constantly add new members. The point here is that the closed-class expression of spatial location is evidence of the conceptual primacy of space, its special status as a basic element of the human conceptual makeup. This point is strengthened by the fact that the human conception of space appears to structure other parts of the conceptual system through spatial metaphor; its influence is therefore not localized to an isolated sphere of experience (Lakoff 1987). In addition, although physical space is objectively measurable, human conceptualizations of space as manifested in language afford a good deal of subtlety in their semantic structure. In this last respect, space resembles the domain of color, another objectively measurable yet conceptually rich semantic domain (Berlin and Kay 1969).

Space is also attractive as a domain of semantic inquiry because spatial systems exhibit considerable crosslinguistic variation. We have seen one example of this already, in the absolute coordinates of Guugu Yimithirr, and we shall see more in chapter 2. In general, crosslinguistic variation of this sort leads us to ask what limits there are to the variation. For despite the wide variability, it is extremely likely that commonalities exist across languages simply because all linguistic spatial systems are based on human experience of space, which is in turn constrained by the nature of the human perceptual system and the nature of the world around us. The point of interest here is that the varying spatial systems all derive from the same neural mechanisms and the same experiences with objects, gravity, and the like.

The domain of space thus suggests itself as an arena for explorations of issues of linguistic universality and variation with a force that few other domains can match: we know both that crosslinguistic variation exists and that the essential sameness of human spatial experience across cultures motivates the search for semantic universals here. At the same time, since space is a fundamental ontological category and since it metaphorically structures many other domains in language, we are assured that inquiries concerning universality and variation in this domain will focus on elements that deeply affect the language as a whole, rather than just space itself. It is for these reasons that a characterization of the human semantic potential in this domain would be significant.

1.3   Negative Evidence and Language Learning

As we saw earlier, the scientific goal of this book is to understand the human semantic potential through investigating the learnability of various semantic contents. It is because learnability is at the heart of the discussion that the model described here is a model of the *acquisition* of spatial semantics. The modeling effort of course derives some of its motivation from those aspects of spatial semantics we have just covered: their fundamental ontological status, and the issues of universality and variation that arise in this domain. In addition, however, any account of the acquisition of spatial semantics will have to confront a very general issue in language acquisition, the problem of learning in the absence of explicit negative evidence. Thus, another source of motivation for the present modeling endeavor is that it necessarily involves an issue known to be generally relevant in language learning.

Researchers in child language acquisition have often observed that the child learns language apparently without the benefit of explicit negative evidence (Braine 1971; Bowerman 1983; Pinker 1989). This introduces the following problem: if children are never told that particular utterances are ungrammatical, how do they learn not to utter them, while still learning to produce grammatical sentences that they have also never heard? How do they know which of these sentences that they have never heard conform to the constraints of the language they are learning, and which do not? In other words, how do children know not to undergeneralize or overgeneralize from the utterances they hear, if nothing has been explicitly ruled out?

Although the above-mentioned researchers have focused on the so-called no-negative-evidence problem as it relates to the acquisition of grammar, the problem is a general one that appears in several aspects of language acquisition, including the acquisition of lexical semantics, with which we are concerned here. It is probably safe to assume that children are rarely, if ever, told that a particular configuration is not a good example of some spatial term, and yet they eventually learn to use these terms in novel situations without overgeneralizing or undergeneralizing. How is it that this learning takes place? Any cognitive model of the acquisition of lexical semantics will have to come to grips with this issue, in addition to the issues of crosslinguistic variability touched on above. As we shall see, the model presented here incorporates a means of learning from positive evidence only, thus addressing the no-negative-evidence problem. The idea is a simple one, building on an idea from the child language literature (Markman 1987): in the absence of explicit negative evidence, take each positive instance for one concept as an implicit negative instance for all other concepts. Although this approach has its problems, particularly in cases in which concepts overlap, these problems are demonstrably surmountable.

1.4   The Modeling Challenge

We have seen that languages differ in their spatial structuring, that space occupies a position of distinct privilege in human conceptual systems generally, and that the problem of learning spatial semantics has embedded in it the more general problem of learning without negative evidence. This leads us directly to the three central questions that will serve as the primary motivation for the computational work presented here. First, what sort of system could adapt itself to the different structurings of space manifested in the world's languages? That is, what kind of capacity is it that allows humans to learn to immediately apprehend and articulate the space around them in terms as profoundly different as those we find in Guugu Yimithirr and English? Second, how could such a system learn without the benefit of explicit negative evidence? If children are never told that one object inside another is not "above" it, how do they come to rule out that possibility? How do children avoid over- and undergeneralization in their acquisition of spatial semantics? Third, what could a model of this system tell us about possible semantic universals and about the human semantic potential? Are there constraints on the scope of human spatial semantics, and if so, can we determine what they are? Or is this human faculty essentially limitless in classificatory power, allowing any sort of spatial relation or event whatsoever to acquire its own name? To caricature this last question for the sake of clarity, is it possible for a human language to have a single spatial term meaning something as unlikely as "wiggling away toward the north-northeast"? If so, why? If not, why not? The connectionist model presented in this book provides preliminary and, I hope, at least partially satisfactory answers to these questions, by giving an account of spatial semantic acquisition that is grounded in perception and that derives its constraints from that source.

What exactly does this model do? Imagine a set of movies of simple two-dimensional objects moving relative to one another, such that each movie has

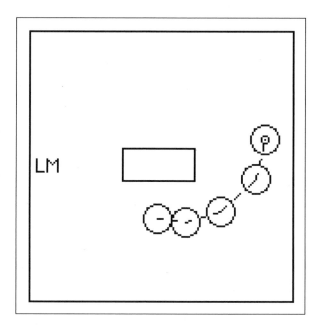

Figure 1.1
A movie: Russian *iz-pod*

been correctly labeled as a positive instance of some closed-class spatial term from a particular language. The movies may be of arbitrary length. For example, figure 1.1 presents such a movie, a positive example of the Russian preposition *iz-pod*, which has no single-word English counterpart but translates to "out from underneath." The connectionist model presented here takes a set of such movies, each labeled as a positive example of some spatial term from some language, and learns the association between words and the events or relations they describe. Once the model has successfully accomplished this task, it should be able to determine which of the spatial terms learned would be appropriate for describing previously unseen movies. The model's task as a whole, then, is learning how to perceive simple spatial relations, both static and dynamic, so as to name them as a speaker of a particular language would.

The movie shown in figure 1.1 was one of many used in training the model described here. Each movie contains a static object here referred to as the *land-mark*, or *LM* (Langacker 1987); this is the reference object with respect to which other objects are located. In this movie it is the horizontally extended rectangle in the middle of the scene. Each movie also contains another object, referred to as the *trajector*, or *TR*; this is the object located relative to the landmark. In this movie the trajector is a circle moving from the region beneath the land-

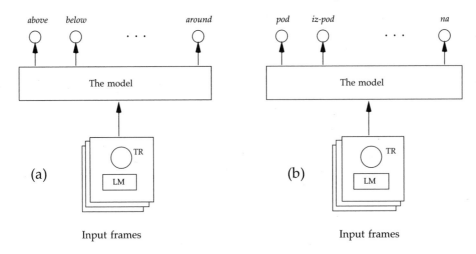

Figure 1.2
Model configurations for English and Russian

mark, to the right and upward. The dashed lines connect successive positions of the trajector as it moves. This particular movie is five frames long, and here the frames are shown superimposed one on top of another. The final frame of the movie is indicated by a small circle located inside the trajector.

Figure 1.2 presents the model, configured to learn a set of English spatial terms in (a) and a set of Russian spatial terms in (b). The input to the model is a movie of the sort shown in figure 1.1, and the model is trained using error back-propagation (Rumelhart, Hinton, and Williams 1986). The result is that when a movie portraying some event is shown, only those output nodes corresponding to closed-class forms that accurately describe the event will be activated. For example, if the movie in figure 1.1 were supplied to the model shown in figure 1.2(b) after training, the *iz-pod* output node would become activated, indicating that the model has classified the movie as a positive example of *iz-pod*.

Clearly, if this system is to be taken as a model of the human capacity for closed-class categorization of spatial relations and events, it must be able to perform this learning task for closed-class spatial terms from any language. Furthermore, it should be able to learn without the benefit of explicit negative instances, since children appear to acquire language under those conditions. As we shall see, the model presented in this book has learned systems of spatial terms from a range of languages with disparate categorizations of space, and it is able to learn using positive evidence only. The primary scientific interest of the model, then, is that it provides tentative answers to the three questions posed at the beginning of this section: (1) it indicates what sort of system could adapt itself to the various structurings of space found in the world's languages,

(2) it is able to learn using only positive evidence, and (3) as we shall see, at the same time it gives rise to predictions concerning semantic universals in the domain of spatial events and relations. In this way, it begins to characterize the human semantic potential.

Having presented what the model is, and what it is about, I am bound by considerations of completeness and clarity to indicate what it is not. Most significantly, it is not a model of concept learning in any nonlinguistic sense, in any sense based exclusively on perceptual and functional nonlinguistic influences. Rather, it is a model of the human semantic potential *for individual linguistic closed-class spatial terms*. So, for example, if the model predicts that a particular concept is unlearnable, this prediction should not be taken to mean that the concept is not conceivable by the human mind; after all, any discussion of the concept will be based on a prior grasp of it. Rather, it should be taken to mean that the concept is not expressible using a single closed-class form, that its expression would necessitate the use of several forms composed according to the syntactic rules of the language under study. For example, as we shall see, the model predicts that no single closed-class lexeme in any language will denote motion of the trajector first through the landmark and then back over it. This does not mean that this motion is inconceivable, or even inexpressible linguistically. I have just expressed it, but in order to do this I had to use the two spatial terms *through* and *over*, composed according to the syntactic rules of English.

1.5 Constrained Connectionism

As we have seen, this is a book with two overarching themes: the search for the human semantic potential, and the place of constrained connectionism as a modeling methodology in cognitive theorizing. Up to this point we have spent most of our time on issues of semantics and a clearer specification of the modeling task itself. Let us now consider methodology.

Connectionist models are by now widespread within cognitive science. These models are made up of networks of simple interconnected processing units, with weights on the interunit connections. The paradigm is based loosely on an analogy with the networks of neurons that constitute the brain, each processing unit being the analogue of a neuron and the connections being the analogues of dendrites and axons. The appeal of building biologically motivated computational models of cognitive processes has been irresistible for many, and there has consequently been a noticeable whiff of reductionism in the air for several years now. This is not to downplay the purely psychological attraction of such models, however. The connectionist framework offers a wide range of desirable features even if one views them strictly as psychological, nonneural, and hence nonreductionist models. One such feature of these models that has seemed particularly valuable is their ability to provide a unified account of a number of psychological phenomena, encompassing both the apparently rule-governed aspects of these phenomena and what appear to be exceptions to those rules. The work of Rumelhart and McClelland (1986) on learning the past tense of English verbs and the work of Seidenberg and McClelland (1989) on visual word recognition are two salient examples of research that has underlined this unificatory strength of connectionist modeling.

At the same time there have been persistent rumblings of discontent (Massaro 1988; Fodor and Pylyshyn 1988; McCloskey 1991), and these definitely bear looking into. Just what is it about this paradigm that leaves some people cold? Are the misgivings that have been expressed valid, but easily addressed and therefore of no deep consequence? Are they simply the result of misunderstanding? Or are there profound, inherent weaknesses in the approach, which we have been overlooking?

We shall look in particular at the assertion that connectionist models as currently constituted are too general, too unconstrained, and too unanalyzable a computational mechanism to hold the explanatory power one should demand of a scientific model. This accusation is generally leveled at models of the parallel distributed processing (PDP) variety, in which flexible, graded, distributed representations are developed as a result of exposure to training data. I shall argue that although this point has some validity, it fails to undermine the connectionist enterprise as fully as it threatens to. Even though the computational power of connectionism per se can translate into an overgenerality that is damaging to the search for scientific explanation, one need not make use of connectionist models in their most unrestricted form. In particular, I shall argue that adopting the modeling methodology of constrained connectionism yields connectionist models that are by their very nature restricted in systematic ways, and whose operation is easily analyzable. It is therefore a far more straightforward task to articulate the explanations they offer, and the predictions they make.

To illustrate these points, let us consider the work of Massaro (1988) and Cybenko (1989). One of Massaro's primary objections to connectionist modeling in cognitive science is that these models—in particular, those based on multilayer perceptrons—are too powerful to be scientifically meaningful. His point is that they are capable of adapting themselves to predict not only those results that are empirically observed but also others that are not observed, and in that sense they say nothing about the learning process that actually gave rise to the observed data in the real world. Since their computational power appears to be more or less unconstrained, it undermines their explanatory power. After all, if they can give rise to both human and nonhuman behavior, they make poor models of human learning. The work of Cybenko (1989) sharpens this argument by proving that a feedforward connectionist network with a sufficient number of hidden units in one hidden layer can produce an approximation of any continuous function whose arguments range from 0 to 1 (and since we can always scale our data down to the 0 to 1 range, this last condition is not particularly restrictive). This is a demonstration of the essential unconstrainedness of these mechanisms, which indicates that Massaro's misgivings were appropriate. For in what sense is it enlightening if we hear that an unconstrained network, which could presumably approximate both human and nonhuman data, has accurately modeled human data? I would agree with Massaro that it is not particularly enlightening, in and of itself. The network in its most general form could accommodate any data set presented to it, provided that data set was generated by a continuous function with arguments in the right range, so its success with human data is irrelevant in the attempt to characterize the human learning process. Or at least this is so unless we assume that the human process is also largely unconstrained. And in some contexts, such as the search for the human semantic potential, such an unconstrainedness assumption is probably not warranted, given that our experience of space is filtered through a particular sort of perceptual apparatus, which is the same for all humans.

Having said that, it is important to point out that this is not the same as saying that no explanations or predictions can be made on the basis of feed-forward connectionist networks with hidden layers, in other words, that they are scientifically empty. They are not, as we shall see in chapter 3. However, if one is searching for a cognitive model with easily articulable constraints on its operation, constraints more restrictive than the rather loose ones Cybenko mentions, one would be well advised to look elsewhere.

Where should one look? An attractive possibility is to incorporate motivated structure into the architecture, constraining the operation of the network in systematic ways. The design philosophy of *structured connectionism* (Feldman, Fanty, and Goddard 1988) advocates the construction of highly structured models, and the current suggestion can be viewed as an application of that philosophy to the domain of PDP. If such a significantly constrained model were to match human data, that fact would be of more interest than the success of a general-purpose mechanism precisely because it would allow us to say that the human process under study is consistent with the constraints built into the model. In other words, we would be able to begin articulating a characterization of the process under investigation, in terms of these constraints.

To make this idea of building in motivated structure more concrete, let us consider a specific example. In particular, let us consider the example most relevant for our purposes: a connectionist model of the human semantic potential in the domain of spatial events and relations. Figure 1.3 presents the constrained connectionist network that we shall be viewing as a provisional model of this human potential. The key to its design is the incorporation of a number of structural devices that are motivated by neurobiological and psychophysical evidence concerning the human visual system. These structures are shown in bold outline in the figure. Their inclusion here serves to constrain the learning potential of the network. This means that not every possible distinction is learnable by this network—as we shall see, there are some distinctions it cannot make. It may be correct or incorrect to attribute these inabilities to the human semantic potential,

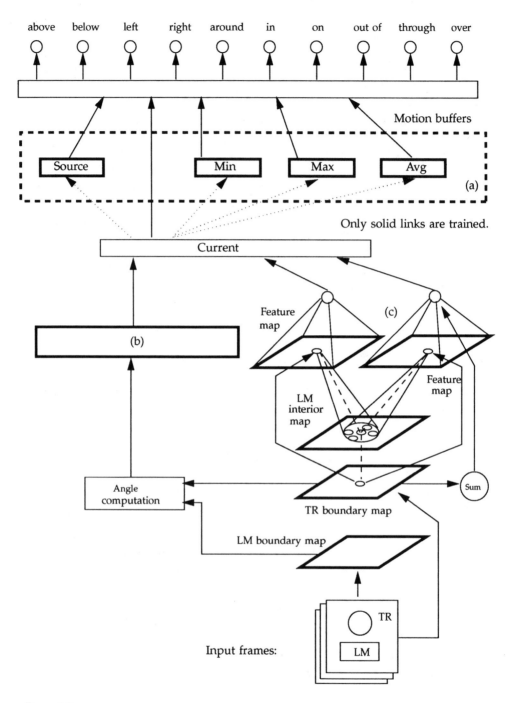

above   below   left   right   around   in   on   out of   through   over

Motion buffers

Source   Min   Max   Avg

(a)

Only solid links are trained.

Current

Feature map

(c)

(b)

LM interior map

Feature map

Angle computation

LM boundary map

TR boundary map

Sum

Input frames:

TR

LM

Figure 1.3
A constrained connectionist architecture

but at the very least it is concrete and falsifiable. Thus, the question is no longer, What can such a network tell us about the process under study?, but rather, as it should be, Is it telling us the right things?

1.6   A Brief Exchange

"Now hold on just a second," the exasperated reader interjects, "I think I can see where you're going with this, and I don't like it. The whole game seems circular to me. You say that your primary interest is in determining whether the human semantic potential is constrained in any fashion. Fine. So you build a model of that potential. Also fine. But then you turn around and build constraints right into the model! So of course you're going to conclude that the human semantic potential is constrained. How could it not be, if that's what the model looks like? You aren't giving the unconstrained option a fair chance."

"Well, yes and no," I respond after regaining my composure. "You're right of course that the so-called unconstrained option isn't getting a fair chance here. But look at it this way: if it turns out that the human semantic potential really is unlimited in scope, that means there will be data out there that will falsify the model. In general, when building a model, you've got to make a concrete hypothesis regarding the nature of the faculty you're trying to characterize. And I decided to build in the structures you see here, based on two considerations. First, the fact that constrained networks are easier to analyze, so at least I'll have a clear idea of what sort of model I'm dealing with. And second, the fact that the structures really are independently motivated: they reflect general architectural principles that are manifested in the structure of the visual system. And since we apprehend space through the visual system, it's reasonable to assume that the structure of the visual system is relevant to our inquiries here. So the structure built in isn't as arbitrary as it might seem at first blush."

1.7   An Overview of the Book

The purpose of this introduction has been to present the general issues that this book will address and to provide the reader with a feel for the spirit of the inquiry. In this section I shall very briefly cover the issues to be discussed in the remainder of the book.

Chapter 2 discusses in further detail the human semantic potential for spatial events and relations and reviews some of the relevant linguistics literature. The primacy of space as a semantic domain is argued for, and examples are given of crosslinguistic variation in the domain of spatial semantics. These and a number of other points are raised in order to motivate the search for the human semantic potential in the spatial domain. This chapter is critical for a proper understanding of the linguistic issues addressed in this book. Chapter 3 supplies an overview of the field of connectionism and its application to cognitive modeling.

The chapter presents the philosophies behind PDP and structured connectionism; it then describes constrained connectionism, an application of the ideas of structured connectionism to PDP networks. It concludes by comparing the merits of various structures for sequence processing—a relevant issue since the movies that the model views are sequences of frames. Chapter 4 presents the general problem of learning without explicit negative evidence, and its specific instantiation in the learning of spatial semantics. A solution based upon the mutual exclusivity learning heuristic is adopted, a solution that relies on the use of implicit negative examples and the deliberate attenuation of evidence from these implicit negatives. Computer simulations demonstrate the feasibility of the concept proposed. Chapter 5 begins with a general discussion of the centrality of structural devices to the constrained connectionist enterprise; it then describes and motivates the three sorts of structures that form the heart of the model. These implement the general principles of orientation combination, map comparison, and source-path-destination trajectory structuring. Chapter 6 describes the overall architecture of the model in which the structural devices are embedded. One critical theme that is addressed here is the manner in which these structures constrain the model's behavior. Results are presented from experiments in learning spatial terms from Mixtec, German, Japanese, Russian, and English, and the model's ability to display prototype effects is discussed. Finally, the chapter presents a number of predictions to which the model gives rise. This chapter is crucial for a real understanding of the operation and ramifications of the model. Chapter 7 describes a number of extensions to the model. Some of these have already been realized; others are merely proposed. Some of the more interesting linguistic issues are in fact addressed by the extensions rather than the core model; these include polysemy, deixis, and the relationship between semantic acquisition and prelinguistic conceptual development. Finally, chapter 8 considers the work as a whole and evaluates the model both with respect to its ability to shed light on the nature of the human semantic potential and with respect to what it tells us more generally about the possible relationship between connectionist modeling and cognitive theorizing. Several possible modes of model failure are examined, along with their consequences, and the results of the book as a whole are examined within that framework. The work is compared with a number of similar efforts, both in semantic inquiry and in connectionist approaches to psychological theory. There is also an appendix, containing some of the technical details of the model's architecture.

I suggest that the reader follow the simplest route imaginable through the book: begin at the beginning, and go on until you reach the end; then stop. However, for those intent on a quick tour, I hope the brief summaries of the individual chapters given above will enable you to piece together an appropriate itinerary.

Chapter 2
The Linguistic Categorization of Space

2.1 Perception and the Human Semantic Potential

This book tries to determine the possible extent of spatial semantic variation through an examination of underlying perceptual mechanisms. This is rather a tall order, and there are two points that bear mentioning in that regard, one cautionary and the other encouraging. The cautionary note is that the work as it stands is preliminary in nature and does not claim to supply a full explication of the human spatial semantic potential. Thus, those insights we may pick up through this endeavor will be of a tentative character. The accompanying point of encouragement is that a similar line of inquiry has been pursued in the past, in another perceptual domain, with considerable success. This earlier work concerned the semantic domain of color, and its primary result was a characterization of the human semantic potential for color naming, in terms of the neurophysiology of the visual system (Kay and McDaniel 1978). Even though the assumptions on which this model was based have been challenged (Hood and Finkelstein 1983; Teller 1991), the model has still yielded significant insights into the manner in which perception can constrain semantics. Let us turn to that earlier work, to get a feel for just how that was done and how similar ideas might be of value here.

The color spectrum provides a smooth gradation of hue, from red through orange through yellow up through violet, and there is nothing in the spectrum itself that dictates its linguistic division into the color terms of English, or those of any other language. One might expect, in fact, that languages could vary without limit in their naming of color, such that any contiguous subsection of the spectrum could be referred to by some color term in some language. Under this view, there would be no semantic universals in this domain, and each language would be free to partition the spectrum in any manner whatsoever.

Berlin and Kay (1969) presented evidence to the contrary. They performed experimental fieldwork on 20 languages, coupled with a literature review of 78 other languages, investigating the crosslinguistic variation of color terms. In their work, they restricted their attention to *basic color terms*. These are color terms with the following four properties: (1) they are single words (unlike *greenish-yellow*); (2) the color range they denote is not a subpart of that denoted by some other

$$\begin{bmatrix} \text{white} \\ \text{black} \end{bmatrix} < \text{red} < \begin{bmatrix} \text{green} \\ \text{yellow} \end{bmatrix} < \text{blue} < \text{brown} < \begin{bmatrix} \text{purple} \\ \text{pink} \\ \text{orange} \\ \text{gray} \end{bmatrix}$$

Figure 2.1
A partial order of basic color terms

term (unlike *crimson*, a kind of *red*); (3) their use is not restricted to particular classes of objects (unlike *blond*, which can be predicated only of hair, and by extension, humans); and (4) they are in frequent, regular use (unlike *magenta*). This confining of attention to the core of the lexical color system is similar in spirit to the idea of examining closed-class spatial terms, as we are doing here, in the expectation that this skeletal subportion of the domain as a whole will reveal whatever fundamental structure may be present.

Through their study, Berlin and Kay arrived at the conclusion that there are substantive semantic universals in the domain of color. When they asked their informants to identify those points on the color spectrum that corresponded to the best examples of color terms in their languages, the so-called foci for those color terms, they found that these foci are essentially the same crosslinguistically. In particular, they argued, there are 11 color foci that seem to structure the human semantic potential in this domain. These correspond roughly to those 11 points on the spectrum that an English speaker would pick out as the best examples of white, black, red, green, yellow, blue, brown, purple, pink, orange, and gray. They argued further that the categories are ordered: all languages contain words meaning *black* and *white*; if a language contains a third color term, that term will be *red*; if a language contains a fourth term, it will be either *yellow* or *green*; if a language contains a fifth term, it will have terms for both yellow and green, and so on. Figure 2.1 presents this ordering in its entirety. Here, $a < b$ means that a term for a is present in all languages in which a term for b is, and also in some in which a term for b is not (i.e., a is in that sense prior to b). The brackets indicate equivalence classes, such that if c and d are bracketed together, no statement is made about which is prior to the other.

These are strong statements, outlining quite clearly a set of empirically determined constraints governing the semantics of color. Although subsequent research has shown that there are minor flaws in Berlin and Kay's hypotheses, it has also substantiated them in general outline (Kay and McDaniel 1978; Kay, Berlin, and Merrifield 1991). There is one critical question that we have not addressed, however: *Why* does the semantics of color in the world's languages look this way? What is the source of these regularities?

Kay and McDaniel (1978) provided a partial explanation for Berlin and Kay's empirical findings, by tying the color foci to the neurophysiology of the visual system. They noted that there is a direct and physiologically observable neural coding for the four categories red, yellow, green, and blue in terms of opponent response cells of the lateral geniculate nucleus, and that there is also an identifiable neural coding for white and black in terms of the responses of other cells. The peak response for each neural coding coincides with the best example, or focus, of the corresponding color. A wavelength of 575 nanometers, for example, corresponds to the peak of one of the opponent cell neural responses, and also corresponds to what English speakers identify as focal yellow. Similarly, the peaks for other opponent cell responses correspond to focal red, green, and blue, and other neural responses correspond to focal white and black. Kay and McDaniel then analyzed the remaining color foci observed by Berlin and Kay in terms of these six neurally established foci, using fuzzy set theory (Zadeh 1965, 1971) as the computational framework for category combination. For example, orange was analyzed in terms of the fuzzy intersection of red and yellow (i.e., a color with a single peak response between those of red and yellow). One intriguing aspect of viewing color data in this manner is that in languages with just two color terms, such as Dani (Heider 1972a, b), those two color terms will each be composed of the fuzzy union of several of the fundamental neural response categories and will consequently each have several foci. Significantly, in her fieldwork, Heider determined that the two-word Dani color system is not well rendered by English *black* and *white*, since fully 69% of her informants indicated that the focus of the lighter of the two categories was at English focal red, rather than white. The category in fact encompasses white, red, orange, pink, yellow, and red-purple. Kay and McDaniel's analysis of such categories is consistent with this view of multiple foci for a single category. In sum, Kay and McDaniel were able to demonstrate that our perception of the color spectrum is implicitly structured by our perceptual apparatus and that this imposes constraints on the human semantic potential for color.

Since the publication of Kay and McDaniel 1978, one of its basic premises has been seriously called into question. Kay and McDaniel assumed, following the color vision research of the time, that the human *psychological* percept of color could be directly linked to the *physiological* response of the opponent cells. The story is unfortunately not as simple as that. Hood and Finkelstein (1983) showed that under some conditions, this "linking assumption" does not hold— that is, the responses obtained psychophysically do not match the ones obtained neurophysiologically. In other words, the reduction of percept to neural response is flawed, or at best incomplete. This in turn means that we do not have a solid reduction of color semantics to the neural level, only an initial model that now requires some updating in the light of more recent research in color vision.

For our purposes here, what is most important about the Kay and McDaniel example? Perhaps the most significant point is that it demonstrates the viability of determining perceptual constraints on semantic potential. Kay and McDaniel were able to explain some of Berlin and Kay's findings, shedding light on what can and cannot appear as a basic color term in human language. This should be heartening for us as we embark on a rather ambitious journey in search of an analogously grounded semantic potential for the domain of spatial relations. A second relevant point is that Kay and McDaniel's work was based on a judicious combination of neurobiological evidence and sensible computational ideas. The neurobiological data available did not take them all the way to an explanation; an additional computationally based category combination step had to be postulated in order to reach that goal. Thus, the lesson here is that even in essentially reductionist enterprises, some form of posited psychological processing may be required. Finally, a third point of interest is that despite the power and elegance of their demonstration, Kay and McDaniel did not succeed in providing a complete explanation of the semantics of color, as evidenced by continuing work along these lines (Kay, Berlin, and Merrifield 1991; Hood and Finkelstein 1983). We have already seen that the percept-to-physiology link is problematic. In addition, the partial order of color foci shown in figure 2.1, one of the most striking aspects of Berlin and Kay's research, was not explained by Kay and McDaniel, leaving open some intriguing areas in color-naming research. This is a point of interest for us primarily since it helps adjust our expectations to the appropriate level: in studies of this sort, we should seek insight into the nature of the human semantic potential, rather than a complete and exhaustive specification of that potential. If we happen upon a complete explanation, so much the better, but we should not count on it.

Having considered a model of perceptually grounded semantics in another domain, let us turn to the linguistic categorization of space. It will help us to keep in mind both the encouragement and the cautionary notes we can draw from this example of modeling the human semantic potential, as we set about examining a different model with similar goals.

2.2   The Primacy of Space

The linguistic description of spatial relations commands an interest one might not at first suspect of such an unassuming topic. This fascination derives from a cluster of reasons, which we shall be reviewing here. Perhaps foremost among them is the relative concreteness of such relations, the fact that they are objectively measurable and hence easily accessible to scientific inquiry. Compare, for example, the amount of room for possible misunderstanding and consequent talk at cross-purposes in a discussion of the semantics of *above* and *below*, on the one hand, with that possible in a discussion of the semantics of *boorishness* and *social grace*, on the other. This relative uncontestability of spatial terms is a major point in their favor, given the potential murkiness of semantic investigation. It is also, of course, an advantage shared with the domain of color. Also, as with color, there is substantial crosslinguistic variation in spatial structuring, together with good reason to suspect that panhuman perceptual processes will give rise to universals in this domain, and this contributes significantly to the attractiveness of both domains.

There is another attraction, however, that is not shared with color or other perceptual domains. The primacy of space, its privileged status, stems from the fact that space serves as a fundamental conceptual structuring device in language. This makes itself apparent in two ways. The first is that spatial terms are often expressed by linguistic forms of the sort that generally carry core conceptual structure, as we shall see. The second is that spatial terms are often used in nonspatial domains, through metaphor, lending a form of spatial structure to these nonspatial domains. Thus, the nature of a language's spatial system will reflect much more of the language than simply its capacity for purely spatial description, and any insights gained into the working of the spatial system may eventually have ramifications throughout the conceptual system of the language.

Spatial relations are often expressed by *closed-class* forms. A *closed class* is a relatively small set of linguistic forms that adds members only rarely; examples are prepositions (such as the spatial prepositions) and verbal prefixes. In contrast, an *open class* is a larger set of elements that constantly adds new members, such as nouns or verbs. The distinction is of interest because closed-class forms seem to be restricted in the semantics they carry. Talmy (1983, 3-4) expresses this as follows:

> They represent only certain categories, such as space, time (hence, also form, location, and motion), perspective point, distribution of attention, force, causation, knowledge state, reality status, and the current speech event, to name some main ones. And, importantly, they are not free to express just anything within these conceptual domains, but are limited to quite particular aspects and combinations of aspects, ones that can be thought to constitute the "structure" of those domains. Thus, the closed-class forms of a language taken together represent a skeletal conceptual microcosm. Moreover, this microcosm may have the fundamental role of acting as an organizing structure for further conceptual material....

There are also open-class forms that capture the same sort of skeletal conceptual structure. For example, English *enter*, a verb and thus an open-class form, describes roughly the same spatial event as English *into*, which is a preposition and thus a closed-class form. For our purposes, however, the important point is that spatial location and motion are often expressed by closed-class forms, regardless of other possible means of expressing the same content. And closed-class forms often express core structural content. Thus, the privileged semantic status of closed-class lexemes for spatial relations is indicated in part by the closed-class company they keep.

Spatial terms are also widely used throughout language, and this is another manifestation of the semantic primacy of space. Consider, for example, such expressions as "*beyond* the call of duty," "the choice *between* these two options," and "worth *over* ten dollars." In each of these, a spatial term is used to express a fundamentally nonspatial concept. One possibility is that the spatial terms contribute a spatial structuring to our understanding of these nonspatial concepts. The phrase "the choice *between* these two options," for instance, can be seen as imposing a spatial structure on our understanding of the decision process, such that the two options are implicitly conceived of as being physically located in different positions, with the choice located between them. Lakoff and Johnson (1980) have championed this view of metaphor and have demonstrated that the phenomenon is widespread. The important point here is that metaphor structures ordinary, everyday speech of the kind used in the examples above. It is by no means the exclusive property of poets or even the imaginative; rather, it deeply pervades all our speech, from the most mundane to the genuinely creative. Interestingly, there are spatial metaphors even for time, which is itself a privileged domain often expressed by closed-class forms. Consider, for example, the temporal sense of completion contributed by *up* in English *burn up* or *drink up*. (This has been interpreted as deriving from the fact that many physical actions of completion involve an upward direction, such as the rising level of liquid in a glass as the glass becomes completely filled—hence *fill up* (Bolinger 1971; Traugott 1978).) In a similar vein, Miller and Johnson-Laird (1976, 375) note that the centrality of spatial organization for human cognition generally "gives this topic an importance that extends far beyond any literal interpretation of spatial locations and directions."

To sum up, then, the primacy of space derives from the fact that spatial relations often carry core conceptual content, as manifested by their expression in closed-class forms, and from the metaphorical use of spatial relations throughout other parts of the semantic systems of the world's languages. In turn, the primacy of space helps motivate the computational modeling work we are centrally concerned with here, since it indicates that a modeling effort directed at the human capacity for spatial categorization would touch on a crucial aspect of language, with ramifications far outside the purely spatial domain.

2.3   Crosslinguistic Variation

Another source of motivation is the remarkable variation in spatial structuring exhibited by the world's languages. Even a cursory glance at linguistic spatial systems, such as we shall necessarily be restricted to, reveals significant crosslinguistic differences. These differences are sometimes quite dramatic, but more often than not, they are rather subtle, particularly when one compares closely related languages. Examples of both striking and subtle crosslinguistic differences in spatial categorization will be given here; the English spatial system will be used as the standard against which others are compared. In general, crosslinguistic variation in spatial systems provides one of the central motivations for the work presented in this book, by implicitly posing the question asked in chapter 1: What sort of system could adapt itself to so many different structurings of space, as the human capacity for categorizing space does?

The spatial system of Guugu Yimithirr, the Australian language introduced in chapter 1, is remarkable because of its reliance on absolute coordinates such as north, south, east, and west, even in situations in which English would use relative notions such as front, back, left, or right. For example, the Guugu Yimithirr speaker who has left some tobacco behind would say the equivalent of "I left it on the southern edge of the western table in your house." Similarly, instead of saying "George is standing in front of the tree," the Guugu Yimithirr speaker would say the equivalent of "George is standing just north of the tree," or south or east or west, as the case may be (Levinson 1992a). This phenomenon becomes much more than just an intriguing semantic oddity when Levinson points out that speakers of Guugu Yimithirr must constantly remain aware of the orientation of the four cardinal directions. Since this is something English speakers frequently do not do, in order to speak Guugu Yimithirr one must *think* in a distinctly non-English way. This conjecture is borne out by both anecdotal and experimental evidence: Levinson has shown that Guugu Yimithirr speakers are far more attuned to the four cardinal directions than are speakers of languages that use relative orientations such as front, back, right, and left. This is true even in nonlinguistic contexts. In this case, then, language may determine experience; that is, the language spoken may have an effect on the speaker's experience of the world (Whorf 1956). This is an interesting reversal for us, since the argument so far has taken the opposite point of view, namely, that experience constrains language, that is, that our shared perceptual apparatus constrains what spatial experiences we may have, and these experiences in turn determine what semantic contents are possible. In fact, there is no logical contradiction between these two outlooks. If our shared perceptual apparatus does not dictate what our experience of space is, but only constrains it, it may well be the case that the language spoken determines the nature of that experience of space, within the constraints set by the human perceptual apparatus. The evidence from Guugu Yimithirr is consistent with this view; the influence of the speaker's language may penetrate through the semantic system into cognition.

Levinson's cognitive tests compared the performance of Guugu Yimithirr speakers with that of Dutch speakers. In an analogous battery of tests Pederson (1994; 1995) found the same sorts of cognitive discrepancies between speakers of two different dialects of the same language, Tamil. One dialect, the so-called urban dialect, uses relative coordinates more or less as English does. The other (rural) dialect uses absolute coordinates in the manner of Guugu Yimithirr. Pederson found that speakers of the rural (absolute) dialect tended to prefer using absolute coordinates over relative coordinates even in nonlinguistic contexts,

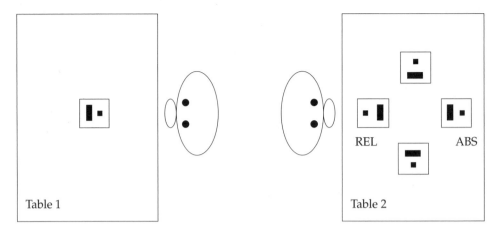

Figure 2.2
Determining the effect of language on cognition. Adapted with permission from Pederson 1994.

whereas speakers of the urban (relative) dialect preferred relative coordinates. Figure 2.2 presents Pederson's experimental paradigm, which is similar to that used earler by Levinson for Guugu Yimithirr. The subject faces table 1 and sees a card on it with a particular spatial configuration on its face. The subject is then asked to turn around 180 degrees and face table 2. There are four cards on table 2, all identical to the card seen on table 1, except for their orientation. The subject must select the card on table 2 with the configuration that matches the card he or she saw on table 1. A subject who is selecting on the basis of relative coordinates, using concepts such as *in front of*, will select the card marked *REL* in the figure, since on that card the small square is in front of the long rectangle from the subject's viewpoint, as was the case for the card on table 1. On the other hand, a subject who is selecting on the basis of absolute coordinates, using concepts such as *to the north of*, will select the card marked *ABS* in the figure, since on only that card does the small square bear the same absolute relation to the large rectangle that it bears on the card on table 1. (The markings *REL* and *ABS* are for our convenience only; they were not a part of the stimulus.) The results of this experiment were that speakers of relative-coordinate Tamil tended to choose the card marked *REL*, and speakers of absolute-coordinate Tamil tended to choose the card marked *ABS*. Pederson is appropriately cautious in his interpretation of these results, noting that what has been demonstrated is simply a correlation between linguistic and nonlinguistic behavior, rather than a causal link. But the results are at least consistent with the hypothesis that language can affect the speaker's apprehension of the surrounding world, with the ramifications discussed above.

There are at least two intriguing issues here. One is the very existence of a spatial system based on absolute coordinates. The other is the Whorfian-like effects we have just seen, in which the language spoken may affect nonlinguistic behavior. The model will account for one of these issues and not the other, and I feel bound to indicate at this point which is which in order to avoid raising false expectations. The basic mechanisms of the model can support an absolute spatial system of the sort found in Guugu Yimithirr or rural Tamil, and in that sense they offer an account of these semantic systems. However, Whorfian effects lie outside the purview of the model; it only provides an account of linguistically founded conceptual structure, without any explicit indication of exactly how that might interact with a nonlinguistically based conceptual system. We shall consider such interactions, and the means by which they might be modeled, when we cover possible extensions to the core model and in the general discussion.

Crosslinguistic variation in spatial systems is by no means restricted to the choice between absolute and relative coordinate systems. To underscore this point, let us turn to the Mexican language Mixtec, whose spatial system is profoundly different from that of English, but different in a different way. Brugman (1983) presents a semantic analysis of spatial terms in Mixtec, spelling out the manner in which the body-part system is metaphorically mapped onto the spatial system, such that body-part terms are used extensively as locatives. For example, to describe the location of a stone under a table in Mixtec, one would say

yuù	wã	híyaà	čìì-mesá
stone	the	be-located	belly-table

which, if translated word for word, would yield "The stone is located at the table's belly." In this sentence Mixtec is schematizing the space underneath the table as the area adjacent to the belly of a quadruped standing on all fours (i.e., the region underneath it). Similarly, to express the location of a bird above a tree, one would say the Mixtec equivalent of "The bird is located at the tree's head." Here the tree is schematized as a biped, with its head at the top. The idea of metaphorical conceptualization of objects as animate beings, and the corresponding use of body-part names for regions of space near parts of objects, is by no means unique to Mixtec. English *in back of* is an instance of the same phenomenon. However, the metaphor is carried much further in Mixtec than in English or related languages. Body-part terms are in fact Mixtec's primary means of expressing spatial relations, and this can lead to some interesting divergences from English spatial structuring. Consider, for example, figure 2.3. This figure presents four scenes, which are grouped differently by English and Mixtec. In English the top two scenes would be classified as *above*, and the bottom two would be classified as *on*. Thus, English divides these scenes as shown by the dotted line labeled *English* in the figure, along a contact/no-contact dimension. Mixtec, on the other hand, is seemingly oblivious to the presence of contact in the scene and instead is sensitive to the nature of the landmark object. In particular, a trajector either above or on a long, wide landmark is considered to be located

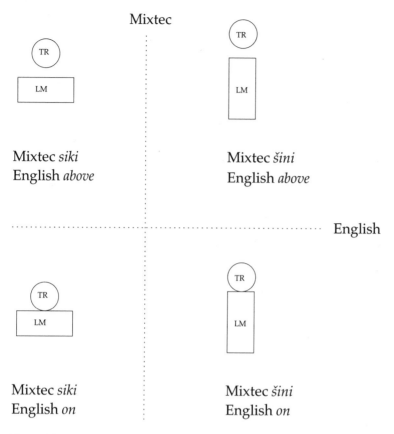

Figure 2.3
Examples of Mixtec *siki* and *šini*

at the landmark's "animal-back" (Mixtec *siki*), by analogy to the dorsum of a horizontally extended quadruped. A trajector above or on a tall, erect landmark is considered to be located at the landmark's "head" (Mixtec *šini*). This division is indicated in the figure by the dotted line labeled *Mixtec*. Interestingly, although the shape of the landmark might at first seem to be a peculiar basis for linguistic distinctions of this sort, a similar phenomenon occurs in English as well, just not in the case of *above* and *on*. Consider the distinction between "Pat walked *across* the corridor" and "Pat walked *along* the corridor"—it is the direction of Pat's motion relative to the long, extended dimension of the corridor that accounts for the difference.

An important point here is that although the body-part foundations of the Mixtec spatial system might lead one to believe that Mixtec spatial categorization involves knowledge of the basic anatomy of quadrupeds and bipeds, this does not seem to be the case. Much of the categorization is based on fairly primitive perceptual features of the landmark object in question, such as the orientation of its major axis, its longer dimension. Thus, the word for head is used in the above examples even though the landmark has no actual head, presumably because the trajector is located above or on a vertically extended landmark. Similarly, the word for animal back is used when speaking about a landmark for which only the slimmest of similarities to a quadruped obtains: the landmark object is horizontally rather than vertically extended. This point has already been made in connection with another Mexican language, Tzeltal, which also uses body-part terms extensively as locatives. According to Levinson (1992b, 23), the process of linguistic categorization of spatial relations in Tzeltal is fundamentally "bottom-up" and relies on rather simple geometric features of the objects, rather than detailed knowledge of the body shapes of various animals. This observation is echoed in the work of Landau and Jackendoff (1993), who note that when expressing object location, language tends to pick up only on gross geometric properties of the object. This is critical for the modeling enterprise we are involved in here, for it indicates that the amount of knowledge the model must have access to, in order to learn to categorize space, may be fairly limited in scope.

Although Japanese does not use body-part terms the way Mixtec does, the two languages do have something in common: they share an apparent insensitivity to contact, in situations in which English would explicitly mark it. For example, the Japanese spatial term *ue ni* can be used to describe either the location of a cup *on* a table, as in the first example, or the location of a lamp hanging *above* a table, as in the second:

kappu	wa	teeburu	no	*ue*	*ni*	aru
cup		table		*on*		exist

ranpu	wa	teeburu	no	*ue*	*ni*	sagatte-iru
lamp		table		*above*		hang

Japanese *ue ni* thus seems to subsume English *above* and *on*, and in that sense it is more abstract than either (Yoko Hasegawa, personal communication). These Japanese examples indicate that the insensitivity to contact that we encountered first in Mixtec is not necessarily tied to Mixtec's use of body-part terms: it may appear in languages that do not structure space in that manner.

Interestingly, even closely related languages can differ substantively, although subtly, in their spatial systems. Figure 2.4 shows two scenes that would both be classified as *on* in English but that do not fall into the same category in German. In German the orientation of the landmark surface supporting the trajector is significant, but in English it is not. If the supporting surface is roughly horizontal, as in the scene on the left, the German preposition *auf* is used to describe the relation. However, if the supporting surface is roughly vertical,

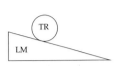

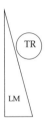

German *auf*

English *on*

German *an*

English *on*

Figure 2.4
Examples of German *auf* and *an*

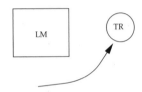

Russian *iz-pod*
English *out from underneath*

Figure 2.5
Russian *iz-pod*

as in the scene on the right, the preposition *an* is used instead. Thus, *auf* is used to describe the location of a cup on a tabletop or a Band-Aid on one's shoulder; *an* is used to describe the location of a picture on a wall or a fly on a windowpane (Bowerman 1989). Another Indo-European language with a spatial system slightly but demonstrably different from that of English is Russian. Figure 2.5 presents a spatial event, the motion of a circle out from underneath a rectangle, which is described by the Russian preposition *iz-pod*. The interesting point here is that Russian expresses in a single word a spatial event that is expressed by a phrase, *out from underneath*, in English.

There are many other languages that differ significantly from English in their structurings of space (Bowerman 1989; Talmy 1983; Casad and Langacker 1985; Denny 1982; Hill 1978), and an exhaustive cataloguing of this variation is well beyond the scope of this chapter. More to the point, a complete listing of that sort is not the goal of this necessarily brief survey. The goal is simply to note that linguistic spatial systems vary in nontrivial ways, and to impart a feel for the details of that variation in a few specific cases. Some of these specific cases will be of special interest later on, since we will be returning to them in evaluating the model. For now, the primary purpose of this review has been to motivate the modeling task, by implicitly asking what sort of system could adapt itself to so many different structurings of space, as the human spatial semantic potential does.

2.4 Cognitive Linguistics

The work presented in this book springs partly from recent work in cognitive linguistics. The purpose of this section is to look at the general philosophy of cognitive linguistics and thus to provide a fuller understanding of the context within which the current work takes place. More specifically, however, the purpose is to present a number of issues that cognitive linguists have concerned themselves with and that are relevant to the modeling of spatial semantics.

From the point of view of cognitive linguistics, language is "inextricably bound up with psychological phenomena that are not specifically linguistic in character" (Langacker 1987, 12). The idea is that since the acquisition and use of language rest on an experiential basis, and since experience of the world is filtered through extralinguistic faculties such as perception and memory, language will of necessity be influenced by such faculties. We can therefore expect the nature of human perceptual and cognitive systems to be of significant relevance to the study of language itself. One of the primary tasks of cognitive linguistics is the ferreting out of links between language and the rest of human cognition. In the domain of semantics in particular, cognitive linguistics seeks to ground meaning not directly in the world, but in mental and perceptual representations of the world. Given that this is the general thrust of the field, it should be no surprise that one of the topics cognitive linguists have focused on is the relation of language to perception, and specifically, the linguistic categorization of spatial relations (Linder 1982; Casad 1982; Vandeloise 1991; Matsumoto 1994; Janda 1984; Brugman 1981, 1983; Talmy 1983). Apart from outlining the structure of a number of non-Western spatial systems and their relation to other cognitive processes, these and other researchers have addressed a cluster of issues that impinge on the work described here. We shall be looking in particular at the phenomena of prototypicality, deixis, and polysemy.

Rosch's work on *prototypicality* in categorization (Rosch 1973, 1977, 1978) has attracted the attention of several cognitive linguists (Lakoff 1987; Langacker 1987). Prototype-based categorization has been attractive because of the serious problems that arise in attempting to define natural language categories by lists of necessary and sufficient conditions for membership. The basic issue here is that some members of a category are better exemplars of the category than others; they are in some manner more central, or more *prototypical* of the category. For example, most native speakers of English would agree that a robin is a better

Figure 2.6
Prototypical and nonprototypical cases of English *above*

example of a bird than is an ostrich or a kiwi, just as a lion is a better example of a mammal than is a platypus. Under a theory of categorization that considers membership in a category to be contingent only on meeting a set of necessary and sufficient conditions, there is no room for such a notion of gradation of membership in a category. We have of course already seen this issue, in the discussion of color terms. The search for color foci, the best examples of particular color terms, amounts to a search for the prototypes of those color categories. The phenomenon of prototypicality appears in the domain of spatial relations as well, as can be seen in figure 2.6. Here, the scene on the left is a prototypical instance of English *above*; the one on the right, although clearly an instance of *above*, is not nearly as prototypical an instance of the concept. The significance of this simple observation is actually fairly profound. It indicates that if we really want to get at the nature of human spatial categorization, we shall require a modeling framework that allows for this sort of graded category membership. A list of simple binary features such as [+above], [−contact], and the like, will not suffice. As we shall see, connectionism is a modeling methodology that accommodates this requirement; thus, this will turn out to be one of several motivations for choosing connectionism as our scientific language.

Deixis is the effect that the physical setting of a speech event may have on the way in which an utterance is interpreted. For example, anyone in Berkeley, which is located just across the Bay Bridge from San Francisco, would be able to truthfully say "San Francisco is just across the Bay Bridge," whereas someone in Los Angeles would not, generally speaking. Notice that Berkeley is never explicitly mentioned in the sentence. It is, however, implicitly the *deictic center*, or center of discourse, for the sentence, and this is why the sentence makes sense when spoken in Berkeley. However, if the speaker were in fact in Los Angeles, but were describing the layout of the San Francisco Bay Area, it would be perfectly legitimate to anchor the description in Berkeley by saying "Berkeley is a city on the east side of the Bay," and then to say that San Francisco is just across the bridge. In the latter case, the deictic center has been shifted to Berkeley, despite the fact that the speaker is actually in Los Angeles.

Consider figure 2.7. Here, the facelike figure denotes an object with an inherent front and back, such as a human being—this convention is adopted from

(a)   **(b)**

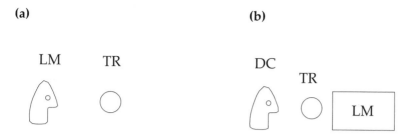

Figure 2.7
Deixis: English *in front of*

Vandeloise (1991). Both (a) and (b) are examples of English *in front of*. In (a) the inherent front of the landmark object is facing the trajector; therefore, the trajector is *in front of* the landmark. This is the nondeictic sense of *in front of*, the one encountered in sentences such as "Kim is standing *in front of* Pat." In (b), however, something different is happening. Here, the deictic center (*DC*) is taken to be at the speaker's location, and the landmark object has no inherent front and back of its own. Instead, the fact that the speaker is facing the landmark imputes a front and back to the landmark, such that the front of the landmark is the side facing the speaker. Now, since the trajector is also on that side of the landmark, the trajector is considered to be *in front of* the landmark. This is a deictically anchored sense of the term, such as one encounters in the sentence "The ball is lying *in front of* the tree," provided there is a speaker on the scene to provide an orientation with respect to the tree.

It is interesting to note that there are languages that handle deixis differently. For example, Hausa, a West African language, treats deictic effects in such a way that figure 2.7(b) would be considered an example of *in back of* (Hill 1978): the side of the landmark object that is facing away from the deictic center is implicitly taken as the front, rather than the side facing toward the deictic center, as is done in English. There are also languages with far more elaborated and intricate deictic systems than that of English. One of these is the Eskimo language Inuktitut (Denny and Issaluk 1976; Denny 1982), which has deictic terms denoting such specific notions as "down there (used for a large trajector)" and "down there (used for a small trajector)," among others. The significance of all this is that deixis is a phenomenon that can affect the construal of even very simple scenes, such as those in figure 2.7. It is thus a relevant issue for the modeling effort at hand.

Polysemy is a linguistic phenomenon whereby a single word has a cluster of distinct but related senses (Brugman 1981; Lakoff 1987; Jurafsky 1993; Regier 1994). Let us consider a simple spatial example to begin with: the polysemy of *in*, as illustrated in figure 2.8. Here, the scene marked (a) depicts a small circular trajector within a square landmark, corresponding to the sense of English *in*

(a)   **(b)**

Figure 2.8
The polysemy of English *in*

(a)   **(b)**   **(c)**

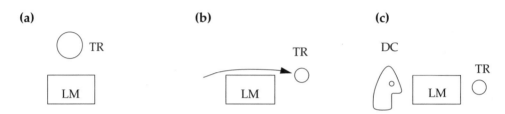

Figure 2.9
The polysemy of English *over*

commonly found in sentences such as "Pat is *in* the room." The scene marked (b) depicts the same trajector moving into the landmark, corresponding to the sense of *in* found in sentences such as "Pat walked *in* the room and said hi." Notice that there is a simple generalization, an abstraction over these two senses, that allows us to differentiate positive from negative instances of *in*: if the trajector ends up inside the landmark, the scenario is an instance of *in*, regardless of whether or not the trajector started there—in fact, regardless of whether or not it moved at all. This means that in this case there is no principled reason to consider the two senses distinct on purely semantic grounds, since the phenomenon can be accounted for using a simpler explanation, namely, the above abstraction over the two senses. As it happens, however, the two senses are grammatically distinguished in a number of other languages. Both German and Russian, for example, use the accusative case to mark the directional sense, the so-called *accusative of motion*, and another case to mark the locative sense.

On the other hand, there are a number of English prepositions for which no obvious semantic abstraction over the various senses exists, and in these cases we need not turn to grammar to find justification for asserting the distinctness of the senses. For example, Brugman (1981) presents a semantic analysis of the English preposition *over*, detailing dozens of different senses. These do not lend themselves to the straightforward sort of analysis offered above for *in*. Rather, this word seems to have a cluster of demonstrably distinct senses. Figure 2.9

illustrates three of these, the ones that correspond to the use of *over* in the following sentences:

(a) "The circle is *over* the rectangle."

(b) "The circle went *over* the rectangle."

(c) "The circle is *over* the rectangle from here."

Notice that there is no obvious abstraction covering these three senses. One possible abstraction that comes to mind takes a scenario to be an instance of *over* if the trajector is ever above the landmark. But this cannot be correct. For one thing, in (c) the trajector is never above the landmark. It could be countered that the scene is classified as *over* because of an *imagined path* from the speaker to the trajector, a path that does go over the landmark and is therefore above it at some point. The point here is that the abstraction should be taken to hold not of the actual situation, but of the mental representation of that situation. This is in fact a reasonable response, but it will not save the abstractionist argument, and to see this we need only look at the first two scenes in the figure. Consider scene (a). Here, if the trajector were to come down to rest on the landmark, to be in contact with it, we would no longer consider that spatial relation to be *over*; rather, it would be *on*. However, in (b) it is perfectly permissible for the trajector to be in contact with the landmark while crossing it—this is still a good example of *over*. We are forced to conclude that contact between landmark and trajector is permissible for *over* in some situations but not in others. There can therefore be no single abstract meaning covering all the senses, because that single meaning would have to either allow or disallow contact. This indicates that a more detailed analysis is required, pointing out the various senses and their relations with one another. In general, the study of polysemy implicitly involves an admission that language use exhibits a wide range of subtleties that are not always amenable to simple analysis. The examples we have seen so far in fact barely scratch the surface of the semantics of spatial prepositions in English (Herskovits 1986), let alone those of other languages. But again, as in the case of our look at crosslinguistic variation, exhaustive coverage was not what we were aiming at here. Rather, the goal was simply to demonstrate that the phenomenon exists and that it merits our attention in our modeling efforts.

2.5 Summary

Let us take stock of our position. What have we seen, and what does it tell us?

We have seen that space can claim a certain conceptual primacy, by virtue of its expression through closed-class terms, and more significantly by virtue of its pervasive influence as a metaphorical structuring device for nonspatial domains. We have also seen that languages vary in the ways in which they structure space, sometimes using spatial structurings that seem quite unusual from the point of view of English. We have seen that there are a number of central issues in linguistic categorization, such as prototypicality, deixis, and polysemy, that appear in the spatial domain. And implicit throughout the discussion has been the notion that spatial semantics are to some degree constrained by universal human perceptual mechanisms.

For these reasons, the domain of spatial relations is a deeply attractive setting for investigations into the human semantic potential, into issues of crosslinguistic semantic variation and possible limits to that variation. We know on the one hand that semantic variation does exist in this domain; and we know on the other hand that the search for spatial universals is well motivated, in that our semantics of space is based on our experience of space, which in turn is filtered through panhuman perceptual mechanisms. Finally, the conceptual primacy of space suggests strongly that whatever insight we gain into the workings of spatial semantics will eventually ripple out to affect our understanding of other domains as well.

Our modeling enterprise, then, is quite well motivated. But what have we learned about that enterprise itself? What have we seen that could do more than just excite our general interest in the semantics of space, that could actually tell us something about modeling in that domain? The answer of course is that we have seen Kay and McDaniel's model of color semantics. That work reassures us that perceptually grounded models of the human semantic potential are at least possible, which is important given the ambitious nature of the task on which we have embarked. At the same time, the model cautions us. Kay and McDaniel were not able to *reduce* semantic structure to perceptual structure; rather, their work indicated how semantics might be *constrained* by perception. Their model included a computational component, based on fuzzy set theory, that was not independently motivated by research in visual neurophysiology. Further, even given this additional component, there were aspects of color semantics that the model did not explain, and indeed the very basis of the model has been called into question. Similarly, in our case, if parts of the model are motivated on independent grounds, we should be prepared to admit other parts that are not. And we should not be either surprised or disappointed if the resulting model does not offer up a complete explanation of spatial semantics, but only a partial one.

Chapter 3

Connectionism and Cognitive Models

This chapter introduces the field of connectionism and its application to the enterprise of cognitive modeling. After a necessarily brief overview of the field as a whole, it considers the computational philosophy of parallel distributed processing (PDP) and its application to cognitive modeling. This includes an exposition of the back-propagation algorithm, since that algorithm will be used in the model presented later. The chapter then takes up the connectionist design philosophy of structured connectionism. This leads to a discussion of what I have come to call constrained connectionism, which amounts to an application of the ideas of structured connectionism to PDP models. I shall be arguing in particular for the utility of constrained connectionist models in cognitive theorizing. The chapter closes with a review of a number of connectionist methods for sequence recognition, situated within the framework of the preceding discourse concerning modeling methodologies, and serving to illustrate some of these earlier ideas. This issue of sequence recognition is relevant here since the movies that will be presented to our model of the human spatial semantic potential are sequences of static frames.

3.1 Overview

Connectionism is a neurally inspired style of parallel computation in which many simple interconnected processors cooperatively perform some computational task (Feldman and Ballard 1982; Rumelhart, McClelland, and the PDP Research Group 1986; Ballard 1987a). This field, also known as the field of neural networks, has had a profound impact in recent years on the way in which computation is conceived of, primarily by providing an alternative to the classic Von Neumann model of a program residing in memory dictating the actions of a central processing unit. Under the connectionist view, there is no single sophisticated central processor; rather, there are a large number of quite simple ones, which correspond roughly to biological neurons. These are interconnected by links, which correspond roughly to axons and dendrites—the fibers by means of which actual neurons transmit and receive signals. Within cognitive science, these models have gained considerable attention because of the reductionist

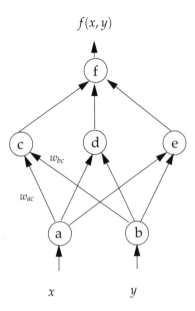

Figure 3.1
A simple connectionist network: a two-layer perceptron

appeal of building neurally motivated models of cognition, and also because of their attractive computational properties of parallelism, flexibility, adaptability, and graded responses.

Figure 3.1 presents a very simple connectionist network of a particular sort known as a *two-layer perceptron*. This network consists of three layers of units, or nodes—somewhat unhelpfully, input units are generally not considered when counting perceptron layers. The bottom layer, consisting of units **a** and **b**, constitutes the *input layer*; these two units receive external inputs x and y respectively. Units **c**, **d**, and **e** make up the intermediate *hidden layer*; these units are neither input units nor output units, but receive signals from the input units, perform some computation on them, and pass signals on to the output unit. Finally, unit **f** constitutes the *output layer*, producing some function $f(x, y)$ of the input by virtue of its connections to the nodes of the hidden layer. At a given point in time, each unit in the network has an activation level, which is affected by the activation levels of those units whose outgoing links lead into it, and which in turn affects the activation levels of those units to which its outgoing links are connected. The links that connect units in the network are typically weighted; for example, the link connecting unit **a** to unit **c** in the figure is shown with weight w_{ac}. Under this scheme, each unit receives as input the weighted sum of the activations of the units that have links leading into it. For example, unit **c** in the figure receives as input $w_{ac}a + w_{bc}b$, where a and b are the activation levels of nodes **a** and **b,** respectively. Unit **c** then produces as its activation level some function of this net input. Commonly, the function of a unit is the sigmoidal squashing function $f(x) = 1/(1 + e^{-x})$, where x is the net input to the unit. The other two hidden units similarly compute their activation levels, and finally, the output unit computes its activation as a function of the activations of the hidden units.

This two-layer perceptron is an instance of a particular sort of network known as a *feedforward* network, since the flow of activation is always in one direction, from input units to output units. The alternative form is a *recurrent* network, one in which there exists a path from a unit back to itself, either directly or through other units. We shall see examples of recurrent networks later in this chapter.

The field of connectionism has had a checkered history. Early work (McCulloch and Pitts 1943; Hebb 1949) held out the promise of a relatively simple and easily understood biological grounding for the characterization of intelligence, and Rosenblatt (1962) in particular excited interest with a proof of convergence for an algorithm to train the weights of simple one-layer perceptrons (i.e., perceptrons without hidden units), so that a given perceptron could learn to adapt itself to various tasks. This excitement was quashed by Minsky and Papert (1969), who pointed out that some very simple computations were in principle unlearnable by one-layer perceptrons. The most famous example of such a function is the *exclusive-or*, a function of two binary arguments that returns 1 when the inputs are different (i.e., one is 0 and the other is 1) and returns 0 if they are the same. A two-layer perceptron, such as the one in figure 3.1, is required for this function. Since no training algorithm for multilayer perceptrons was known at the time, this served to dampen a good deal of the earlier enthusiasm engendered by Rosenblatt's proof.

This state of affairs continued until the recent resurgence of interest in multi-layer perceptrons, brought about by the development of an algorithm that is able to train weights in such a perceptron. This is the *back-propagation* algorithm (Rumelhart, Hinton, and Williams 1986). (It is interesting to note that the algorithm had actually been discovered previously by Werbos (1974), but not publicized widely. The rediscovery of the algorithm over ten years later had a much greater impact than the original discovery.) This algorithm, together with somewhat earlier work in neurally inspired computational models based on ideas from statistical mechanics (Hopfield 1982, 1984), led to a renewal of interest in the field of connectionist or neural network models generally. In recent work connectionist networks have been applied to a wide variety of tasks, such as neurobiological modeling (Lehky and Sejnowski 1988; Zipser and Andersen 1988; O'Reilly et al. 1990), speech recognition (Waibel et al. 1987; Morgan and Bourlard 1989; Renals, Morgan, and Bourlard 1991; Waibel et al. 1991; Oster-holtz et al. 1992), natural language processing and inference (Waltz and Pollack 1985; Cottrell 1985; Elman 1988; Shastri and Ajjanagadde 1993; Weber 1989b;

Miikkulainen 1993; Stolcke 1990; Jain, Waibel, and Touretzky 1992), vision (Ballard 1987b; Sejnowski and Hinton 1987; Olson 1989; LeCun 1989; Hummel and Biederman 1990; Poggio and Edelman 1990; Ahmad and Omohundro 1990; Ahmad 1991; Mozer, Zemel, and Behrmann 1991; Keeler, Rumelhart, and Leow 1991). There has also been theoretical work probing the limits of connectionist networks as computational devices (Cybenko 1989; Kruglyak 1990; Siegelman and Sontag 1991). Computational mechanisms similar in flavor to connectionist networks, such as Markov random fields, have also enjoyed widespread attention (Cross and Jain 1983; Geman and Geman 1984; Chou and Raman 1987; Cooper 1989; Regier 1991). Hertz, Krogh, and Palmer (1991) provide an excellent overview of the field of connectionism as a whole, and Hinton (1990) presents a review of connectionist learning mechanisms. Anderson and Rosenfeld (1988) and Anderson, Pellionisz, and Rosenfeld (1990) provide useful collections of influential papers in the field.

3.2   Parallel Distributed Processing

Parallel distributed processing, or PDP, is a connectionist modeling methodology encompassing a number of techniques, all of which share a commitment to those basic principles manifest in the methodology's very name: the utilization of massive *parallelism* in processing, and the *distributed* nature of representations. The concept of parallelism is self-explanatory: many computations proceed in parallel. The concept of distributed representations is that there is no obvious symbolic interpretation of the function of an individual computing unit. Rather, each unit plays a role in a number of different higher-level functions and is itself best characterized at the *subsymbolic* level—at a conceptual level more fine-grained than that conveyed by the symbols of natural language. By contrast, representations in which each computing unit has a clear symbolic interpretation are referred to as *localist* representations.

What are the benefits of PDP? One simple yet powerful advantage is the computational efficiency gained by using inherently parallel representations, such that only a few time steps are required in order to complete a complex task. In addition, representations of this sort very naturally allow the representations of similar things to be similar in form. The power of this is that it allows generalizations to be made, on the basis of representational form, that capture the intuitive notion of conceptual similarity. Also, such representations, when damaged, yield graceful degradation of performance since no single unit is responsible for a given symbolic entity. Since there is no unit representing the concept "grandmother," for example, the network will not lose all knowledge of grandmothers upon losing a single unit. Finally, and perhaps most attractively, with learning tools such as back-propagation at our disposal, distributed representations need not be explicitly coded in by hand, but may develop as a result

Output

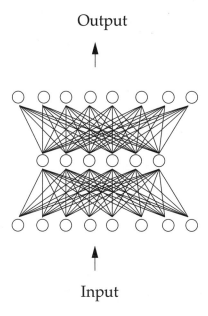

Input

Figure 3.2
A two-layer perceptron, trainable under back-propagation

of the learning process. Figure 3.2 presents a two-layer perceptron with full connectivity between layers, of the sort one might train under back-propagation. This is the sort of network I have in mind when I refer to PDP. The units in the hidden layer will come to develop a distributed representation of the input in the process of producing the desired output—thus, the modeler is relieved of the task of constructing these representations.

In general, the back-propagation algorithm has had a profound effect on connectionism, by enabling the training of multilayer perceptrons, which are not as restricted in representational power as one-layer perceptrons. Let us look at exactly what this algorithm does, and how it does it, before turning to its use in cognitive modeling.

Back-propagation is a *supervised learning* algorithm for connectionist networks. This means that it is given a *training set* of input patterns paired with desired output patterns; it then trains the network to produce the input-output associations given in the training set. One may also keep a *test set* of input and desired output patterns, to which the network is never exposed during training, and then test the network's *generalization* to the test set after training. If it has captured the regularities in the training set well, it should respond appropriately to previously unseen items in the test set. For example, one might train a network to respond with a 1 if and only if the leftmost bit of a 3-bit input vector is a 1. A simple training set might look like this, where $a \rightarrow b$ means that input a should result in output b:

$$0 \ 0 \ 0 \rightarrow 0$$
$$0 \ 0 \ 1 \rightarrow 0$$
$$0 \ 1 \ 0 \rightarrow 0$$
$$1 \ 0 \ 0 \rightarrow 1$$
$$1 \ 0 \ 1 \rightarrow 1$$
$$1 \ 1 \ 1 \rightarrow 1$$

A test set for this same function, containing the two possible combinations not covered by the test set, would look like this:

$$0 \ 1 \ 1 \rightarrow 0$$
$$1 \ 1 \ 0 \rightarrow 1$$

The degree to which the network yields the desired results on the test set, after training on the training set, is an indication of its generalization capability.

When being trained under back-propagation, a network takes a training set input vector as input and produces an output vector at the output node or nodes. This output pattern is then compared with the desired output given in the training set for that input pattern; the overall goal is to reduce the difference between the desired and actual outputs for all patterns, that is, to reduce the *error*. The formula for the error is

$$E = \frac{1}{2} \sum_{i,p} (t_{i,p} - o_{i,p})^2, \tag{3.1}$$

where i indexes over output nodes, and p indexes over training patterns. Here, $t_{i,p}$ is the desired output, and $o_{i,p}$ is the actual output, for node i on pattern p. Thus, the above quantity is simply the difference between the observed and desired outputs, squared, and summed over all output nodes and all patterns. This amount is then multiplied by $\frac{1}{2}$—this last factor has no conceptual content and is often introduced simply to make the associated mathematical derivations cleaner.

The essence of the back-propagation algorithm is that it reduces error by performing *gradient descent* in this error measure. For each weight w_{ij} in the network, it computes the gradient $\frac{\partial E}{\partial w_{ij}}$ (i.e., the partial derivative of the error with respect to that weight). This is the amount that the error E would increase given an incremental increase in w_{ij}, with everything else held constant. The algorithm then changes the weight by a small amount in the opposite direction, so as to decrease the error:

$$\Delta w_{ij} = \epsilon \times -\frac{\partial E}{\partial w_{ij}}, \tag{3.2}$$

where ϵ is the *learning rate*, a constant factor. Thus, with each weight update, the overall error should decrease, eventually reaching an amount so small as to be negligible. At this point the network has learned the training set. The back-propagation algorithm gets its name from the fact that in order to compute the gradient, it must *back-propagate* an error term backward through the net.

How can back-propagation be used in the service of cognitive modeling? For purposes of illustration, let us focus on a particular example: the model of Seidenberg and McClelland (1989). They modeled the psychological phenomenon of visual word recognition using a PDP model that was built much along the lines shown in figure 3.2. In fact, their model differed from the one shown only in that there were many more units per layer, and in that it was required to reproduce the input, in addition to the output specified by the training set. This model took as input a representation of the orthography of a word, that is, its written form, and produced as output a phonological representation of that word's pronunciation—together with a reproduction of the orthographical input. The model was trained under back-propagation on a large set of English word-pronunciation pairings, that is, pairings of orthography with pronunciation. This means that the weights on the model's links were adjusted by the learning algorithm until it was the case that when the model was presented with a representation of the written form of a word, it would produce as output a representation of the word's pronunciation, together with a reproduction of the input orthographical representation.

Seidenberg and McClelland point out that the visual word-recognition task derives a significant amount of its interest from the fact that the pronunciation of written English is partially but not completely regular: the word ending *-ave* is usually pronounced as in *gave*, *save*, and *cave*, which one might be tempted to consider a general rule, but this does not hold for the word *have*. This observation had led earlier researchers to posit separate pronunciation mechanisms for regularly and irregularly pronounced items: the irregular words require lexical lookup since they do not obey the rules; at the same time, the pronounceability of nonwords such as *mave* rules out a purely lexical answer and indicates that there must be a rule-governed component as well. The primary theoretical point made by Seidenberg and McClelland is that there need not be two separate mechanisms: in empirical simulation, their single homogeneous PDP model successfully matched a broad range of empirical data on visual word recognition, including both those aspects that appear to be rule-governed and those that appear to be exceptions to the rules. The distributed representations in the hidden layer captured the *quasi regularity* of English pronunciation in a single mechanism. This is very similar to the point made by Rumelhart and McClelland (1986), regarding their undifferentiated PDP model of the formation of the English past tense, which also exhibits apparently rule-driven aspects and exceptions to the rules—for example, *bake – baked*, *rake – raked*, *fake – faked*, but *take – took.* Their model was similarly able to produce both regular and irregular forms within a single mechanism. These past tense results have since been the focus of considerable controversy (Pinker and Prince 1988; Plunkett and Marchman 1988; Marchman 1993; Forrester and Plunkett 1994; Kim et al. 1994), some of which seriously challenges the basic assumptions of the model. But the model and its descendants have at least brought another viewpoint on the phenomenon into serious consideration. Thus, both Seidenberg and McClelland's model and Rumelhart and McClelland's model contributed to cognitive theorizing by calling into question the dual-mechanism conclusions that earlier researchers had reached. More generally, the attractiveness of PDP models in psychology can be seen as deriving from their ability to inspire reinterpretations of old findings and to provide a cohesive, unified account of a wide range of different empirical results (McClelland 1988). PDP modeling has also been used, in a similar manner, to suggest a number of theoretical points in neurobiology, (Zipser and Andersen 1988; Lehky and Sejnowski 1988) and neuropsychology (Farah and McClelland 1991).

For our purposes, one important point regarding these models is that their analysis is to a significant degree *empirically based*. That is to say, once such a network has been trained to exhibit a particular cognitive faculty, our understanding of its operation is largely founded on empirical observation of the network's behavior during simulation. This is the case since analysis of its function without resorting to simulation would be difficult in the extreme. There are methods one can use, such as principal components analysis of the hidden-unit activation vectors, or hierarchical cluster analysis of the same, but these are merely tools of interpretation, which assist in the process of empirically determining what the network is doing during simulation. We shall discuss the implications of this facet of the models later—for the time being, it is simply a point to keep in mind, since we shall see alternatives to this way of doing things.

3.3   Structured Connectionism

Two general views on the prestructuring of connectionist networks can be distinguished. One viewpoint holds that with learning algorithms such as backpropagation at our disposal, we need not put much effort into network design, but may rather let the algorithm induce whatever structure is inherent in the training set. Recent work in neuroscience, demonstrating the plasticity and flexibility of structures found in the brain, provides a possible source of inspiration for this view (Merzenich and Kaas 1982; Métin and Frost 1989). If actual neural structures change upon exposure to training stimuli, the argument would run, shouldn't connectionist networks also allow that possibility? PDP networks of the sort displayed in figure 3.2 and discussed in the section above are the sort of model one might use if one advocated this position. Note that there is full connectivity between layers here; this unrestricted interlayer connectivity leaves the representations formed in the intermediate hidden layer free to adapt themselves to the training set in any of a very large number of ways, thus capturing the flexibility that is central to the appeal of this viewpoint.

The opposing viewpoint is that of *structured connectionism* (Feldman, Fanty, and Goddard 1988; Feldman 1989). Although not denying the appeal of the notion of flexible representations, this approach holds that it is unrealistic to expect unstructured networks to be able to learn to solve large, complex problems in inherently structured domains, such as language and vision, and that a more promising route is the incorporation into the network architecture of knowledge regarding the target domain. In connectionist networks of this sort, units usually have interpretations at the symbolic, rather than the subsymbolic, level, and the structure of the network itself reflects the cognitive or neural structure that the modeler is positing. Work in structured connectionism has addressed the classification of structured objects (Cooper 1989), inference (Shastri 1988), the use of figurative language (Weber 1989a), and the interpretation of visual motion (Goddard 1992). In addition, Shepard (1989), in presenting a challenge for current connectionist models, comes quite close to articulating the structured connectionist philosophy.

Let us look at a concrete example, to help illustrate the general idea. Figure 3.3 presents a structured connectionist network from the work of Shastri and Ajjanagadde (1993), which addresses the phenomenon of *reflexive reasoning*. Reflexive reasoning is the human capacity to carry out inferences over a large body of knowledge almost instantaneously. This allows us to piece together the various parts of a story, follow a conversation, generate predictions about the intentions of various characters in a narrative, and so on. Each step of this reasoning process could potentially involve anything the listener knows, and yet the inference process as a whole is accomplished extremely quickly and without effort. Shastri and Ajjanagadde present a structured connectionist model that shows how it is possible to encode millions of facts and rules in long-term memory and still perform a certain class of inferences within a few hundred milliseconds, about the amount of time available in conversation or reading. Inferences in their system proceed in parallel. One of their central ideas is that variable bindings are maintained through the synchronous firing of sets of nodes. For example, figure 3.4 presents the activations over time of a set of nodes in their system, representing the statement "John gave Mary a book," together with the resulting inferences that Mary now owns the book and can sell the book. These inferences were obtained through the network fragment shown in figure 3.3. The fact that the nodes for *John* and *giver* are firing synchronously represents John's filling the role of giver in the *give* relation. Similarly, the fact that the node for *Mary* is firing synchronously with that for *recipient* in the *give* relation means that Mary was the recipient. Note that the network has propagated this synchrony of firing from the recipient in the *give* relation to the owner in the *own* relation, representing the inference that Mary now owns the book. This use of temporal synchrony

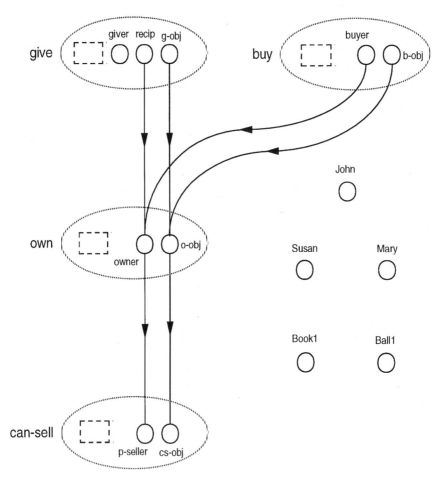

Figure 3.3
A structured connectionist network, from Shastri and Ajjanagadde 1993. Reprinted with the permission of Cambridge University Press.

to express the notion of two entities being bound has some neurophysiological foundation and enables the sort of reflexive inference with which the authors are concerned.

Shastri and Ajjanagadde's model gives rise to psychological predictions; let us consider one in particular. The authors point out that if the units in their system obey the timing properties of actual neurons, this will place a constraint on the *number of distinct items that can participate in relations in the inferential process.* This follows since the neuronal timing properties will dictate the number of distinct phases that can be represented in a single cycle on the model's units.

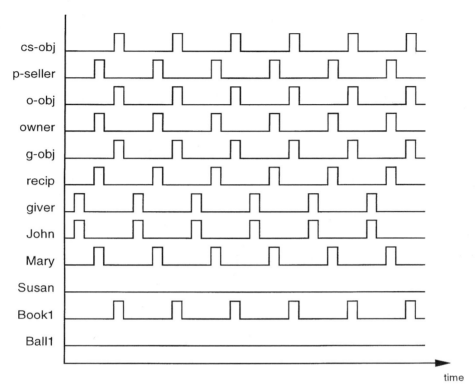

Figure 3.4
Binding through temporal synchrony, from Shastri and Ajjanagadde 1993. Reprinted with the permission of Cambridge University Press.

And the identity of actors in their system is encoded by temporal phase. So a constraint on the number of possible phases translates into a constraint on the number of possible actors that the model can keep track of. Thus, the authors predict that although the human inferential capacity allows a large number of facts to be involved in inference, these facts have to concern a relatively small number of actors. Under this view, a long story involving only a few characters should be perfectly comprehensible, whereas a comparatively short story that involves many distinct characters will be confusing. They predict, on the basis of evidence from neurophysiology, that an upper bound on the number of distinct entities that may be involved in the inferential process at a given time is around ten. They note that this number coincides quite well with the results of Miller (1956), indicating that the number of entities that can be maintained in human short-term memory is seven plus or minus two. Although more recent work has suggested that Miller's formulation may be an inadequate characterization of memory capacity (Crowder 1976), there is still a rough match with the predicted upper bound.

It is instructive to compare this prediction, and this form of analysis, with that more commonly used for comparatively unstructured PDP networks. Since the use of temporal phase in Shastri and Ajjanagadde's model is relatively easy to understand, the analysis is not empirically based here—it is possible to analytically determine constraints on the model's operation that are translatable into psychological terms, without running the network. This analyzability is a distinct advantage from the standpoint of cognitive modeling, since it makes it possible to articulate exactly why the network behaves as it does and thus supports credit and blame assignment: we can tell which aspects of the model are responsible for which aspects of the behavior, a situation that does not always obtain in the case of PDP networks (McCloskey 1991) (McCloskey 1991).

On the other hand, some of the attractive features of PDP modeling are absent in structured connectionist networks of this sort. The representations here are not learned—they had to be painstakingly wired up by the designers. This clearly translates into greater design effort. More significantly, it also translates into a lack of flexibility and plasticity: the model cannot adapt itself to different environments, since there is no adaptive mechanism to subserve this process. Although some efforts have been directed at learning within the structured connectionist framework (Fanty 1988), the state of affairs we see here is more or less typical of such networks.

3.4   Constrained Connectionism

Is there a way to retain the benefits of PDP while gaining the simple analyzability of structured connectionism? The design philosophy I have been calling *constrained connectionism* is an attempt to do just that. I view constrained connectionism as an application of structured connectionism to the realm of PDP. The essence of the idea is to build PDP networks that have built-in structural devices that constrain their operation. Ideally, these operational constraints can then be translated into psychological terms just as easily as in the case of Shastri and Ajjanagadde's work. To make these ideas somewhat more concrete, consider figure 3.5, which presents the constrained connectionist network we shall be examining in detail in this book. For the time being, a quick comparison with the PDP and structured networks we have seen shows that it has elements of each. The portions of the network displayed in dashed outline are psychophysically and neurophysiologically motivated structural devices, which constrain the network's operation. In contrast, the layer labeled *Current* and the unlabeled box beneath the output units are hidden layers of the type one might find in a PDP network, which support the formation of distributed representations. The network as a whole is trained under back-propagation.

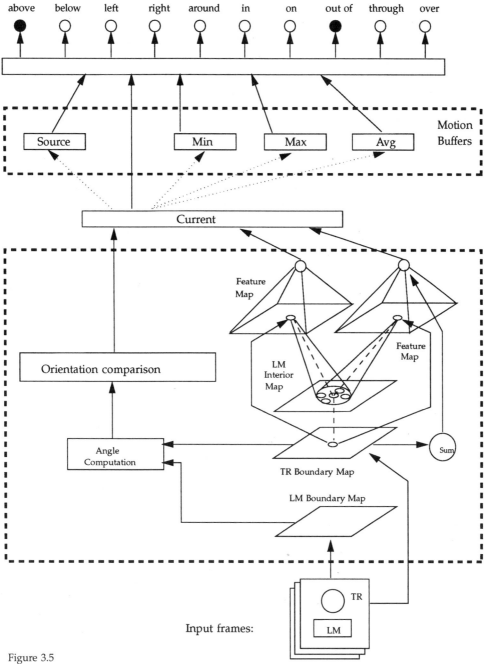

above below left right around in on out of through over

Motion Buffers

Source   Min   Max   Avg

Current

Feature Map

Orientation comparison

LM Interior Map

Feature Map

Angle Computation

TR Boundary Map

Sum

LM Boundary Map

Input frames:

TR

LM

Figure 3.5
A constrained connectionist architecture

What merit is there to this approach? What assurance do we have that this hybrid will exhibit the best, and not the worst, of each of its parents? One answer is to point to the track record. Although the incorporation of structure into learning networks is not as widespread in cognitive science as it might be, the technique has a history, and we can take heart at the success of our predecessors. This very general idea has been used in the construction of handwritten digit recognizers (LeCun 1989; Keeler, Rumelhart, and Leow 1991), visual recognition systems (Ahmad and Omohundro 1990; Mozer, Zemel, and Behrmann 1991; Hummel and Biederman 1990; Poggio and Edelman 1990), natural language systems (Jain, Waibel, and Touretzky 1992; Miikkulainen 1993), and the perceptually grounded lexical semantics acquisition systems of Nenov (1991) and Nenov and Dyer (1988). Nenov and Dyer (1988) In addition, Nowlan (1990) and Jacobs, Jordan, and Barto (1990) have investigated the use of modular structure in more general-purpose learning networks. These lists of course do not approach being exhaustive; they are merely meant to indicate the variety of connectionist models that embody this notion of prior structuring of the architecture and to encourage us in following a similar path. There are in principle at least three benefits to constrained connectionism that we can consider right at the outset, however. First, constrained learning devices such as these lead to superior generalization from the training set. Second, if the structures built in are independently motivated in some manner, this helps to motivate the model as a whole. Third, as we have seen, these devices provide ease of analyzability coupled with the advantages of distributed representations. Let us consider each of these in turn.

It has been known for some time that incorporating appropriate structure into a connectionist network leads to superior generalization from the training set. For example, LeCun (1989) has pointed out that the view of back-propagation as a general-purpose learning rule, applicable to a wide range of problems without any prior structuring of the network, is simply wishful thinking: an unstructured network cannot be expected to generalize in an appropriate manner from the training set. The generalization performance of judiciously structured networks is much greater, and for good reason. Prior structuring of the network can be thought of as reducing the dimensionality of the search space, thereby reducing the number of solutions being considered. This in turn reduces the number of false solutions—those solutions that result in low error for the training set but not for the test set. The work of Denker et al. (1987) and Patarnello and Carnevali (1987) has indicated that the likelihood of correct generalization depends on the number of alternative solutions being considered, the number of solutions that are acceptable, and the size of the training set. Thus, if everything else were held constant, better generalization from the training set could be obtained through decreasing the number of networks being considered (i.e., reducing the number of free parameters in a given architecture)—and this means prestructuring the architecture. This argument for constrained connectionism therefore essentially rests on the relative impracticality of the unstructured approach, in that it is unreasonable to expect good generalization performance from a network in a complex domain without building in knowledge of the domain so as to constrain the search for solutions. Of course, this need for prior structuring, or biasing, in generalizing learning systems is by no means restricted to connectionist learners—it affects any machine learning system (Mitchell 1980). The structural devices shown in dashed outline in figure 3.5 serve precisely the role described above: they reduce the dimensionality of the space that the network must search through, in the process of learning, to find a solution. Thus, the way in which these structural devices are designed is critical to the success or failure of such a network. If they are designed well, accurately incorporating knowledge of the domain into the network architecture, the hypotheses considered during the learning process will be restricted to those that are consistent with the knowledge of the domain that the network designer was trying to capture.

Building structure into a network can also help to motivate the network as a cognitive model, provided there is independent motivation for the structure. In the particular network we are considering here, the structural devices are motivated by neurophysiological and psychophysical evidence concerning the human visual system. Thus, these structures make the model's design somewhat less arbitrary than it might have been otherwise. In addition, this incorporation of nonlinguistically motivated structures is very much in keeping with the spirit of inquiry into issues of semantic universality and relativity that motivates the work as a whole. After all, the central tension is between crosslinguistic variation on the one hand, and on the other, the knowledge that all languages share general human perceptual constraints on semantics and are therefore very likely to have some semantic structure in common. The model presented here fits in as an element of this line of inquiry, since it is a linguistic learning system whose architecture is inspired by neurobiological and psychophysical insights into the workings of the human visual system. Thus, although the model can learn to adapt to any of a number of different structurings of space, as a language-learning human being does, there is an unchanging core of structure underlying the learning mechanism, corresponding to the perceptual structure that is common to all humans. These independently motivated structural devices thus play a central theoretical role.

Finally, let us turn to analyzability. The issue of exactly what role connectionist models should play in cognitive theorizing has a rich and contentious history (Broadbent 1985; Rumelhart and McClelland 1985; Smolensky 1988; Fodor and Pylyshyn 1988; McClelland 1988; Massaro 1988; McCloskey 1991; Seidenberg 1993), and part of the dispute has centered on the analyzability of these models. McCloskey (1991) in particular has pointed out that even the most complete description of a PDP model will not constitute a theory of the cognitive function modeled by that network. This is so because the model's architecture does not lend itself to straightforward analysis; there is no obvious way to translate the model into a set of general principles governing the cognitive capacity under study. Rather, as we have seen, the model may *simulate* the function, and we may draw our theoretical conclusions from its empirically observed output behavior. A particularly uncharitable interpretation of this state of affairs is that it is no more enlightening to build a simulation of this type than it is to beget a child. After all, your child will certainly exhibit the cognitive function you are interested in—more accurately than the model, for that matter—and then rather than empirically observe the model, you may empirically observe the child. Unanalyzable or unanalyzed simulation misses the point entirely: it does not matter whether the network accurately models the data as long as we cannot say *why* it does. McCloskey in fact comes quite close to this point of view, and moves from there to assert that the proper role for PDP networks to fill in cognitive theorizing is the same role currently filled by animal research: one may do things to networks that ethical considerations would prevent one from doing to humans, and then observe the results. These networks have a role to fill as simulators, but they should not be taken as theories.

There are a number of possible responses to this. One is that general psychological conclusions can be drawn from the overall character of a network. For instance, the homogeneity of Seidenberg and McClelland's (1989) network led them to question the dual-mechanism assumption for visual word recognition. Interestingly enough, this defense is the PDP counterpart to the constrained connectionist idea of building in structure and then drawing theoretical points from that structure: in the PDP case, no structure is built in, and the theoretical point made is that a single unstructured mechanism can account for data that were thought to require a more differentiated one. Another possible response is that interpretation tools such as cluster analysis or principal components analysis over hidden-unit activation patterns allow us to analyze networks after they have been trained, and that the rather bleak view of PDP networks as inherently unanalyzable is therefore unjustified. This is only partially true, however, since these tools aid only in interpreting the simulation and in that sense still lead to empirically rather than analytically based understanding of the network's operation. Finally, a third response is that accurate modeling of cognitive processes may in fact *require* of us that we specify our models at the level of hundreds of interconnected units—a level that initially appears a hopelessly uninterpretable tangle, such that simulation is the only recourse left to us. In other words, we should not shy away from complicated models simply because they are complicated (Seidenberg 1993)—they may be on the right track even if it is difficult for us to understand them completely. This is certainly a valid point, but it brings up another one in turn: if this level of indecipherability is *not* required of us in modeling some process, we should certainly not default to it simply because these models that are so inconvenient to analyze are so very convenient to put together and train.

There is a related thread of argumentation, which holds that PDP networks with hidden units are "too powerful to be meaningful" (Massaro 1988, 213)—in other words, that they are essentially unconstrained and therefore scientifically unenlightening. The point here is that one should expect of a cognitive model not only that it match human data, but also that it fail to produce data that a human would not produce. If a model learns to exhibit humanlike performance, but that same model could also have been trained to exhibit performance very much unlike that of a human being, in what sense does this tell us anything about the human learning process that the model simulates? This concern was voiced by Minsky and Papert (1969) as well when considering such networks: "... if there is no restriction except for the absence of loops [i.e., recurrent connections], the monster of vacuous generality once more raises its head" (p. 232). (It is interesting to encounter this objection coming from this source, since these authors were the ones who originally pointed out the *over*constrainedness of one-layer perceptrons.) This line of argument is sharpened by the work of Cybenko (1989), showing that a feedforward multilayer perceptron with a sufficient number of hidden units in a single hidden layer can approximate any continuous function whose arguments range from 0 to 1. We can always scale our data down to the 0 to 1 range, so this last condition is not particularly restrictive. Not every function *representable* in such a network will necessarily be easily *learnable* through back-propagation (Kruglyak 1990), but it is unfortunately unknown exactly how the relevant parameters, such as the number of hidden units, limit the range of learnable functions. In any event, the point remains that such networks can still learn to represent a wide range of functions, and this computational power limits their explanatory power.

A possible counterargument would be that PDP models will not exhibit non-human data because the training sets, derived from human data, will not include it. According to this view, it is incorrect to view the network by itself as the model—the model is really the network together with its environment, the training data. This brings up the general nature/nurture question: to what degree are the regularities in human behavior due to the structure of the organism, and to what degree are they due to the structure of the environment? An implicit claim of those who advocate fully unstructured PDP models is that these regularities are due almost entirely to the structure of the environment; an implicit claim of structured or constrained connectionists is that they are at least partially due to the makeup of the organism. Either approach may constitute a reasonable working hypothesis, depending on the particular cognitive faculty under study.

In sum, even if PDP models are not impossible to analyze, they are certainly difficult to analyze. Whether this is because we lack the wherewithal or because they themselves are underconstrained, the fact remains and must be dealt with. And a large part of the appeal of constrained connectionism stems from the fact that the analysis of networks with clearly specified constraints on their operation is a far simpler and clearer undertaking. As we have seen, the approach also has attractions based on the computational consideration of enhanced generalization, and on the fact that independently motivated structure in a model may help to motivate the model as a whole.

3.5   Learning Sequences Using Back-Propagation

The issue of learning sequences using back-propagation is relevant here. After all, a movie portraying an event, of the sort that will be provided as input to our model, is simply a sequence of static frames, and the model will be trained under back-propagation to recognize such sequences. In this section we shall review three methods commonly used for sequence learning under back-propagation, so as to have some idea of what our options are later on when we discuss the model's architecture. As we shall see, the actual method used will not be any of these more general methods, but rather one tailored to the task at hand, in line with the philosophy of constrained connectionism. In this section we shall be referring back to the general notion of operational constraints imposed through prior structuring while viewing these off-the-shelf methods, noting how their structure makes them appropriate for some tasks and inappropriate for others. This section thus serves double duty in a sense: on the one hand, it familiarizes us with some common methods for sequence learning, setting the stage for a later comparison with the method actually used; on the other hand, it serves as a forum in which we may note the effects of prior structuring on network function and analyzability. The three methods we shall examine are *time-delay neural networks, back-propagation through time,* and *back-propagation with state units.*

Figure 3.6(a) presents an example of a time-delay neural network, or TDNN (Waibel et al. 1987; Waibel 1989; Weigend, Huberman, and Rumelhart 1990; Guyon et al. 1991). Here, the current input $x(t)$ is fed directly to the leftmost input node; successive input nodes in the network receive the input signal after it has passed through a number of delays, each shown as a box marked δ. Thus, at a given point in time, the input nodes at the bottom of the network receive as input, from left to right, $x(t), x(t - \delta), x(t - 2\delta), x(t - 3\delta)$, and $x(t - 4\delta)$. In other words, the idea is to splay time out over space across the input units. The network as a whole is then trained using standard back-propagation. The input to the network shown here is a single scalar value. The extension to vector inputs is straightforward and is shown in (b): instead of having a single input node for each time step, we have a full input vector of nodes for each time step. This is a simple and elegant solution to the problem of processing time-varying patterns, but it has one serious limitation: a fixed time window. The use of time delays in this manner means that only a fixed number of time steps of the input sequence can be brought to bear on the response the network gives at any point in time. This is a form of structuring that sharply constrains the operation of the network, making it clearly inappropriate for some uses. For

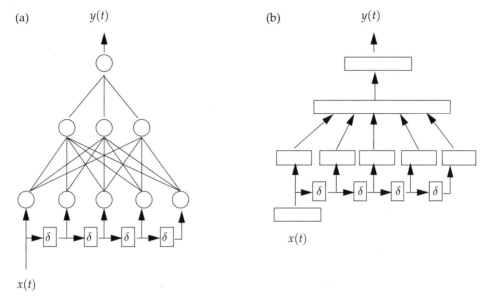

Figure 3.6
Time-delay neural networks

example, consider a task as simple as determining whether the binary input string as a whole has at least one 1 in it. If we allow input sequences to be of arbitrary length, TDNNs are obviously the wrong choice, for their output will be a function only of the input currently visible at the input nodes, whereas this function requires sensitivity to the presence of a 1 anywhere in the sequence as a whole. On the other hand, if it is not critical that the entire sequence be considered as input, TDNNs may be appropriate. These networks are often used in speech recognition, for example (Waibel et al. 1987; Waibel 1989), where the identification of a phoneme is presumed to depend on only a fixed temporal window of input. Notice the sharpness of the constraint that is imposed by the structure here, and the ease with which it can be articulated and related to the network's behavior—if a TDNN were to be used as a cognitive model, the model would implicitly predict that no more than n time steps are relevant to the categorization under study, where n is the width of the network's time window. If the value for n were independently motivated, this constrainedness would be a desirable state of affairs, rather than simply an ad hoc solution. It would be an analytically determined prediction, requiring no simulation, which can be tied directly to one particular aspect of the model's structure: the fixed time window.

Let us next look at networks that can bring more than a fixed-width subportion of the input sequence to bear on their operation. Consider figure 3.7 (a),

(a)   (b)

Figure 3.7
Two recurrent networks

for example. This single node with a single recurrent link is the simplest possible recurrent network, that is, the simplest possible network that has a path from a unit back to itself. Although this network is exceedingly limited in computational power, with the appropriate weight on its single link, it would be able to distinguish certain sorts of sequences. For example, if the weight were set correctly and the activation function of the net shown were the usual sigmoidal squashing function, the network would be able to discriminate between arbitrary-length binary sequences that have at least one 1 in them, and those that do not. To see this, imagine that w_{aa} is some large positive number. Once the activation of a goes high, because of a 1 in the input stream, the recurrence will cause it to stay high, always feeding a large positive input back to node a. So this sort of network would be appropriate for the task for which we showed TDNNs to be inappropriate. The extension to several units in the layer with recurrent connections is shown in (b)—here, each unit in the layer connects to itself and to every other unit in that layer.

The back-propagation algorithm assumes a feedforward architecture; since these are recurrent networks, they cannot be trained using a straightforward application of back-propagation. Given this, one approach to training such a network to recognize sequences is to unfold the network over time (Rumelhart, Hinton, and Williams 1986), as shown in figure 3.8. Here, the recurrent network of figure 3.7(a) has been transformed into a feedforward network of depth $t + 1$, where $t + 1$ is the length of the input sequence, by replicating node a once for each step in the sequence. Thus, node a_0 corresponds to node a in the recurrent net at time step 0, node a_1 corresponds to node a at time step 1, and so on. Notice that each node a_i accepts input $x(i)$, which corresponds to input x at time i in the original recurrent network. Finally, note that in the feedforward case, the weights on the links connecting the nodes corresponding to different time steps are all the same: w_{aa}. This is the counterpart of the recurrent link in the original network. This network will respond as the recurrent network would

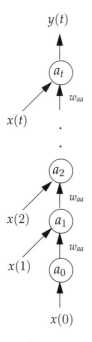

Figure 3.8
Back-propagation through time

to a sequence of length t, but since it is feedforward in nature, we can apply back-propagation to it, with the constraint that the links between nodes must all have the same weight. This constraint is easily enforced using the technique of *weight sharing* (Rumelhart, Hinton, and Williams 1986; LeCun 1989). Note that the unfolded version of the network is required only for training; once this has been completed, the learned weights may be transferred back to a functionally equivalent, and much smaller, recurrent network.

Back-propagation through time has the disadvantage that it consumes a good deal of memory by replicating network nodes. Furthermore, the resulting unfolded networks can be quite deep—that is, they may have many layers—particularly for long sequences. This is a disadvantage since back-propagation tends to be more successful at learning in relatively shallow networks (Pollack 1990a). As we have seen, however, there are at least some functions that are learnable by these networks that are not learnable by TDNNs. This increased power goes hand in hand with a decrease in analyzability: general recurrent networks of the sort shown in figure 3.7(b) are generally analyzed empirically, through simulation, using the standard tools of the trade: principal components analysis and hierarchical cluster analysis. The distributed representations formed across the hidden units do not lend themselves to any more straightforward analysis.

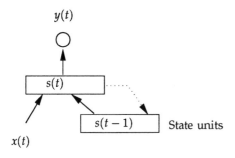

Figure 3.9
The Elman architecture

A popular approach to connectionist sequence learning is the use of state units (Elman 1988; Jordan 1986; Cleeremans 1993; Miikkulainen 1993). This is perhaps best exemplified by the work of Elman (1988); the network architecture he suggests is presented in figure 3.9. Probably the most significant aspect of this sort of network is that it is a recurrent network that can be trained using a simpler method than back-propagation through time. As we shall see, this network is functionally equivalent, once trained, to a trained recurrent network of the sort shown in figure 3.7(b). Here, each box represents a layer of units. Thus, this is a standard two-layer perceptron, with one addition, namely, the state units. The solid arrows connecting layers in the network represent full connectivity between layers; the dashed arrow from the hidden layer down to the state layer represents one-to-one connections, each of weight 1, such that the state layer contains an exact copy of the contents (i.e., the state) of the hidden layer at the previous time step. Here, the hidden layer is marked $s(t)$, and the state layer is marked $s(t - 1)$, indicating that at time t the state layer holds whatever the contents of the hidden layer were at time $t - 1$. This network is functionally equivalent to the recurrent network we saw earlier since the fixed copy-back connections to the state layer together with the connections from the state layer to the hidden layer take the place of the recurrent connections in the network without state units. In either case, the hidden layer will receive as input its own activation vector on the previous time step, weighted by a set of connection strengths. The two networks differ only in the manner in which these connection strengths are trained. In contrast to the earlier recurrent network, this architecture may be trained using ordinary back-propagation, keeping the one-to-one downward connections fixed, and treating the contents of the state buffer as if they were external input to the network. The one-to-one downward links are thus essentially ignored by the training algorithm. Technically, ignoring these links means that only an approximation to the gradient $-\frac{\partial E}{\partial w_{ij}}$ is obtained, and that "gradient" descent is then performed using that approximation. We can see how this approximation is obtained: here we do back-propagation only one step back in time, instead of all the way back to the beginning of the sequence. Thus, training under this paradigm can be viewed as a simple approximation to back-propagation through time, an approximation in which the network is unrolled for only one time step rather than the length of the sequence as a whole. In effect, this amounts to capturing the dependence of $s(t)$ on $s(t-1)$, but ignoring the dependence of $s(t-1)$ on $s(t-2)$—together with $s(t-2)$'s dependence on earlier time steps. It is in this sense that the gradient obtained is only an approximation. Given this, it should not be surprising that this method has difficulty learning long-range temporal dependencies. Consider for example the two strings

PSSSP and TSSST,

and view them as sequences of characters, each of length five. These two strings are identical except for their first and last characters. Imagine that a network with state units is trained on these two strings, so that at each time step it outputs a prediction of the next character in the string. Error is calculated based on the difference between the predicted and actual next characters, and this error is back-propagated through the network. Once trained, after seeing PSSS as input, the network should produce P, and after seeing TSSS, it should produce T. But the fact that these networks ignore the dependence of $s(t-1)$ on earlier states during training leads us to suspect that they may not be able to retain a representation of the first character of the input string in their state. After all, there is nothing in the predictions for the SSS portion of either string that requires memory of the first character of the string, and this means that back-propagation for these intermediate predictions will not force the state representation formed to include the first character. It is only when the network reaches the final character that it needs some memory of what occurred at the beginning of the string. By then, back-propagation will be able to adjust weights based only on the state for the last time step and the time step before—it will not be able to trickle back to the first time step the way it would under back-propagation through time. The important point here is that there is no pressure for the state vector to carry a representation of the first character until it reaches the final character—and by then it may be too late. Cleeremans (1993) reports that although increasing the number of hidden units partially alleviates this problem, learning becomes exponentially difficult with the length of the intervening SSS...S sequence. This underscores the limitations of these networks in handling long-range temporal dependencies.

In general, this method yields convergence if the learning rate is relatively low, since the algorithm will never commit itself to a large step in the wrong direction. However, methods based on the second derivative of the error with respect to the weight, which do take large steps, will be misled by the approximate gradient. These tend to perform poorly on Elman networks. Despite this, networks of this sort have become a standard connectionist tool for the learning of sequences.

They have in their favor simplicity and the ability to learn sequences without unfolding input in time out over space, as both TDNNs and back-propagation through time do. Thus, they are somewhat less memory-expensive than these other two methods.

On the subject of analyzability, it is worth pointing out that Elman networks, and the recurrent networks that they mimic, are similar in form to finite-state automata: at a given point in time, the output and next state depend on the current input and current state. Given this similarity, it is not surprising that networks of this sort have had some success in the induction of regular grammars (Servan-Schreiber, Cleeremans, and McClelland 1988; Cleeremans 1993). This general formal similarity is unfortunately not enough to indicate clearly the limits of what will be learnable by such a network—the distributed representations that develop in the hidden layer and are copied to the state layer are not a finite set of states. In fact, Pollack (1990a) has coined the term *infinite-state machines* to denote those recurrent networks that develop their own distributed state representations. Analysis of such networks is often carried out through simulation.

The three methods outlined above are by no means the only ways in which back-propagation, or indeed the general idea of gradient descent, can be applied to the learning of temporal sequences. In fact, there exists a wide array of methods (Williams and Zipser 1989; Fahlman 1991; Mozer 1988; Pollack 1990a; Watrous 1990). The interested reader may find reviews in Hertz, Krogh, and Palmer 1991 and Pearlmutter 1990. Nonetheless, these are three of the most commonly used connectionist approaches to sequence learning. When presenting the details of the model with which we are primarily concerned here, I shall consider these possibilities before moving on to a solution more customized, and therefore more appropriate, to the particular learning task we are considering. That solution, as we shall see, will have the additional advantage of being fairly easily analyzable.

3.6   Another Brief Exchange

"You know, there's something that's been bothering me," says my not-so-gentle reader. "You've been arguing for your so-called constrained connectionism, for building structure into PDP networks, in part because it allows one to determine exactly what's going on in the model, exactly what the constraints are on the model's operation, and therefore exactly what those translate into in psychological terms. No problem so far. What makes me uncomfortable is that you say this as if it does away with the need for simulation, for empirically based understanding of the model. Look, if that's the case, and if that's what you're aiming for, why do computational modeling at all? If you're interested in understanding your models analytically, why not just write them down on paper, analyze them, and save yourself the bother of coding up the simulation?"

"I'm glad you brought that up," I say, getting used to the idea of being stopped short in my stride from time to time. "Here's my take on the situation. If it were possible to do away with simulation entirely, then I agree that that's what we ought to do. Because analysis will by its very nature give you a clearer apprehension of what the forces at play are than will empirical observation of a simulation. However, I don't believe that's possible. Which is to say that there are some domains for which it simply is not feasible to build easily analyzable models. And in that sort of situation, as you point out, computational modeling comes into its own. But—and this is the critical part—the fact that you will be building models whose operation must be understood *in part* through simulation doesn't mean that these models have to be understood *solely* through simulation. There may be no need to swing over to the other extreme. If you can build in constraints on the model's operation, then you ought to be able to articulate, prior to simulation, what broad parameters the model's behavior will lie within. To determine just what it will do within those broad parameters will still require simulation, however. This is the kind of model, and the accompanying kind of analysis, I've been advocating."

Chapter 4
Learning without Explicit Negative Evidence

It has often been noted that children learn language almost entirely without the benefit of negative evidence (Braine 1971; Bowerman 1983; Pinker 1984, 1989). Children are only very rarely told that an utterance is ungrammatical or inappropriate, rarely enough that it seems unlikely that this occasional feedback plays a pivotal role in their acquisition of language. This raises a serious problem in the study of language acquisition: if children do learn language without being explicitly told that some forms are inappropriate, how do they learn to avoid using those forms? Of all the sentences a child has never heard, which are grammatically acceptable and which are not? The child will learn to make this discrimination, but it is not clear just how this is done. In short, how can the child generalize from the input without *overgeneralizing* to include inappropriate usages, if these usages have never been explicitly flagged as infelicitous?

The "no-negative-evidence" problem has primarily been investigated in the context of grammar acquisition, but it is general in scope, affecting any acquisition process in which one cannot rely on a consistent source of negative evidence. In particular, it affects the acquisition of lexical semantics for spatial terms, since we cannot assume the existence of a reliable source of negative evidence for semantic acquisition here any more than we can in the case of the acquisition of grammar. In this chapter we shall consider the no-negative-evidence problem as it arises in the domain of learning the meanings of spatial terms, and we shall see that even if one takes the most conservative stance possible, assuming that children receive absolutely no negative evidence in the learning process, semantic acquisition is still possible, using an adaptation of a heuristic proposed in the child language literature. Thus, the primary theoretical role of the simulations we shall see here is to verify that this heuristic approach is viable and that it can enable accurate semantic acquisition even under the assumption that the child receives no negative evidence whatsoever.

Although our discussion will center on the no-negative-evidence problem in the domain of spatial terms, the learning heuristic we shall adopt as a solution is not particular to this domain. Rather, it is a very general solution to the no-negative-evidence problem, one that could well be applicable far outside this domain.

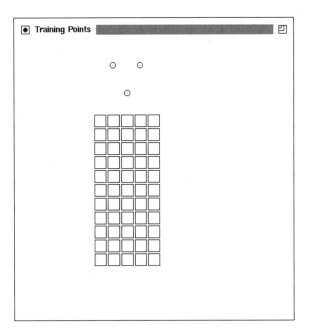

Figure 4.1
Three point trajectors *above* a landmark

4.1   The Problem

This section illustrates the no-negative-evidence problem as it arises in the learning of perceptually grounded semantics for spatial terms. To simplify exposition, only *static* terms are considered, that is, terms that do not involve motion and can thus be represented visually in a single frame. Furthermore, only *punctate* trajectors are used, that is, trajectors consisting of a single point each. Later chapters will cover nonpunctate trajectors, motion, and the integration of the techniques presented here with those other methods.

Imagine a system that is presented with punctate trajectors located relative to nonpunctate landmarks, as illustrated in figure 4.1. Here, the placement of each of the three punctate trajectors, indicated by small dotted circles, constitutes a positive example of English *above*, relative to the tall landmark shown. The system is to learn to associate data such as this with natural language terms for spatial relations. Thus, once it has learned, the system should be able to indicate, for a point trajector at any location relative to a given landmark, how good an example of *above* the relation between that point trajector and the landmark is.

The no-negative-evidence problem arises here, because it is not clear just how to generalize from the positive examples seen. To help illustrate this point, figure 4.2 shows three possible generalizations from the training data shown in

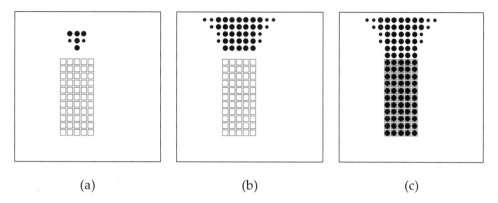

Figure 4.2
Three possible generalizations from the training set for English *above*

figure 4.1. The size of each of the black circles indicates how good an example of *above* the relation between a point at that position and the landmark would be considered. The very small region shown in (a) consists roughly of the convex hull of the training points. (The convex hull of a set X of points is the smallest set of points that is convex and contains X. Intuitively, if one were to stretch a rubber band around a set of points, the rubber band would provide the outline of the convex hull of the set of points.) This, an obvious undergeneralization, is a valid generalization from the training set. The region shown in (b), which generalizes further from the training data than the region in (a), corresponds fairly closely to an English speaker's notion of *above*. Finally, the region shown in (c) generalizes still further, including the interior of the landmark, another valid generalization—and yet an inappropriate overgeneralization—from the training data. Thus, the three figures show undergeneralization, correct generalization, and overgeneralization, all of which are valid given the training data shown in figure 4.1.

The essence of the problem is that without negative evidence, the system will have no way to know where to stop generalizing. Clearly, some generalization is called for, since the correct answer (b) does involve generalizing from the training data. However, since there is no negative evidence to explicitly rule out including the interior of the landmark in the region considered to be *above* the landmark, the system may well include that region as well, as in (c).

Despite this problem, humans do learn to map words onto these concepts, apparently in the absence of negative evidence. The computational work presented in this chapter indicates how that learning might take place and makes contact with relevant work in the child language literature. Although the central ideas discussed here were first developed by others in the context of word learning, and then adapted here in the same context, there is nothing about the

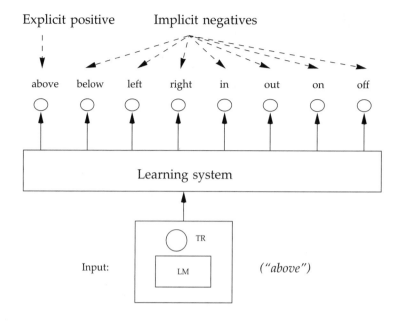

Figure 4.3
The principle of mutual exclusivity

ideas themselves that necessarily restricts their scope to the domain of lexical semantic acquisition. They could easily be applied to any domain characterized by the need to explain learning in the absence of negative evidence. Thus, both the problem and its solution are quite abstract in nature and general in scope.

4.2   A Solution: Mutual Exclusivity

One solution to the no-negative-evidence problem is to take every *positive* instance for one spatial concept to be an *implicit negative* instance for all other spatial concepts being learned. There are problems with this approach, as we shall see, but they are surmountable. Figure 4.3 illustrates this idea by showing how the principle might be applied to a learning system of the sort presented in this book. The input scene is shown at the bottom; this particular scene has been classified by the teacher as a positive instance of English *above*. Therefore, in this one scene we have an explicit positive instance of *above* and implicit negative instances for all other terms being learned. This is indicated at the output nodes at the top of the figure.

This idea and a number of closely related ones may be found in the child language literature. Markman (1987) posits a *principle of mutual exclusivity* for object naming, whereby a child assumes that each object may have only one name. This is to be viewed more as a heuristic learning strategy than as a hard-and-fast rule: clearly, a given object may have many names (*an office chair, a chair, a piece of furniture,* etc.). The method being suggested here really amounts to an application of the principle of mutual exclusivity to the domain of spatial terms: since each spatial relation is assumed to have only one name, we take a positive instance of one to be an implicit negative instance for all others.

In a related vein, Johnston and Slobin (1979) point out that in a study of children learning locative terms in English, Italian, Serbo-Croatian, and Turkish, terms were learned more quickly when there was little or no synonymy among terms. They note that children seem to prefer a one-to-one meaning-to-morpheme mapping; this is similar to, although not quite the same as, the mutual exclusivity notion we are examining here. The two proposals are not the same since a difference in meaning need not correspond to a difference in actual reference. When we call a given object both a *chair* and a *throne,* these are different meanings, and this would thus be consistent with a one-to-one meaning-to-morpheme mapping. It would not be consistent with the principle of mutual exclusivity, however. Johnston and Slobin's principle of one-to-one meaning-to-morpheme mapping also appears as the principle of contrast (Clark 1987) and the principle of uniqueness (Pinker 1989); these are thus also close relatives of Markman's principle of mutual exclusivity. Similar ideas can also be found elsewhere (Bolinger 1965; MacWhinney 1989). The idea is also well established among connectionists. It is often used when training networks on tasks such as handwritten digit recognition (LeCun et al. 1990), in which we are guaranteed that a positive example of a *1,* for instance, will be a good negative example of all other digits. However, it is not generally used when we have no such guarantee. As we shall see, we have no such guarantee here, but we shall still find a way to apply this heuristic.

4.3   Difficulties with Mutual Exclusivity

We shall be seeing illustrations of the principle of mutual exclusivity using simulations run on a prototype version of the computational model with which this book is primarily concerned. Presentation of the model itself will be covered later—for the time being, we shall be examining the manner in which it is trained, and how that can affect its ability to learn without explicit negative evidence. In particular, we shall be considering the learning, in consort, of the eight English spatial terms *above, below, to the left of, to the right of, inside, outside, on,* and *off.* Note that all eight are static; that is, they do not involve motion. These correspond to the terms that label the output nodes in figure 4.3. Bearing this set of terms in mind, let us consider figure 4.1 again. Under mutual exclusivity, if the three dotted circles are considered as positive instances of *above,* they are implicit negatives for all other spatial terms in our contrast set. It is certainly the case that a trajector cannot be both *above* and *in* a landmark; thus, it is reasonable for a positive instance of *above* to yield an implicit negative for *in*

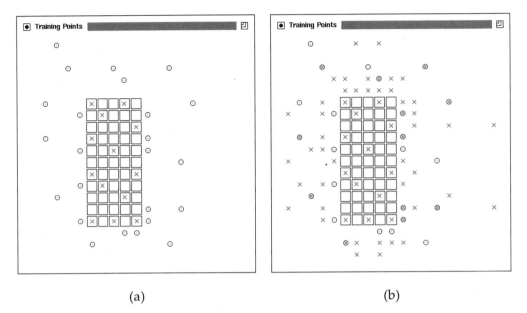

(a)   (b)

Figure 4.4
Ideal and realistic training sets for English *outside*

(and for *below*, among other terms). However, a trajector can be both *above* and *outside* a landmark, or both *above* and *off* a landmark. As an example, all three positive instances for *above* shown in the figure could also be perfectly good positive instances of *outside*, and labeling them as implicit negatives through mutual exclusivity leaves us with a training set that has many *false negatives* in it, that is, implicit negative instances that really should be positives. More generally, any time the principle of mutual exclusivity is applied to a domain in which there is overlap among concepts, the problem of false implicit negatives will arise. This is of course the same problem that we considered briefly in the context of object labeling—the same object can be a chair, a throne, a piece of furniture, a thing, and so on.

Outside is a spatial term that is particularly seriously affected by this problem of false implicit negatives: all of the spatial terms listed above except for *in* (and *outside* itself, of course) will supply false negatives to the training set for *outside*.

The severity of this problem is illustrated in figure 4.4. The two figures shown, which represent two possible sets of training data for the spatial concept *outside*, depict tall, rectangular landmarks, and training points, that is, trajectors consisting of a single point each, relative to the landmarks. Positive training instances are marked with circles; negative instances are marked with Xs. In both (a) and (b) the positive instances were supplied by a teacher. In (a) the negative instances were positioned by the teacher, showing exactly where the region *not* outside the landmark is. This produces a clean training set, but the use of teacher-supplied explicit negative instances is precisely what we are trying to get away from. In (b), on the other hand, the negative instances shown were derived from positive instances for the other spatial terms listed above, through the principle of mutual exclusivity. Thus, this is the sort of training data the model will actually be exposed to, whereas (a) is an idealization we can never hope to encounter in a realistic training situation. Note that in (b) there are many false negative instances among the positives, to say nothing of the positions that have been marked as both positive and negative—these are the positions that have been marked with both a circle and an X.

False implicit negatives pose a critical problem for the principle of mutual exclusivity, one that researchers in child language are quite aware of. Their response has been, very appropriately, to view mutual exclusivity not as an absolute rule governing acquisition, but as a probabilistic bias that can be overridden (Woodward and Markman 1991). As we shall see, the computational work described in this chapter takes this notion of mutual exclusivity as a critical but violable constraint and demonstrates how that conception of the heuristic can in fact account for semantic acquisition in the absence of explicit negative evidence. Thus, the work functions as a proof of concept for an independently existing theory.

4.4   Salvaging Mutual Exclusivity

The basic idea used here, in salvaging the idea of mutual exclusivity, is to treat positive instances and implicit negative instances differently during training. In particular, implicit negatives are viewed as supplying only *weak* negative evidence and in that sense are taken less seriously than the explicit positive evidence encountered. The intuition behind this is as follows: since the implicit negatives are arrived at through the application of a fallible heuristic rule (mutual exclusivity), they should count for less than the positive instances, which are all assumed to be correct. Clearly, the implicit negatives should not be seen as supplying excessively weak negative evidence, or we revert to the original problem of learning in the (virtual) absence of negative instances. Equally clearly, though, the training set noise supplied by false negatives is quite severe, as seen in figure 4.4. This approach is therefore to be seen as a compromise, so that we can use implicit negative evidence without being overwhelmed by the noise it introduces in the training sets for the various spatial concepts.

This amounts to a concrete proposal regarding just how to think about the notion of mutual exclusivity as a violable bias rather than a hard-and-fast rule. As we have seen, child language researchers have acknowledged that mutual exclusivity is profitably viewed as a soft rather than a hard constraint, and the idea of deliberately weakening evidence from implicit negatives is one possible way in which this general idea might be implemented.

The details of this method, and its implementation under back-propagation, are covered below. Note, however, that this is a very general solution to the no-negative-evidence problem, and that it can be understood independently of the actual implementation details. Any learning method that allows for weakening of evidence should be able to make use of it—although nonevidential symbolic systems cannot, which is an argument against their use in this domain. In addition, it could serve as a means for addressing the no-negative-evidence problem in other domains. For example, this implementation of mutual exclusivity as soft constraint rather than hard-and-fast rule could be used for object naming, the domain for which Markman originally suggested the mutual exclusivity heuristic.

4.5   Implementation

The actual network architecture used in the experiments reported in this chapter is a simplified version of the architecture that we shall review fully in the next two chapters. For our purposes here, we need not consider its internal structure in detail; it suffices to note three elemental aspects of its form and function. First, it is important to keep in mind that it accepts input in the form of training points (i.e., punctate trajectors) relative to landmarks, as was shown previously. Second, it must classify its input into one or more of the spatial categories that label the output nodes, as shown at the top of figure 4.3. Third, it is trained under back-propagation (Rumelhart, Hinton, and Williams 1986). The notion of "weakening of evidence from implicit negative instances" is of course very abstract, and we shall see one possible implementation of the general idea, an implementation that makes use of the basic training paradigm for back-propagation. In this sense, the presentation will be back-propagation-specific, although the basic ideas involved are so elementary that they could be trivially transferred to other learning algorithms.

It is assumed that training sets have been constructed using mutual exclusivity as a guiding principle, such that each negative instance in the training set for a given concept results from a positive instance for some other concept.

Evidence from implicit negative instances is weakened simply by attenuating the error caused by these implicit negatives. Thus, an implicit negative instance that yields an error of a given magnitude will contribute less to the weight changes in the network than will a positive instance of the same error magnitude. Referring back to figure 4.3, note that output nodes have been allocated for each of the concepts to be learned. For a network such as this, the usual error term in back-propagation is

$$E = \frac{1}{2} \sum_{i,p} (t_{i,p} - o_{i,p})^2, \tag{4.1}$$

where i indexes over output nodes, and p indexes over training patterns. Here, $t_{i,p}$ is the desired output, and $o_{i,p}$ is the actual output, for node i on pattern p.

We modify this by multiplying the error at each output node by a value $\beta_{i,p}$, dependent on both the node and the current input pattern. In general, $\beta_{i,p}$ corresponds to the amount by which the error signal from node i on pattern p is to be attenuated:

$$E = \frac{1}{2} \sum_{i,p} ((t_{i,p} - o_{i,p}) \times \beta_{i,p})^2. \tag{4.2}$$

For positive instances, $\beta_{i,p}$ is 1.0, so that the error is not attenuated. For an implicit negative instance of a concept, however, $\beta_{i,p}$ takes on some value less than 1.0, such that error signals from implicit negatives are deliberately attenuated. Let us consider a concrete example. If input pattern p is marked as a positive instance of *above*, then the target value for the output node for *above* is 1.0, and the target value for all other output nodes is 0.0—they are implicit negatives. Since we are not weakening evidence from positive instances, $\beta_{above,p} = 1.0$. For all other output nodes however, we deliberately weaken the effect of the error term: $\beta_{j,p} < 1.0, \forall j \neq above$. This is done since the target value for these nodes is determined through the fallible mutual exclusivity heuristic. In this example, then, $\beta_{outside,p} < 1.0$, since *above* is taken less than completely seriously as an implicit negative instance of *outside*.

This idea of differential weighting of evidence from sources of different reliability is used elsewhere in connectionist modeling, in particular in *reinforcement learning*. Under reinforcement learning, the network is simply told whether its output is correct or not; it is not told what the correct answer should be for each of its several output nodes, as is done under supervised learning algorithms such as back-propagation. This introduces an asymmetry into the training process. If the network is told that its output is correct, it knows that the outputs of *all* of its output nodes are correct. On the other hand, if it is told that its output is incorrect, it does not know which of its output nodes are incorrect, and which may be correct—after all, it takes only one incorrect output node to cause the answer as a whole to be wrong. The *associative reward-penalty* algorithm (Barto and Anandan 1985) handles this problem by assuming that if the answer as a whole is wrong, then each individual output node is wrong, a clearly fallible assumption. The evidence obtained on the basis of this assumption is then weighted much less strongly in the training process than is evidence derived from correct answers.

The question of how to set the $\beta_{j,p}$ attenuation values in the case of implicit negatives now arises. There are two general approaches to this issue that have been investigated, and a third that seems promising but has not yet been followed up on. The two methods that have been investigated are *uniform attenuation* and *incorporation of prior knowledge*; the as-yet-untried option is *attenuation adaptation*. Let us examine each of these in turn.

Uniform attenuation is the obvious approach: set the β attenuation value for all implicit negatives to the same quantity, somewhere between 0 and 1. Thus, if pattern p is a positive instance of concept j, set all $\beta_{i,p}$ where $i \neq j$ to the same predetermined value, B. This value B will then be an external parameter that can be set prior to training, much the way learning rate and others usually are. As we shall see, despite its simplicity, this approach has yielded positive results. Uniform attenuation is the only recourse open if one has no prior knowledge whatsoever regarding the relations of the various concepts to be learned.

On the other hand, if prior knowledge is available regarding the manner in which the various concepts interrelate, this can be used to guide the learning process. In particular, if it is known which concepts are disjoint, this knowledge can assist the learning. This is easily done by setting $\beta_{i,p} = 1.0$ for all concepts i that are known to be completely disjoint with the current positive concept j in pattern p. Thus, these concepts will receive strong, rather than attenuated, negative evidence from positive instances of concept j. Analogous treatment is easily arranged if one concept is known to include another. This approach can of course be used in conjunction with the one above, should it be the case that one has only partial knowledge of the ways in which the target concepts interrelate. In this case, certain pairs of concepts will have their β values set according to prior knowledge regarding their distribution relative to one another, and the remainder will take $\beta_{i,p}$ where $i \neq j$ to be the uniform value B, as a default.

Let us consider a concrete application of this idea. One possible source of knowledge regarding which concepts are disjoint comes from *antonyms*. It is at least conceivable that language-learning children are aware that *above* and *below* are opposites before they actually know what the words mean. In other words, they may know that the words form an antonymic pair and therefore that any spatial configuration that is a positive instance of one must be a negative instance of the other. Notice the infallibility of the mutual exclusivity heuristic in this restricted case: if the two words are antonyms, it is not just a good rule of thumb to assume that they are disjoint, it is a certainty. This can be reflected in the β values in the manner described above: any positive instance of *above* would supply unattenuated negative evidence for *below*, and vice versa. The psychological plausibility of this approach of course hinges on the idea of children knowing, prior to learning the semantics of individual spatial terms, that the terms are antonymically paired. There is some suggestive evidence supporting this notion. For example, it is interesting to note that the opposite of *above* is *below* and not *under*, even though *under* is roughly synonymous with *below*. This is of possible relevance since it indicates that it is the words themselves, rather than the meanings, that are antonymically paired. If this lexical pairing were known to children before the word meanings were, the knowledge could be used in acquiring the word meanings, in the manner we have been discussing. In addition, Tomasello (1987) presents psycholinguistic data indicating that English prepositions that are members of antonym pairs (e.g., *in, out, over, under*) are learned earlier than other prepositions that are not (e.g., *by*, *at*). One might suspect that knowledge of which word pairs are antonyms would facilitate learning, and as we shall see, simulation results are consistent with this expectation. Thus, Tomasello's data are consistent with the hypothesis that children bring this knowledge to bear when learning the meanings of spatial terms. Under this interpretation, the antonyms are learned earlier precisely because they are antonyms, and a positive example of one member of the pair can supply unattenuated negative evidence for the other member.

An appealing idea that has not been fully investigated is that of adapting the values $\beta_{i,p}$ during learning. This is a delicate business: it would be possible to learn the β values under back-propagation, but simply following the gradient given by $-\frac{\partial E}{\partial \beta_{i,p}}$, following equation (4.2), will tend toward a solution in which $\beta_{i,p} = 0.0, \forall i \neq j$, where j is the positive concept in pattern p. This is easily shown. Note that $-\frac{\partial E}{\partial \beta_{i,p}} = -\beta_{i,p}(t_{i,p} - o_{i,p})^2$. Since $0 \leq (t_{i,p} - o_{i,p})^2 \leq 1$, following the gradient will result in taking a step of size smaller than or equal to $\beta_{i,p}$ in the negative direction if $\beta_{i,p}$ is positive, and in the positive direction if $\beta_{i,p}$ is negative. This will cause $\beta_{i,p}$ to approach 0. This essentially takes us back to the original situation, in which we had no negative evidence whatsoever—here, we have negative evidence, but it is being given vanishingly little weight. Thus, this will tend to yield overgeneralization from the positive examples. A possible remedy is to add a term in the cost function penalizing trivial solutions of this sort.

Another approach is to set all $\beta_{i,p}$ where $i \neq j$ to a uniform value B, as above, have the system learn the concepts to the best of its ability, and then use observed output correlations between concepts to estimate what the actual overlap in concepts is and thus to estimate what the optimal β values would be. These estimates would then be used in further training, to improve upon the initial results obtained with uniform attenuation. As learning progresses, β estimates closer and closer to the ideal would be obtained from interconcept output correlations and used in further learning.

4.6   Results

The system was trained, using the techniques described in this chapter, on the eight English spatial terms mentioned earlier: *above, below, to the left of, to the right of, inside, outside, on*, and *off*. Figure 4.5 and figure 4.6 show positive training instances for the eight concepts being learned, relative to a vertically extended landmark, and figure 4.7 and figure 4.8 show positive instances for these concepts relative to a horizontally extended landmark; these constitute the positive training data used for the concepts. The principle of mutual exclusivity was used to obtain implicit negative instances in addition to the explicit positive instances supplied by the training sets, and the system was trained on all concepts in parallel.

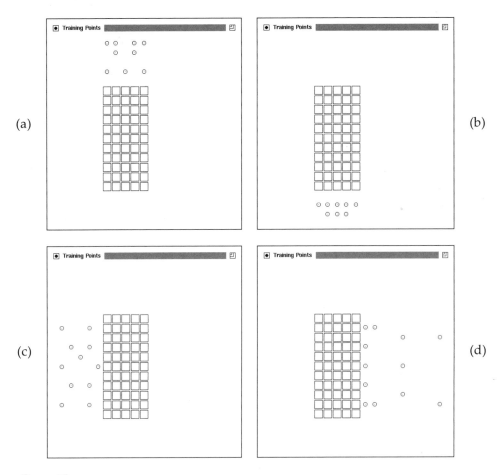

Figure 4.5
Positive instances for English *above, below, to the left of,* and *to the right of* relative to a vertically extended landmark

The first method used was uniform attenuation of error signals from all implicit negative instances. In other words, all $\beta_{i,p} = B$, for some B, where i is not the concept of which pattern p is a positive instance.

Figure 4.9 shows the results of learning the spatial term *outside,* under three different conditions. The term *outside* is of interest because of its particular susceptibility to the problem of false implicit negatives under mutual exclusivity. The size of the black circles indicates the appropriateness, as judged by the trained network, of using the term *outside* to refer to a particular position, relative to the landmark shown. Figure 4.9(a) shows the results of learning without any negative instances whatsoever. As one might expect, this yields gross over-

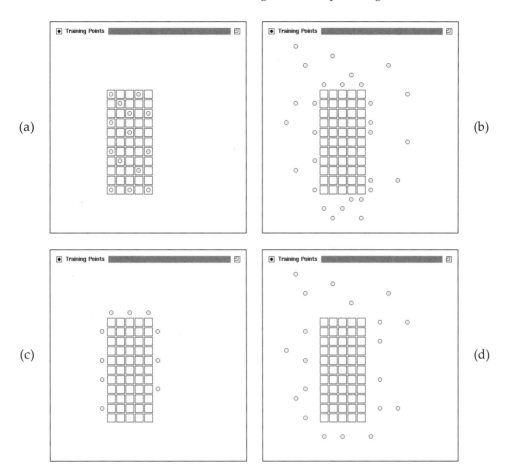

Figure 4.6
Positive instances for English *inside, outside, on,* and *off* relative to a vertically extended landmark

generalization from the positive instances, such that all points inside as well as outside the landmark are considered to be *outside.* Figure 4.9(b) shows the results of learning with implicit negatives, obtained through the mutual exclusivity heuristic, but without weakening the evidence from these negatives—that is, without attenuating the error signal resulting from them. Clearly, the concept is learned very poorly, since the noise from the false implicit negatives hinders the learning process. In general, when mutual exclusivity is used without weakening the evidence given by implicit negatives, the results are not always identical with those shown in figure 4.9(b), but they are always of approximately the same quality—namely, rather poor.

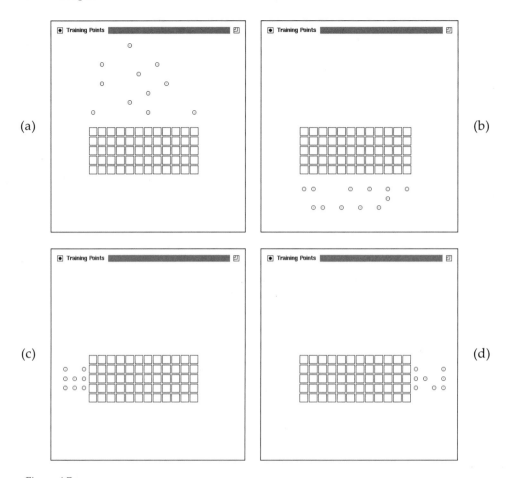

Figure 4.7
Positive instances for English *above, below, to the left of,* and *to the right of* relative to a horizontally extended landmark

Finally, figure 4.9(c) shows the results of learning with implicit negative instances, obtained through mutual exclusivity, such that the evidence from the negatives is weakened, following equation (4.2). The uniform attenuation value $B = 0.03$ was used in the experiment reported here. The concept *outside* is learned far more accurately in this case than in the other two cases, demonstrating the utility of the techniques used here. Having implicit negatives supply only weak negative evidence greatly alleviates the problem of false implicit negatives in the training set, enabling the network to learn without using explicit, teacher-supplied negative instances.

Figure 4.10 and figure 4.11 show the results of learning for all eight concepts in this experiment.

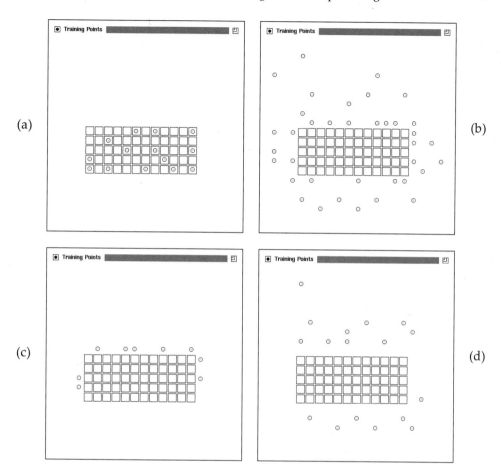

Figure 4.8
Positive instances for English *inside, outside, on,* and *off* relative to a horizontally extended landmark

Experiments were conducted varying the value of B, the uniform attenuation value, with a learning rate of 1.0. For each value of B, the learning was allowed to proceed until the error on an accompanying test set, which included both positive and negative instances of each concept, fell to 0.99. This technique of using the error on an accompanying test set as a criterion for stopping training is known as *cross-validation* (Morgan and Bourlard 1989; Weigend, Huberman, and Rumelhart 1990). The idea is that error on a test set tends to give a better indication of the capability of the trained network to generalize than does error on the training set, since the network has never seen the actual data in the test set. The fact that the total summed squared error on this test set, which contained 593 positive and negative instances in total, reached as low as 0.99 (and indeed as low as 0.86

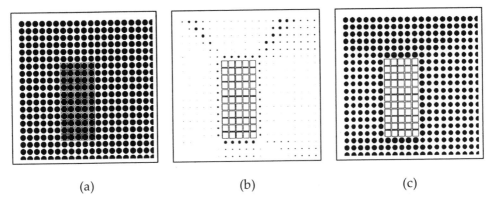

(a)   (b)   (c)

Figure 4.9
English *outside* learned without negatives, and with strong and weak implicit negatives

for $B = 0.03$) indicates that the concepts were learned quite accurately. Note that there was no attenuation of error from negative instances in the test set, only in the training set. Thus, this is evidence that the system neither undergeneralized nor overgeneralized. This can also be seen from figure 4.10 and figure 4.11.

The success of this scheme is somewhat sensitive to the particular value chosen for B, although a fairly broad range was found to be acceptable. Figure 4.12 plots the number of epochs required for the total test set error to reach 0.99 against the value chosen for B. Note that the x-axis scale for B is logarithmic and runs from 0.005 to 0.5. For values of B greater than 0.035, the learning never converged. This indicates that although a range of values for B will yield convergence in fairly short order, the range is definitely limited. Moreover, these results are all for the particular training set described earlier—some change in the value of B may be necessary for other training sets.

Thus, although it would be possible to empirically try to find an acceptable value for B for each training set one wanted the network to learn, a more reasonable approach would be to use this technique in conjunction with others, which may alleviate this problem of sensitivity to the specific B value chosen. Two possibilities are the incorporation into the $\beta_{i,p}$ values of prior knowledge regarding the domain, and some means of adapting the $\beta_{i,p}$ values during learning, as discussed above. Of these two, only the former has been investigated in any detail. Let us consider it now.

If the learning system had access to knowledge that certain concepts were disjoint, this knowledge could be brought to bear on the learning process. We have seen that antonyms can provide a source of such knowledge. For example, if we knew that *above* and *below* were antonyms, and therefore disjoint, we could set $\beta_{above,p} = 1.0$ for all patterns p that were positive instances of *below*, and $\beta_{below,p} = 1.0$ for all patterns p that were positive instances of *above*. All remaining $\beta_{i,p}$ values would be set to the uniform attenuation value, B. Intuitively, this

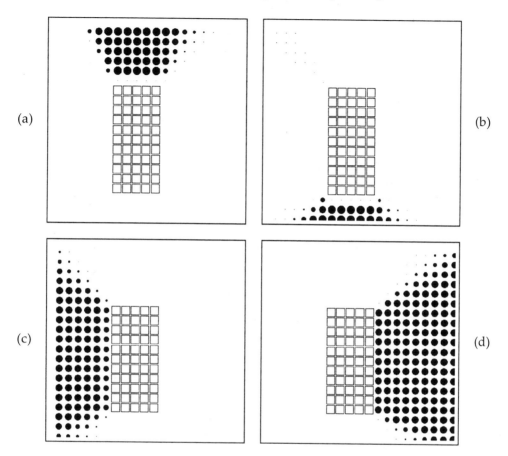

Figure 4.10
English *above, below, to the left of,* and *to the right of* learned with weakened implicit negatives

means taking implicit negative evidence seriously, provided it comes from a source we know to be reliable, and otherwise, taking it less seriously.

A set of experiments was conducted in which this technique was used. Specifically, *above* and *below* were treated as antonyms, as were the pairs *left/right, in/out,* and *on/off.* Thus, negative evidence was unattenuated within these pairs. The results are displayed in figure 4.13. Here we see the dependence of convergence time on *B* in two cases. The first is the case of uniform attenuation, as described above. Thus, the solid line in figure 4.13 is identical to the one in figure 4.12. The second is the case of no attenuation in the case of antonym pairs, and uniform attenuation otherwise; this is the dotted line in the figure.

It is clear that incorporation into the system of knowledge about which terms are antonyms assists the learning, helping the system reach a test set error of 0.99

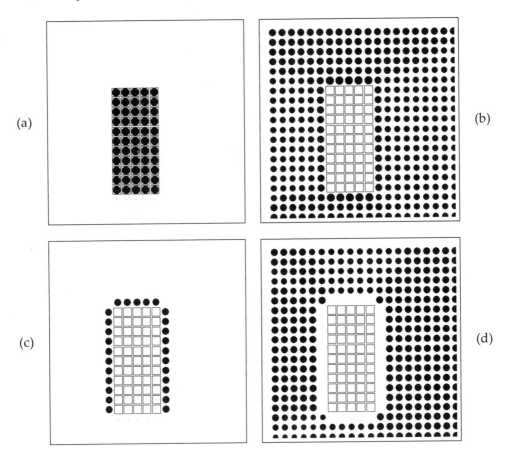

Figure 4.11
English *inside, outside, on,* and *off* learned with weakened implicit negatives

in a shorter amount of time than is required without this built-in knowledge. In addition, the system is less sensitive to the exact value of B chosen. This can be seen from the gentler slope in the case of antonym knowledge. As we saw earlier, there is psycholinguistic evidence indicating that those lexemes that are members of antonym pairs are learned earlier by children, suggesting that knowledge of antonym pairings may facilitate learning (Tomasello 1987). These simulation results are consistent with that interpretation, since they indicate a facility in learning conferred by knowledge of antonyms.

The learning is somewhat more accurate, as well. Figure 4.14 presents the concept *outside,* learned first without knowledge of antonym pairings, then with this knowledge. As can be seen from the figures, the concept is more accurately learned in the latter case—the black circles are larger in the area outside the

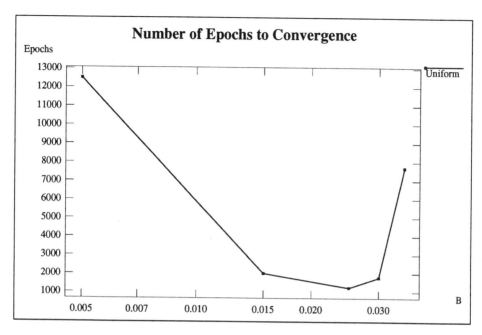

Figure 4.12
Epochs to convergence as a function of B: uniform attenuation

landmark in (b) than in (a), indicating a stronger response to a point trajector at that location. This fact is also reflected in the minimum total summed squared error over the test set obtained in the two cases: using knowledge of antonym pairings, the minimum test error obtained was 0.37 over 593 test instances, as compared with 0.86 without this knowledge. Thus, incorporation into the learning system of prior knowledge regarding the distribution of concepts relative to one another can lessen the problem of sensitivity to the particular attenuation value B chosen and can yield more accurate learning of the concepts overall.

We have seen in this chapter that the technique of mutual exclusivity using weak implicit negatives provides a means for learning in the absence of explicit negative evidence. Although knowledge of antonyms facilitates the learning, perhaps the most important point made here is that learning is also possible in the absence of any such knowledge, on the strength of the mutual exclusivity heuristic alone. As we have seen, the idea of mutual exclusivity as a violable bias has been addressed in the child language literature, and the work presented here amounts to a concrete demonstration that that general idea does in fact provide a workable solution to the problem of learning without negative evidence. In the process, it also provides a specific interpretation of the notion of mutual exclusivity as a bias rather than a hard constraint, an interpretation shown to be effective.

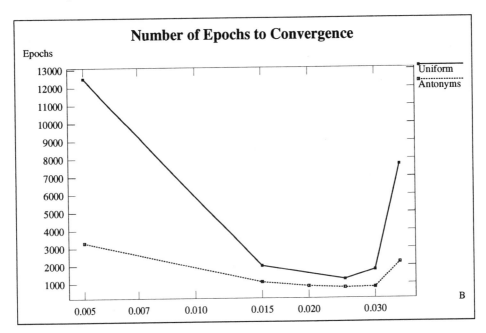

Figure 4.13
Epochs to convergence as a function of *B*: uniform attenuation versus antonym pairings

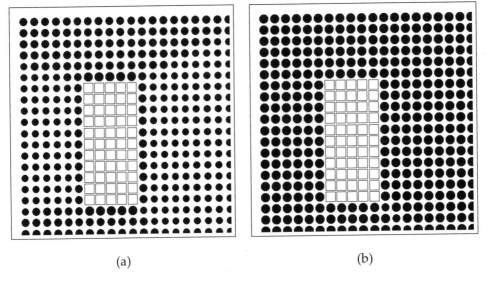

Figure 4.14
English *outside* learned without, then with, knowledge of antonyms

As noted at the outset of this book, one of its central themes is the intimate interrelatedness of two general frameworks, the scientific and the methodological, within which a model such as the current one might be viewed. In particular, it is claimed that a computational modeling effort directed at a particular line of scientific inquiry can, in the modeling process, produce techniques of general applicability. The method presented in this chapter, the use of weak implicit negative instances arrived at through the principle of mutual exclusivity, provides an example of such a general technique springing from a very specific modeling effort. The technique is general enough in character that it could be used in a straightforward manner in domains having nothing to do with spatial relations or semantics, to effect learning without the benefit of explicit negative instances.

Chapter 5
Structures

5.1   *Structures and Constrained Connectionism*

Constrained connectionism is best thought of as the incorporation of a significant amount of domain-specific structure into a parallel distributed processing (PDP) network. As we saw earlier, this is done with a number of very general but significant goals in mind. Prior structuring can enhance the generalization capacity of the network, by excluding obviously inappropriate solutions from consideration during the learning process. In addition, it can make the network more easily analyzable, in that the structures will allow some things to be learned but not others—and we will generally be able to articulate clearly what those things are. Finally, if the structures themselves are independently motivated, they can help to motivate the model as a whole. Thus, this incorporation of structure is central to the constrained connectionist enterprise generally; and this means that the choice and design of these structures are critical in the building of such a model. If they are well designed and independently motivated, the result will be an easily analyzable and well-motivated model of the process under study. On the other hand, if they are unmotivated and designed in a manner inappropriate for the task at hand, they will not help to motivate the overall model in any way and will hamper, rather than facilitate, the learning process. In this sense, the design of these structures is the scientific crux of the model as a whole—the model will either stand or fall on the strength of these structures.

With this in mind, then, let us look at three general architectural principles concerning the linguistic categorization of space. These principles will be realized in the structures of the model. They will therefore provide the primary constraint on the model's operation, and their theoretical importance stems from this fact. The principles are *orientation combination, map comparison,* and a *source-path-destination* structuring of motion trajectories. We will be able to adduce some form of motivation for each of these principles and the corresponding structures in the model. In each case we will start by examining a few examples and the general principles they suggest, and then move on to the corresponding structures. We will also consider independent motivation for these structures.

Before we dive into the specifics, however, one brief caveat: the analysis presented here concerns spatial relations between *convex* objects. This should

82   Chapter 5

not be taken to mean that nonconvex objects lie outside our realm of discourse. Rather, convex objects provide a psychologically motivated and convenient starting point. The motivation for considering convex objects first comes from evidence that nonconvex objects are perceptually parsed into their constituent convex subparts (Hoffman and Richards 1985). This indicates that convex objects have a perceptually privileged status and are therefore a reasonable place to begin analysis. In chapter 7 we shall extend the analysis proposed here to nonconvex objects as well.

5.2   Orientation Combination

The idea of orientation combination is extremely simple. As we shall see, it seems to be the case that a number of different orientational features play a role in linguistically characterizing the overall orientation of a trajector relative to a landmark. In other words, the categorization of a given configuration as *above*, or *below*, or some other relation, relies on a convergence of evidence from a number of sources. No single one of the features involved seems to be sufficient on its own. One point of interest here is that this sort of mechanism very naturally gives rise to prototype effects: a prototypical instance of some spatial term is one for which there is strong evidence from each of the various features, whereas less prototypical cases do not exhibit this sort of unanimity across the relevant sources of evidence.

Let us make this discussion more concrete by looking at some simple examples of the English preposition *above*. Figure 5.1 presents two scenes; the one on the left is a good example of English *above*, whereas the one on the right is not, at least not in my estimation. The only difference between the two is the absence of the "supporting" triangle in the scene on the right. Thus, it is clear that the physical context in which a spatial relation occurs can profoundly influence the way it is categorized linguistically. Herskovits (1986) provides several other examples

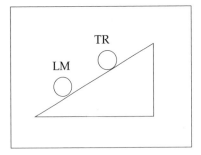 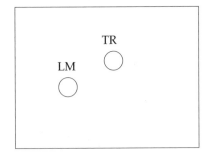

Figure 5.1
The role of context

illustrating the effect of physical context on the linguistic categorization of spatial relations, so we can be assured this is not an isolated phenomenon. This example is interesting because it helps to weed out some naive first-cut characterizations of *above*, such as "the center of mass of the trajector is located higher in the visual field than the center of mass of the landmark." This characterization is clearly not correct, since it is unaffected by physical context.

A more satisfying approach is suggested by some recent work in perceptual psychology. Freyd, Pantzer, and Cheng (1988) present intriguing evidence that humans viewing static scenes (such as the ones in figure 5.1) mentally represent the forces that are acting on the objects, keeping them where they are. They presented subjects with three pictures of a potted plant, first supported from below (sitting on a table), then hanging in midair without support at the same height as in the first picture, and finally once again in midair without support, either in the original position or slightly above or below the original position. Subjects were asked whether the final frame showed the plant at the same height as the first two. The results indicated that subjects had a tendency to misjudge the position of the plant in the final frame, often judging it to be at the original position when it was in fact slightly lower. The authors also conducted an analogous experiment in which the plant was first shown supported from above (hanging from a hook) rather than from below, and obtained the same results. The authors take this, along with the results of similar experiments, as evidence that subjects represent the forces implicit in static scenes: when they are shown a situation in which a force that was previously present has been removed, they mentally represent the unfreezing of potential motion that is enabled by the removal of the counterbalancing force. This notion of unfreezing of potential motion is helpful in considering the case of figure 5.1; for if balanced force and potential motion are part of what humans mentally represent when they perceive static scenes, then English *above* could well have a component of such potential motion in it. On this view, part of what *above* denotes is the possibility of the trajector striking the landmark if it is allowed to fall under the influence of gravity. More specifically, if the *direction of potential motion*, illustrated in figure 5.2, tends to lead the trajector to the landmark, this could be taken as evidence for *above*. This would explain figure 5.1, since the direction of potential motion leads the trajector to the landmark in the scene on the left, but not in the scene on the right, and it can also explain some more straightforward instances of *above*.

The direction of potential motion does not suffice for characterizing even as simple a term as *above*, however, although it may well play an important part in the overall story. Its insufficiency can be seen by considering figure 5.3, which presents one good and one poor example of English *above*. Note that in both cases, the direction of potential motion of the trajector, were it to suddenly be released from its position, would lead it downward to strike the landmark. The

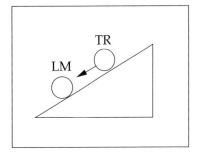

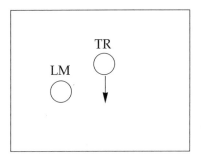

Figure 5.2
Direction of potential motion

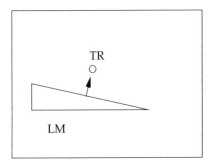

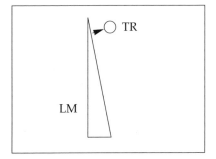

Figure 5.3
Good and poor examples of English *above*

fact that these two cases are not equally good examples of *above* thus indicates that there is more to the concept than the simple characterization outlined above, relying exclusively on the direction of potential motion of the trajector.

The idea, then, is that even very basic spatial concepts such as *above* in fact involve a combination of evidence from various sources, the direction of potential motion being only one of these. Let us consider two others.

Two perceptual primitives that seem to play a role in the linguistic categorization of space are the *proximal orientation* and *center-of-mass orientation* of a scene. These both specify the location of the trajector with respect to the landmark, but in different ways. The proximal orientation is the orientation of the imaginary directed line segment connecting the landmark to the trajector where the two objects are closest. The center-of-mass orientation, on the other hand, is the orientation of the imaginary directed line segment connecting the center of mass of the landmark to that of the trajector. Figure 5.4 illustrates both the proximal and center-of-mass orientations in a single scene.

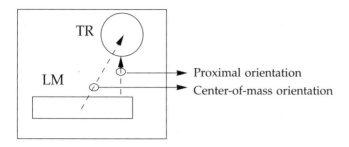

Figure 5.4
Proximal and center-of-mass orientations

A motivation for introducing the proximal orientation as a primitive comes from figure 5.3. Recall that the direction of potential motion did nothing to differentiate these two cases, one of which is a good example, and the other a poor one, of English *above*. The proximal orientation, on the other hand, is very different in the two cases: in the scene on the left, it is very nearly upright vertical (and this corresponds to our intuitive notion that *above* is intimately related to upright vertical), whereas in the scene on the right, the proximal orientation is far from upright vertical. Thus, it is at least possible that this difference is what causes the scenes to be judged differently as examples of English *above*.

However, this cannot be the entire story either. Figure 5.5 presents two more examples of English *above*, again, one good and one poor. The one on the left is essentially identical to the left-hand scene in figure 5.3. The one on the right, on the other hand, was produced from the one on the left by sliding the trajector down the slope of the triangle until it was near the bottom. Notice that the direction of potential motion and the proximal orientation do not vary across these two scenes. Thus, some other feature must account for the difference in judgment. The center-of-mass orientation does vary, and may well be the deciding factor.

Implicit in the discussion so far has been the notion of *orientational alignment:* the degree to which one orientation, such as the proximal orientation, aligns with another, such as upright vertical. In general, I shall call orientations that describe the location of the trajector relative to the landmark *relational orientations;* examples are the proximal and center-of-mass orientations. I shall call those orientations to which these are compared *reference orientations;* examples of these are upright and downward vertical, left and right, and the major and minor axes of the landmark object. We shall be examining, in general, the degree to which a relational orientation aligns with a reference orientation. For example, we might want to know how well the center-of-mass and proximal orientations align with upright vertical. Consider figure 5.6. This figure shows the proximal and center-of-mass orientations between the landmark and the trajector (in dashed lines),

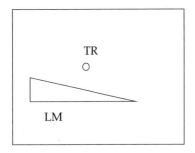 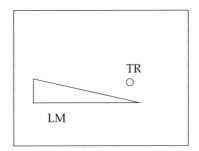

Figure 5.5
More good and poor examples of English *above*

and the degree to which each of these two relational orientations aligns with upright vertical, a reference orientation. The general idea being proposed here is that this notion of focusing on the degree of alignment between relational and reference orientations is a useful way to approach the issue of the spatial orientation of two objects. More particularly, the principle of orientation combination holds that the degrees of alignment between a number of relational orientations and a number of reference orientations will combine to yield a characterization of the overall orientation of the trajector relative to the landmark.

Let us make this concrete by considering *above* again. The orientational features being posited here are the center-of-mass orientation, the proximal orientation, and the direction of potential motion. How would these enter into *above* judgments? We would begin by calculating the degree of alignment of these relational orientations with these reference orientations:

> proximal orientation with upright vertical
> center-of-mass orientation with upright vertical
> proximal orientation with direction of potential motion plus π
> center-of-mass orientation with direction of potential motion plus π

Notice that when comparing the proximal and center-of-mass orientations with the direction of potential motion, we really want to be comparing them with the direction of potential motion plus π (i.e., that direction 180 degrees opposed to the direction of potential motion). This is so because the direction of potential motion describes potential motion of the trajector, possibly toward the landmark, whereas the proximal and center-of-mass orientations describe orientations originating at the landmark and headed toward the trajector. To make the two sorts of orientational features compatible, we need to reverse the directionality of one set or the other, and I chose to do this with the direction of potential motion.

In any event, the important point here is that the principle of orientation combination suggests that *above* judgments will involve a weighted combination of the four alignments listed above. No statement is made regarding the

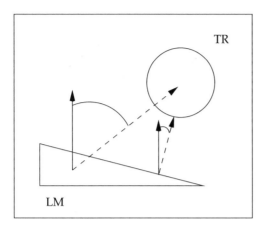

Figure 5.6
Orientational alignment

relative weights of these four orientational sources of evidence—in the model, these weights will be set by back-propagation. But the sources of evidence are specified, and we know we will be taking some weighted sum over them. This, then, is the basic idea of orientation combination.

What sort of mechanism could do this for us? Let us start by focusing on orientational alignment, that is, the determination of how well a given relational orientation lines up with a reference orientation. This can be easily measured using a simple Gaussian of the sines and cosines of the two orientations:

$$f_\theta(r) = \exp\left[-\frac{(sin(\theta) - sin(r))^2 + (cos(\theta) - cos(r))^2}{\sigma^2} \right]. \tag{5.1}$$

Here, r is the relational orientation, and θ is the reference orientation with which it is being compared. Both orientations are represented in radians, such that the values 0, $\pi/2$, π, and $3\pi/2$ correspond to the four cardinal directions "right," "up," "left," and "down." In practice, this function is tuned through the θ parameter for a particular reference orientation value, such as upright vertical, and measures the degree to which the input relational orientation r aligns with that reference orientation. The function will return its maximal value of 1.0 when r is perfectly aligned with the reference orientation θ and will drop off as r deviates from θ. The overall shape of the function can be seen in figure 5.7, which plots the function $f_\theta(r)$ against the relational orientation r, for $\theta = 0$. In other words, the figure shows the response of this function, which has been tuned to respond maximally to a reference orientation pointing directly to the right, to a range of relational orientation values. Clearly, the function responds maximally when the relational orientation r is aligned with the reference orientation, in this case at the value 0. The σ parameter in the equation controls the width of the Gaussian.

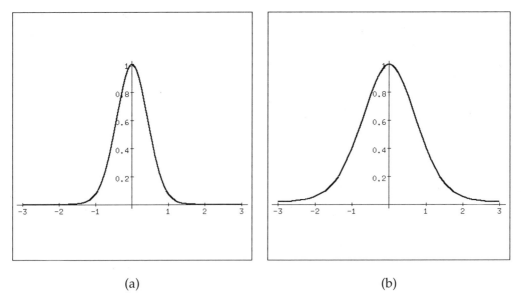

(a)   (b)

Figure 5.7
Gaussians for determining orientational alignment

In the figure, (a) and (b) show the shape of the function with σ set to 0.6 and 1.0, respectively. A smaller value for σ yields a more sharply peaked response. Thus, by adjusting this parameter, we can control how closely the two orientations must align in order to yield a response of appreciable strength.

This fairly simple construct will measure orientational alignment. But what does it have to do with connectionism? Can it be implemented in a manner allowing straightforward incorporation into a connectionist network? It can, using a simple node of the sort illustrated in figure 5.8. This type of node, which I shall call a θ-node, compares an input relational orientation r with the reference orientation θ for which the node is tuned and returns the value $f_\theta(r)$ as defined above. For example, the node might be tuned to respond rather sharply to a relational orientation value of 0, in which case the response profile as a function of r would be similar to that shown in figure 5.7(a). Note that the relational orientation r is supplied as input to the node, whereas the reference orientation θ and the σ width parameter are stored in variables internal to the node. This means that once nodes of this sort are embedded in a network trained under back-propagation, the learning algorithm itself can adjust the values of the internal variables shown here, just as it adjusts the weights on interunit connections. In the model we shall be examining, the σ values for all θ-nodes in the system acquire their values through training under back-propagation. As the figure also indicates, the reference orientation θ may be supplied externally. This will be

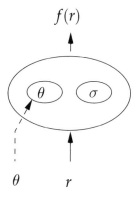

Figure 5.8
Internal structure of a single θ-node

the reference orientation is itself extracted from the image—for ex-
he case of the direction of potential motion, since that may change
to frame. In contrast, other reference orientations such as upright
fixed and unchanging.

n, is an implementation of the idea of orientational alignment. But the
al notion we have been pushing for is that of orientation combina-
mbination of evidence from several sources of information regarding
tion of the trajector relative to the landmark. This is easily accom-
taking a weighted sum of the outputs of a number of θ-nodes. Since
isely what the interlayer connections in a multilayer perceptron do
e combination aspect follows quite naturally from the connectionist
. In fact, orientation *combination* in and of itself does not require any
lt structures—the only such structures required here are the θ-nodes
for orientational alignment.

Let us consider how a set of θ-nodes might work in consort, and combine
their evidence. Figure 5.9 presents the simplest possible example of orientation
combination. Here we see two θ-nodes connected to a unit labeled c above
them—unit c receives the weighted output of the θ-nodes. The activation function
of c is the usual sigmoidal squashing function $f(x) = 1/(1 + e^{-x})$ customarily
used in networks trained under back-propagation. Thus, c is an ordinary hidden
unit like any other in a multilayer perceptron, except that it receives its input
from θ-nodes. The θ-nodes here are each labeled $f_\uparrow$, indicating that their reference
orientation is upright vertical. One of the θ-nodes compares the center-of-mass
orientation to upright vertical, and the other compares the proximal orientation
to it (recall from figure 5.6 that the degrees of alignment of these two relational
orientations with upright vertical will not necessarily be the same). Orientation
combination is achieved at c, which takes the weighted sum of the outputs

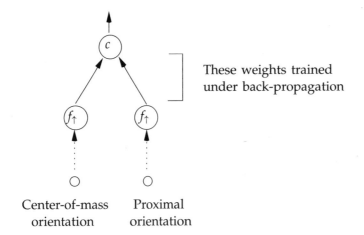

These weights trained
under back-propagation

Center-of-mass   Proximal
    orientation   orientation

Figure 5.9
Combination of evidence from two θ-nodes

of the two θ-nodes as input to its activation function. As we saw earlier, this combination appears to play a role in categorizations such as English *above*. Note that the weights on the connections from the θ-nodes to c are trained under back-propagation, as are the σ variables controlling the width of the Gaussian in each of the θ-nodes. This means that although we can specify in broad outline what this structure will do—namely, orientation combination—we cannot ascertain in advance exactly what form the combination will take—that will be determined by the training algorithm. This is a specific instantiation of a more general constrained connectionist idea: building in architectural constraints so that one may determine the general parameters of the model's behavior ahead of time. One cannot foresee exactly what the behavior of the model as a whole will be, however. Determining that will require simulation.

This was the simplest possible example. In actuality, more than this enters into categorizations of *above* and related words. We saw earlier that there is good reason to believe that the direction of potential motion also plays a role. We also saw that in Mixtec the major axis orientation of the landmark is significant. These and other reference and relational orientations may all have a role to play. But the way in which they play that role will be precisely the same as that outlined here: θ-nodes checking for alignment between relational and reference orientations, and combination of evidence from these θ-nodes.

This, then, is the manner in which orientation combination will be implemented in the model. Now, what independent motivation is there for all of this? Is there any indication that structures such as these might guide human perception, apart from the informal demonstrations we considered above? Are such structures present in the brain? Although there are no known neuroanatomical structures that correspond directly to θ-nodes, it is well known that the majority of cells in visual cortex are sensitive to the orientation of visual stimuli (Hubel and Wiesel 1959, 1962). These cells respond maximally to a visual stimulus at the orientation for which they are tuned, and response drops off as the stimulus deviates from that preferred orientation, much in the manner of θ-nodes. Thus, the basic principle of orientation sensitivity of visual cortical cells is well established. The difference is that the cells found in visual cortex respond to the orientation of physical luminance discontinuities in the image itself, rather than to the orientations of more abstract (indeed, invisible) entities such as the center-of-mass orientation. However, in this regard, it is worth noting that von der Heydt, Peterhans, and Baumgartner (1984) have shown that cells in area 18 of monkey visual cortex are sensitive to the orientations of *illusory contours*. These are contours that are perceived by human observers of particular visual stimuli, but that do not correspond to physical luminance discontinuities in the image (see Kanizsa 1979 for a review of this phenomenon). These results are striking because they indicate that there are cells in visual cortex that respond to orientations that are not physically present in the image. Thus, the principle of sensitivity to nonphysical orientations has a precedent, even if not for the particular nonphysical orientations we are concerned with here. These results can be viewed as a general, loose form of motivation for θ-nodes. The motivation is perhaps strengthened somewhat by the observation that orientation-sensitive cells with response profiles qualitatively similar to those of θ-nodes can be found in other areas of the brain as well, responding to the directions of arm movements (Kalaska, Caminiti, and Georgopoulos 1983; Georgopoulos, Schwartz, and Kettner 1986), eye movements (Henn and Cohen 1976), and head position (Suzuki, Timerick, and Wilson 1985). This indicates that the mechanism is a very general and widely used one. Thus, although there is no direct evidence for cells corresponding exactly to θ-nodes, there is a good deal of evidence that the general principle they embody is used in a number of cortical areas.

There is some evidence supporting the particular choices of relational and reference orientations made so far. Hirsch and Mjolsness (1992) present psychophysical data suggesting that the human visual system represents the center of mass: the precision of discrimination in a random dot displacement task was well captured by a model based on the extraction of the center of mass of the random dots and only rather poorly captured by other, more local, models. This provides motivation for the use of the center-of-mass orientation as an orientational feature. Another source of motivation comes from the work of Huttenlocher, Hedges, and Duncan (1991). They presented subjects with a dot randomly located within a circle and asked the subjects to indicate in a second blank circle where the dot was located in the first circle. They found that subjects exhibited a consistent radial bias away from the center of the circle, and to a lesser extent away from the circumference of the circle, and also a consistent angular bias away from the horizontal and vertical axes. Neither the center nor the axes were explicitly marked on either circle. This suggests that subjects structure the circle by imposing the horizontal and vertical axes on it, providing some motivation for the choice of directions along these axes as reference orientations in the model. It also suggests that subjects similarly represent the center of mass of the circle, which again motivates the use of the center-of-mass orientation as a relational orientation here. There are also very general arguments one can make to the effect that it is evolutionarily advantageous for an organism to be able to detect the center of mass of an object, so as to be able to effectively manipulate it. Similarly, one might argue that it is advantageous to keep track of the closest point on an object for obstacle-avoidance purposes, and this provides an equally loose form of motivation for the use of the proximal orientation. In the case of proximal orientation, this is the extent of the motivation. However, as we saw earlier, there is psychophysical evidence supporting the idea that the visual system encodes the direction of potential motion (Freyd, Pantzer, and Cheng 1988). In sum, there is some motivation for these relational and reference orientations, enough that I would be remiss not to mention it, despite its incomplete and sometimes informal character.

Interestingly, there is neurophysiological evidence suggesting something similar to the idea of orientation combination. Georgopoulos, Schwartz, and Kettner (1986), in studying the motor control of arm movements in the monkey, discovered a situation reminiscent of that proposed here for the linguistic categorization of spatial configurations. In particular, they identified a population of direction-sensitive cells, each tuned to a preferred direction, and each with a response profile similar to those of the θ-nodes described above. Thus, each cell responded maximally to an arm movement in its preferred direction, and less strongly to movements in other directions. So far, this finding is similar to the others we saw above, showing the general principle of orientation sensitivity in a number of areas of the brain. The aspect of this finding that distinguishes it from the others is that Georgopoulos, Schwartz, and Kettner found that although no single one of these cells predicted the direction of movement of the monkey's arm, the direction of movement could be very accurately and consistently predicted by a *weighted vector sum* over the population as a whole: if the preferred direction of each cell was weighted by the output of the cell, the resulting vector sum was in the same direction as the arm movement. This is not the same as the sort of orientation combination proposed above and illustrated in figure 5.9, but it shares some features with it. In both cases, the output o_i of each of a set of orientation-sensitive cells is multiplied by some quantity a_i and summed: $\sum_i o_i a_i$. In the case of the cells observed by Georgopoulos, Schwartz, and Kettner the quantity a_i was the vector corresponding to cell i's preferred direction, whereas in our case the quantity a_i is a scalar, a weight whose value is determined under back-propagation. Another important difference of course is that the findings of Georgopoulos, Schwartz, and Kettner concern motor cortex rather than visual cortex. Nonetheless, they indicate that something similar to the principle we are adopting here characterizes known neural structures, and thus they help to motivate the structures actually used here.

This is of course a far cry from a complete reductionist grounding for the spatial semantics task. I simply do not believe that such a thorough reduction is feasible at this time, although I would be delighted to be proven wrong. What I have done instead is outline a number of disparate sources of motivation for the orientation combination structures, each of which indicates that the general ideas adopted here are similar to functional principles characterizing actual neural structures. Therefore, the motivation is kept at that level, rather than at the level of a more specific structure-to-structure isomorphism. In considering the validity of motivation of this sort, it is perhaps worthwhile keeping in mind what the alternative is: no motivation—structure called into existence primarily to fit the data, rather than on other, more independent grounds.

5.3   Map Comparison

The second architectural principle that we shall see instantiated in network structures is map comparison, which is used in the detection of such topological features as contact and inclusion. The basic idea here is that these topological features may be detected by observing the trajector boundary and seeing if it or portions of it lie within, or immediately adjacent to, the landmark. For example, if each point on the trajector boundary is located within the landmark, then we know that the trajector as a whole lies within the landmark, as in figure 5.10(a); and if at least one point of the trajector boundary is immediately adjacent to the landmark, but none of the trajector boundary is actually within the landmark, then we know that the trajector as a whole is in contact with the landmark, but has not penetrated it, as in figure 5.10(b). Thus, the very general idea being suggested here is that these topological features can be detected by attending to the *boundary* of the trajector and determining the relation of each point along this boundary to the *interior* of the landmark.

It is important to distinguish two different cases here. There are situations in which the fraction of the trajector boundary along which some perceptual feature occurs is not relevant—rather, all that is relevant is that the feature occurred at some point. Consider English *on*, for example, as illustrated in figure 5.11. It makes no difference how much of the trajector boundary is in contact with the landmark; (a) and (b) are equally good examples of *on*. What is significant is that there is contact at some point. Of course, the underlying reason for this is that it is critical to *on* that the landmark *support* the trajector. And visually, support

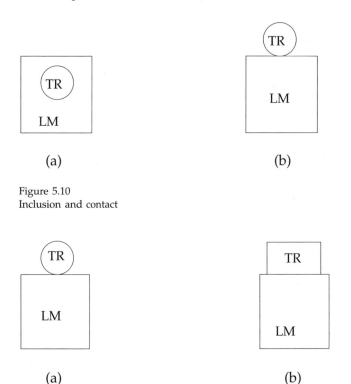

Figure 5.10
Inclusion and contact

Figure 5.11
English *on*: contact at at least one point along the trajector boundary

may be manifested by contact at a single point, or along a larger part of the trajector boundary. The point here is that even though the semantics for words such as *on* appear to involve the nonvisual notions of support and force, and even though we know from our discussion of the direction of potential motion that there is evidence that humans do mentally represent forces when viewing static scenes, the actual categorization of a spatial configuration as either *on* or not must rely ultimately on the visual correlate of support, an important element of which is contact. This is the case since support is not directly perceptible. And since support can be manifested in contact at a single point or along a longer stretch of the trajector boundary, our model will have to be constructed so as to be able to learn to respond equally to scenes (a) and (b).

On the other hand, there are cases in which the fraction of the trajector boundary along which a perceptual feature occurs is linguistically significant. As an example of this, consider English *in*, illustrated in figure 5.12. Here, (a) is an excellent example of *in*, (b) is a fair one, and (c) is a poor one. This graded

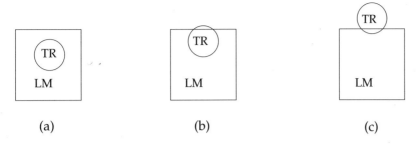

(a)   (b)   (c)

Figure 5.12
English *in*: inclusion along the length of the trajector boundary

response varies directly with the proportion of the trajector boundary that lies within the landmark, in contrast with the insensitivity that we saw in the case of English *on*. The model should be able to learn to exhibit behavior of both sorts.

What sort of structure might underlie this behavior? The very general notion of comparison along the trajector boundary can be easily effected if the landmark and trajector are held in separate topographic maps that are kept in register with each other. Figure 5.13 illustrates an input frame containing a circular trajector above a rectangular landmark, and the separation of these two objects out into their respective *boundary maps*, maps containing each object's outline. The figure also shows the landmark *interior map*, a map in which both the landmark's outline and its interior are activated. In the figure, the trajector boundary map is shown in line with the landmark interior map since these two maps are the ones that will be compared in the detection of the topological features we are concerned with here. All three maps are kept in register, such that the objects keep the same position within the maps that they had in the original input frame.

As we shall see, this configuration of separate topographic maps helps us in the detection of features such as inclusion and contact. Before we look at just how this is done, though, let us pause to consider a question that is implicitly raised by even the minimal amount of structure we have posited so far—namely, how is the interior of the landmark computed? How is the landmark boundary filled in to yield the landmark interior?

This filling-in operation is accomplished using a simple spreading mechanism, similar to the *visual routine* of spreading activation proposed by Ullman (1984). The actual method used is illustrated in figure 5.14. We begin by activating every pixel in the landmark interior map, such that the entire map is black. We then pick some point on the perimeter of the scene, which is assumed to lie outside the object, and deactivate the pixel at that point. Each neighbor of this deactivated pixel in the map is then deactivated, and the deactivation spreads out from pixel to pixel, until the object boundary is reached. We can tell we have reached a pixel that corresponds to the object boundary because the corresponding pixel in

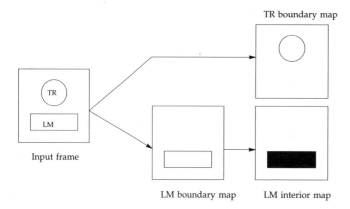

Figure 5.13
Separate landmark and trajector maps

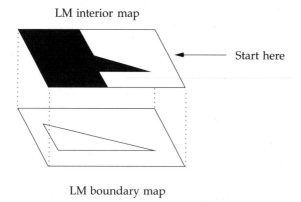

Figure 5.14
Computing the interior of an object

the landmark *boundary* map is activated. The boundary is never deactivated, and therefore the interior of the object is never deactivated either. The resulting map contains a filled-in copy of the original outline. (Note that the algorithm assumes that everything inside the landmark boundary is interior. This means that if it were applied to a "doughnut" outline, that is, to a landmark boundary that consisted of a circle with a smaller circle nested within it, the interior detected by the algorithm would be the interior of the larger surrounding circle, rather than an annulus.)

Now, how can the various maps just introduced be of use to us? How can they implement the general idea of feature detection along the trajector boundary?

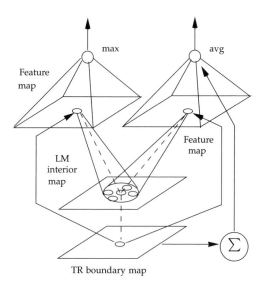

Figure 5.15
Map comparison structure

The map comparison structure that does this is illustrated in figure 5.15. To begin with, notice that the trajector boundary map and the landmark interior map lie within this structure. Directly above the landmark interior map, and receiving input from both it and the trajector boundary map, are two *feature maps*. These feature maps, together with their connections to the maps below, constitute the core of this structural device. Let us zoom in to take a closer look, so as to understand the operation of the structure as a whole. Figure 5.16 presents a single feature map and its connections to the other maps. The feature map is simply a map of units, with a *head node* at the top taking some function of the entire map; this function is either the maximum or the average value of the nodes in the feature map.

Three forms of structuring are built into the feature map. In the first place, each node in the feature map is gated by the node in the corresponding position in the trajector boundary map, such that the feature map node responds only if the node in the trajector boundary map is activated. In addition, each feature map node has a very highly localized receptive field, examining only the node directly beneath it in the landmark interior map and that node's four nearest neighbors. This in general yields a very simple center-surround receptive field. Finally, the weights of corresponding links at all different positions are constrained to be identical, through weight sharing. This implies that there are actually only five *weights* to be adjusted for a single feature map, despite all the links: one for the center links and four for the surround links. In fact, the four surround links may

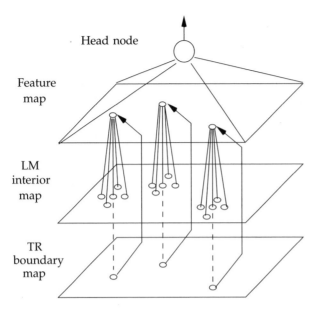

Figure 5.16
A feature map and its connections

be tied together as well. This without fail yields a center-surround receptive field and reduces the number of free parameters to only two: one for the center and one for the surround.

Thus, the function of a given feature map node at position i is

$$f_i = \left[\sigma \left(\sum_{j \in N(i)} l_j w_{ij} \right) \times t_i \right], \tag{5.2}$$

where $\sigma()$ is the usual sigmoidal squashing function, and $N(i)$ is the set of visual field positions that constitutes the neighborhood of a unit at position i, namely, position i together with its four nearest neighbors. l_j and t_i are, respectively, the activations (either 0 or 1) of the landmark interior map unit at position j and of the trajector boundary map unit at position i. Position j is in the neighborhood of position i. In other words, the function of a feature map unit at position i is the usual sigmoid of the weighted sum of its inputs, from i's neighborhood in the landmark interior map, but gated by the trajector boundary map unit at position i.

What is the intuition behind the wiring? The effect of structuring the network in this way is that whatever function the feature map receptive fields are trained to compute given their input from the landmark interior map, that function is computed at every point in the visual field that is a part of the trajector boundary, and only at those points.

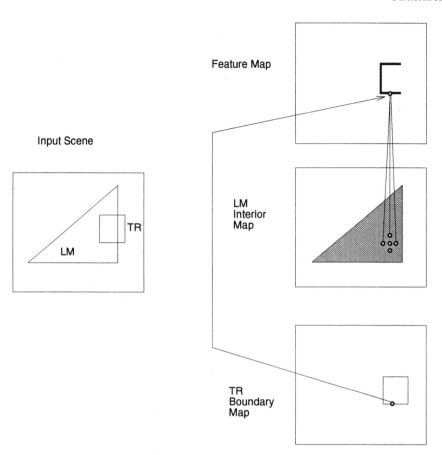

Figure 5.17
Detecting inclusion

Let us make this concrete by considering some examples. Imagine that the receptive field for feature map units has been trained so as to respond strongly to the presence of the landmark interior at the central point being examined. This situation would obtain if we had a strong positive weight on the central connection of the receptive field, and weights of 0 on the surrounding connections. Then we might expect to see situations like the one portrayed in figure 5.17. Here, the input scene shows a small square trajector partially inside a triangular landmark. The receptive field within the landmark interior map for a single unit in the feature map is shown (in fact, only three of the five links are shown, to avoid an excessively cluttered exposition). The gating input from the trajector boundary map to that feature map unit is also shown. The feature map as a whole will contain a strip of activation, one unit wide, corresponding to that portion of the trajector boundary that is inside the landmark. This is because the receptive field has been trained to cause feature map units to respond strongly to the presence of the landmark interior at the central point of the receptive field, but since the feature map units are gated by the trajector boundary map, only those feature map units that are both within the landmark interior and a part of the trajector boundary will be strongly activated: this gives us the C-shaped strip of activation we see. In essence, the feature map is detecting *inclusion* of parts of the trajector boundary in the landmark interior.

Let us consider another example, using the same structure. Let us now assume that training has led the pointwise feature map receptive field to respond strongly at locations for which the landmark interior is not visible at the central point of the field, but for which it is visible at one of the four peripheral receptive field points. This could be implemented by a strong negative weight for the central connection of the field and positive weights for the surrounding connections (off center, on surround). This situation would result in configurations of the sort portrayed in figure 5.18. Here, the feature map contains a single straight strip of activation, corresponding to those points on the trajector boundary that are immediately adjacent to, but not within, the landmark. Thus, the feature map is now essentially detecting *contact* between trajector boundary points and the landmark.

Thus, the same structure could learn to detect either inclusion or contact. For that matter, it could also learn to detect any function of the five points viewed in its receptive field, and it would detect that function all along the trajector boundary. Of course, if the trajector is nowhere near the landmark, as in the case of English *above,* the result is a completely empty feature map, since the landmark does not lie within the receptive fields of any feature map units that correspond to trajector boundary points. This is true regardless of the localized feature the receptive fields have learned to detect. Figure 5.19 illustrates this situation.

As we saw above, one may distinguish at least two ways in which features of this sort may be dealt with in language. On the one hand, for terms like English *on,* it does not matter how much of the trajector boundary is in contact with the landmark; all that matters is that contact exists at some point along the trajector boundary. On the other hand, for terms like English *in,* the amount of the trajector boundary that is contained within the landmark makes a difference in the judged applicability of the term to a scene. Thus, we have one situation in which all we care about is the simple presence or absence of a feature, and another in which we care about the amount of the trajector boundary along which a feature is present.

This distinction provides the motivation for the two sorts of head nodes that exist in the system, taking a function of all the units in the feature map below. Some feature maps will be headed by a node taking the *maximum* response over the nodes in the map below: $F = \max_i f_i$. Others will be headed by a node that

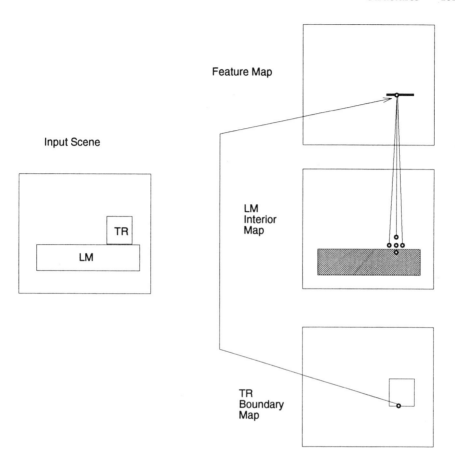

Figure 5.18
Detecting contact

takes the *average* response of the nodes in the map below it, averaged over only those positions corresponding to trajector boundary points: $F = [\sum_i f_i]/n$. Here, n is the number of points in the trajector boundary (i.e., the number of units that are activated in the trajector boundary map). These are summed, and this sum is supplied as input to the averaging head node. This can be seen in figure 5.15, the figure of the structure as a whole. Since f_i is 0 when there is no trajector boundary point at i (recall equation (5.2)), we are actually averaging over those points in the visual field that are part of the trajector boundary, not over the entire map.

The idea here is that a head node that takes the maximum response over the feature map units in the map below it allows the system to respond equally to, for example, contact at a single point and contact over a large extent of the trajector

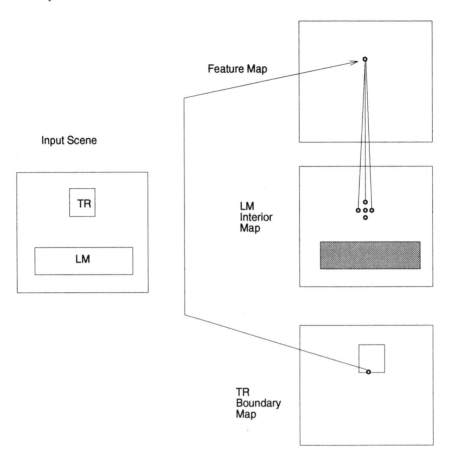

Figure 5.19
Landmark not within receptive fields of trajector boundary

boundary. This is so because the maximum is insensitive to the number of nodes in the feature map that actually reach that maximum. On the other hand, a head node that takes the average of the feature map units allows the system to deliver a graded response depending on the fraction of the trajector boundary along which a given feature occurs. The overall structure shown in figure 5.15 contains two feature maps, one headed by a node returning the maximum over the map, the other headed by an averaging node. The receptive fields within the structure are trained under back-propagation, as is the rest of the network within which the structure is embedded (some minor deviations from straightforward back-propagation were required because of the nondifferentiability of the maximum head node—these are covered in the appendix). The end result is that the head nodes of the feature maps learn to detect topological features such as contact and inclusion, when the training set requires this. Note that the map comparison structure is trained together with all the other structures and hidden layers in the network. There is no off-line training of individual structures.

Now that we have seen the map comparison structure and understood its operation, let us move on to the issue of motivation. Is there independently based motivation for structures of this sort? Although there are, to my knowledge, no neural or psychological structures of exactly this form, a number of the basic structural principles used here definitely do appear in the visual system. These are *multiple topographic maps, center-surround receptive fields, gating,* and *perceptual filling-in.* Thus, there is independent motivation for the subparts of the map comparison structure, for the elements that make it up, if not for the particular manner in which they are arranged here.

It has been known for some time that visual cortex contains topographic maps (Hubel and Wiesel 1977). These are generally retinotopic in character, holding some transformation of the retinal image. There is no evidence for the separation of trajector and landmark into separate maps. However, the architectural principle of hierarchical organization of such maps, which informs the structure we have been examining, also appears to characterize visual cortex (Essen and Maunsell 1983), so we can consider that very general principle to be independently motivated.

Center-surround receptive fields of the sort we saw above are known to exist in primary visual cortex (Hubel and Wiesel 1977), as well as in the ganglion cells of the retina (Kuffler 1953). These receptive fields consist of opposing centers and surrounds, such that an excitatory center is paired with an inhibitory surround, and vice versa. Within the structure presented here, the circular receptive fields of units in the feature maps are similar in overall flavor to such receptive fields, although much simplified. In particular, once trained to detect inclusion (recall, for example, figure 5.17), the receptive fields in the model tend to have an excitatory center paired with an inhibitory surround. These thus supply another source of motivation.

The phenomenon of gating that we saw, whereby the activity of one unit may be either enabled or squelched by the activity of another, also has some neurophysiological basis (Bushnell, Goldberg, and Robinson 1981; Moran and Desimone 1985). Interestingly, these researchers have implicated the *psychological* process of attention in *neural* gating. They noted that an animal's attention to a particular location in its visual field could gate the firing of neurons whose receptive fields covered that location. This is intriguing in its own right, in that it is evidence of a mental process affecting a neural one, and it is consonant with the use to which gating is being put here. After all, the primary function of gating in the model is to restrict the network's focus to those points corresponding to the trajector boundary, to ensure that only those points are considered when it detects topological features on a point-by-point basis. Although this is not a process I would want to identify with the psychological phenomenon of attention, it is at the very least similar in overall function: weeding out some incoming information so as to focus on an aspect of particular interest.

Finally, the spreading activation process that detects the interior of objects, as in figure 5.14, also has some support. To begin with, Treisman and Gormican (1988) have presented empirical psychophysical data indicating that inside/outside discrimination is not a preattentive parallel process. Their results show that this discrimination appears to require attention to the objects themselves. Although this does not directly support the particular spreading activation approach suggested by Ullman and adopted here, it rules out a possible competitor, namely, the idea that inclusion is among those visual properties that can be simply detected in parallel, simultaneously at all locations across the visual field, without requiring attention. Since this is not the case, the spreading activation theory becomes more plausible. Another piece of evidence in favor of the spreading activation method used here concerns the psychophysical phenomenon of perceptual *filling-in* of blind spots (Ramachandran and Gregory 1991; Ramachandran 1992). Each eye has a blind spot at the position in the visual field corresponding to the location at which the optic nerve connects to the eye. Although we might expect to see a black spot at that location, instead the color and texture of the area immediately surrounding it fill in the blind spot, making it invisible. Figure 5.20 illustrates this phenomenon. On the left, we see a dark annulus. Here, the blind spot is indicated by the dashed outline—this means that the outer perimeter of the annulus lies outside the blind spot, and the inner ring lies within it. The resulting percept is a dark circle: the dark immediately surrounding the blind spot has filled it in (Ramachandran and Gregory 1991). It is not known that this is accomplished via precisely the same spreading activation mechanism adopted here, but Ramachandran and Gregory's experiment does at any rate indicate that there are filling-in processes operating in the visual system. This motivates the use of similar processes in the computation of object interiors.

In general, then, the motivation we are able to adduce for the map comparison structure is of a piecewise character. Although there is no motivation for the structure exactly as it was presented above, a number of the building blocks of which it is constituted are independently motivated, some on neurophysiological grounds and some on psychophysical ones.

5.4 Motion: Source, Path, and Destination

The linguistic categorization of motion seems to involve a particular structuring of motion trajectories, whereby the path of an object through space is characterized in terms of the starting point or *source* of the motion, the endpoint or *destination*, and the *path* from the source to the destination (Miller and Johnson-Laird 1976; Jackendoff 1983, 1990; Lakoff 1987). This intuitively natural-seeming decomposition of the motion event is illustrated in figure 5.21. We can see these

 is perceived as

Figure 5.20
Perceptual filling-in at the blind spot

three elements reflected in those aspects of the event that are picked out and focused on in the semantics of closed-class spatial terms in language. For example, consider figure 5.22(a), which displays a small square trajector moving into a larger circular landmark. There are many aspects of this motion event that are entirely irrelevant for classifying it as an example of English *into*, such as the trajector's velocity, whether the trajector wiggled from side to side while moving, and whether it entered the circle broadside first or corner first. In fact, all that is really necessary for a motion event such as this to be categorized as *into* is that the trajector begin its motion outside the landmark and end its motion inside the landmark—the source must be outside and the destination must be inside. This provides an example of the manner in which source and destination are selected as particularly relevant in linguistic categorization. An entirely analogous situation obtains for such words as English *onto* and a number of other directionals: the starting point and ending point of the trajectory are critical elements in determining which spatial term is appropriate.

  If that were the entire story, our lives would be significantly less complicated— and less interesting—than they actually are. This is most easily seen by considering figure 5.22(b), which presents an event that would be classified as *through* in English. It is clear that the source and the destination are not the only elements in the trajectory that are essential here. In particular, the fact that the trajector was inside the landmark in midpath is also significant, and this causes us to broaden our scope, to include some representation of the path from source to destination when modeling spatial language. Figure 5.22(c) underscores this point as well, since here it is the nature of the path itself that is critical to the event's classification as *around*—the locations of the source and destination are not relevant, as long as they give rise to a path of this general shape. Although these examples are all from English, similar examples can be found in many other languages. The Russian word *iz-pod,* which translates as "out from underneath" and thus has no single-word English counterpart, highlights the importance of source and destination in the linguistic structuring of space. This is shown in figure 5.22(d). For *iz-pod* the critical points are that the trajector must begin its motion underneath the landmark and must end its motion somewhere both outside and not underneath the landmark. Returning briefly to English *through,* it is interesting

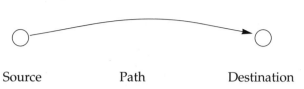

Source   Path   Destination

Figure 5.21
Source, path, and destination

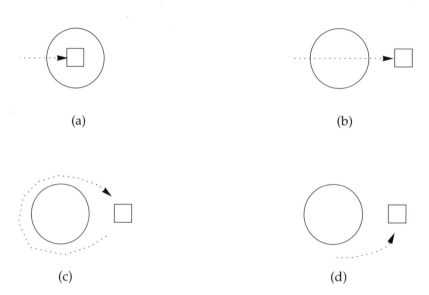

(a)   (b)

(c)   (d)

Figure 5.22
The salience of source, path, and destination

to note that although it is critical that the trajector be inside the landmark at some point during the path, that is, after the source and before the destination, the exact spot along the path is not at all critical. This insensitivity to precise position along the trajectory is illustrated in figure 5.23. The important point here is that in all of these cases, the exact timing of events, velocity, wiggling, and most other details of the motion trajectory do not appear to be relevant.

I shall be assuming that all that is required for the closed-class categorization of spatial events is a tripartite representation of source, path, and destination. As it turns out, there is some independent motivation for leaning toward this schematization of trajectories, motivation not deriving immediately from linguistic studies of spatial language. In particular, psychophysical motivation for this structuring comes from the visual phenomenon of apparent motion (Kolers 1972a, b). Human subjects, when presented first with an object displayed briefly at one position in the visual field and then with another copy of the object

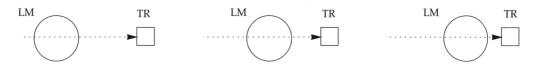

Figure 5.23
Three equally good examples of English *through*

$t = 0$ $t = 1$

Figure 5.24
Apparent motion

displayed at another position, often perceive the object moving smoothly from the first point to the second. In the terms we are using here, given the source and then the destination, subjects perceptually infer the path. Thus, source and destination serve as anchor points of sorts, from which the path is computed. This is illustrated in figure 5.24, where the dashed line indicates that the motion is perceived but not actual. This motivates the source-path-destination structuring we are adopting since it is an example of one of these three elements being inferred from the other two, in a nonlinguistic domain. An attractive although as yet unsubstantiated interpretation is to view both apparent motion and the linguistic focus on source, path, and destination as springing from a single underlying perceptual tendency to parse events into these three elements. Another source of motivation is the serial position effect in memory (Crowder 1976). In most learning tasks that involve sequences of items, performance is better at the beginning and end of the sequence than it is in between. This is therefore another demonstration that the beginnings and ends of sequences have a psychologically privileged status. Yet another indication of this distinctive status comes from the work of Slobin (1985), who suggests that attention to the beginnings and ends of linguistic forms may serve as a learning heuristic in the process of language acquisition.

We shall be considering a particular implementation of the very general idea of source-path-destination structuring, an implementation guided by considerations of simplicity and computational efficacy. We shall also be comparing it with other possible solutions.

Since the motion of the trajector is captured here in a sequence of frames, we require some means of temporal integration over the separate frames in order to arrive at a classification of the movie as a whole. More specifically, we shall be looking for a temporal integration method that captures the three-part breakdown of trajectory into source, path, and destination. In chapter 3 we reviewed a number of techniques for sequence learning under back-propagation, but as we shall see, none of these is appropriate for the particular task we have undertaken. This is because the structures involved do not highlight the aspects of the sequence that we are identifying here as most significant. Let us first consider the actual mechanism used and then turn to comparisons with other options.

Figure 5.25 presents the structure that we shall eventually see incorporated into the model. The three-part decomposition of the motion trajectory is reflected directly in this structure. To see this, let us first focus on the input and then consider the rest of the structure. The input, in the layer labeled *Current*, consists of a hidden-layer representation of the current input frame. For example, if we were viewing a movie of a circle moving out from underneath a square, and if this were the first frame of the movie, this buffer would contain some representation of the position of the circle underneath the square at the outset of the movie. The exact nature of the representation in the Current layer is determined by training. Thus, training sets for different languages will cause different representations to be formed here, corresponding to the different structurings of space implicit in the spatial systems of the languages. For our purposes now, the most important point is that this buffer contains all the information that the model has extracted from the current frame, information that the model has determined will play a role in spatial categorization for the language being learned. The contents of this buffer are therefore perhaps best thought of as a compressed representation of all that is linguistically relevant in the single input frame currently being viewed—relevant, that is, from the standpoint of the particular language being acquired.

Given input of this sort, what kind of temporal integration mechanism will capture the source-path-destination structuring of the motion trajectory? How can we handle a sequence of such representations of the input frames so as to deliver a response that considers the sequence as a whole, and that also emphasizes the three aspects of the trajectory we are focusing on here? The answer is rather simple.

Let us consider first the semantic role of source, or starting point for the motion trajectory. This is most simply represented by the hidden-layer representation for the first input frame of the movie, that is, a copy of whatever the Current buffer contained at the first time step of the movie. The buffer labeled *Source* in the figure contains exactly that, and remains unchanged throughout the course of the movie. In other words, the contents of the Current buffer are copied to the Source buffer on the first time step only, and they stay there for the duration of the movie. The link connecting the Current buffer to the Source buffer is shown as a dotted line, indicating that this link is not trained; rather, it performs the simple copy operation just described. This, then, is the representation of the semantic role of source.

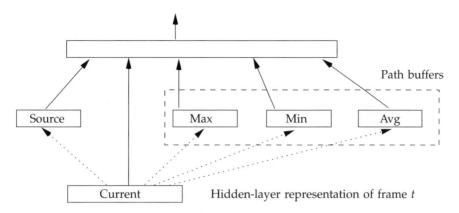

Figure 5.25
Motion using source and path buffers

The role of destination is even simpler to represent. At the last time step of the movie, the contents of the Current buffer itself are a representation of the configuration of the trajector relative to the landmark at end-event. Thus, no copy operation is required, and no representation must be preserved on the side, as was the case with source.

Of course, this is an idealized situation. In a more realistic environment, with several events occurring within the span of a single movie, determining source and destination will be more complex than simply selecting the first and last frames of the movie. But for our purposes now, representing source and destination is quite straightforward. The remaining problem is representing the path, or trajectory, that the trajector traces out as it moves. This is done by the path buffers, the buffers labeled *Max, Min,* and *Avg* and shown in dashed outline in the figure. Note that the links leading into these buffers are shown as dotted lines, indicating that they are not trained. However, they do not perform a simple copy operation either, as was the case with the Source buffer—their operation is slightly more complex.

The basic assumption behind the design of these path buffers is that it suffices to keep track of what events have occurred over the path as a whole, without necessarily recording the exact time when they occurred. Recall from figure 5.23 that English *through* is not particularly sensitive to just where along the path the trajector entered the landmark, as long as the entry occurred during the path. This insensitivity to precise timing is also characteristic of many other terms (e.g., English *over,* in the over-and-across sense). I shall be elevating this observation to the status of theory, in that the temporal integration technique used here will deliberately avoid recording the exact timing of events along the path. In order to record events in this manner, we track each of the nodes of the Current buffer, each of which comes to represent some linguistically relevant aspect of the current input frame. For each node, we record the minimum, maximum, and average activations it attained over the course of the movie. There is a one-to-one correspondence between units in the Current buffer and units in each of the path buffers, such that a given unit in one of the path buffers computes some function of the values seen in the corresponding Current buffer unit over the course of a movie. In particular, units in the Max path buffer record the maximum value attained by the corresponding Current buffer unit over the course of the movie. Similarly, units in the Min buffer record the minimum value attained, and units in the Avg buffer record the average value.

To make this somewhat more concrete, consider figure 5.26. This figure illustrates the operation of the Max path buffer, which receives its input from the representation of the current input frame in the Current buffer. Since each unit of the Max buffer records the maximum value ever attained by the corresponding unit in the Current buffer, at the end of the event the Max buffer will contain a representation of the maximum value attained by each of the Current buffer nodes, which comprise the representation of individual input frames. More specifically, the function for node i in the Max buffer at time step t is

$$Max_i(t) = \begin{cases} Current_i(t) & \text{if } t = 0 \\ Current_i(t) & \text{if } Current_i(t) > Max_i(t-1) \\ Max_i(t-1) & \text{otherwise.} \end{cases} \qquad (5.3)$$

The Min and Avg buffers similarly record the minimum and average values, respectively, attained by Current buffer nodes over the course of a movie.

Let us consider an example. Imagine the network is learning a language such as English, for which location *inside* the landmark is linguistically significant. Imagine further that the weights below the Current buffer have been shaped through training such that some node—say, node i—in the Current buffer now encodes location of the trajector inside the landmark. In other words, partial training of the network has resulted in node i in the Current buffer being strongly activated if and only if the trajector is inside the landmark in the current input frame. Now pretend that this network is exposed to a movie of a trajector going *through* a landmark. At the beginning of the movie, the trajector is not inside the landmark, meaning that node i will have some low activation level at the first time step, and therefore node i of the Source buffer will have that same low activation level; it will stay at that level throughout the movie. At the end of the movie, the trajector will again fail to be inside the landmark, meaning that node i of the Current buffer at the last time step will again have a low activation level. However, since the trajector was inside the landmark at some point in the middle of the movie (it is after all a movie of motion *through* the landmark), node i will have been highly activated at some point, marking that temporary inclusion. This fact will be captured by the Max buffer—node i of this buffer will hold the maximal value ever held by the inclusion-detecting node i of the

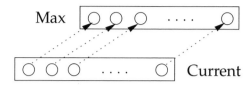

Figure 5.26
The Max buffer

Current buffer. At the end of the movie, then, we have a static representation of the path as a whole, distributed across the path buffers: the low value of node i in the Source buffer indicates that at the beginning of the movie the trajector was outside the landmark, the low value of node i in the Current buffer indicates that at the end of the movie it was outside the landmark, and the high value of node i in the Max buffer indicates that at some point it was inside the landmark. This representation is then used to determine which spatial terms appropriately describe the movie as a whole.

Note that the nodes in the Current buffer may not at first come to represent inclusion or other spatial features in so localist a manner. Once they do, however, it will be simple for the network to encode not just inclusion, but motion through.

Thus, we are left with representations of the starting and ending configurations, and a static representation of all that occurred over the path. The path representation does not record the exact timing of events along the path. I postulate that this is sufficient for closed-class categorization of spatial events. Temporal integration over these representations occurs in the hidden layer to which the representations of source, path, and destination all project. The links connecting the source, path, and destination representations to this hidden layer are trained under back-propagation, so that those aspects of the event that are relevant to the particular language being learned can be brought to bear on the classification of each movie.

The structure introduced here is relatively simple and is well suited to the task. Although its simplicity is fairly evident, establishing its appropriateness requires a comparison of this method with some of the more common sequence-learning methods that can be employed under back-propagation. Let us consider such a comparison now.

Figure 5.27 illustrates how these more traditional methods might be used in place of the motion buffers we have adopted here. In both cases, the input is the Current buffer, as it was in the case of the motion buffers. The network shown in (a) is a time-delay neural network (TDNN), which passes the input through a number of delays and computes a function of the input over a fixed time window. In the diagram shown here, the time window is of length five, so that the output of the network at time t is a function of the input at times t, $t - 1$, $t - 2$, $t - 3$, and $t - 4$. The network can process sequences of length greater than

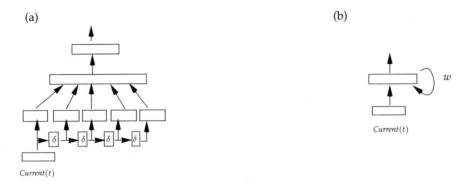

Figure 5.27
Traditional sequence-learning methods: TDNNs and recurrent networks

five, but with a very sharp constraint on its operation: the output at a given moment will not reflect any element of the input that is further than five steps back in time. There are two things to say about this. One is that this sort of a priori analyzability of networks is precisely what constrained connectionism is all about. After all, we are able here to identify a very clear constraint governing this network's operation, and we need not resort to empirical observation of its behavior when seeking to understand it. This sort of clarity is exactly what we are looking for. The other point, however, is that this clarity reveals that the mechanism is completely inappropriate for the task at hand. In the general case, the number of steps back in time will be n instead of five, but it will still be fixed. We will always be able to generate an input sequence of length greater than n, that is, a movie more than n frames long, and when processing that movie, this network will not be able to consider both the initial and the final frame at the same time. This may not be problematic for domains such as speech recognition, in which it is extremely unlikely that the identification of a phoneme will depend on speech data that are arbitrarily distant in time from the current moment. Nonetheless, it clearly rules out this network design for a task such as ours, in which the semantic roles of source and destination, or beginning and end, play a central role. It is worth pointing out, however, that the motion buffer approach we have adopted bears some similarity to a TDNN. In both cases, time is copied out over space, in the sense that we keep physical copies of the input at earlier time steps. The difference is that in the case of TDNNs, we keep copies of the input over the last n time steps, whereas in the motion buffer approach, we keep a copy of the input at the first time step, since we have reason to believe that that element of the sequence will be of particular relevance.

The very general point being made, of course, is that different cognitive tasks often require different architectures. We saw this in the case of TDNNs; let us now compare the motion buffer approach we are using with simple recurrent networks of the sort illustrated in figure 5.27(b), to underscore this point. These networks and others that are similar in design have gained considerable currency in connectionist sequence-processing applications generally, despite their being appropriate for only a limited range of tasks. Simple recurrent networks supply their hidden-unit representations back around to the hidden layer at the next time step. This makes them similar in overall form to finite-state automata: at a given point in time, the output and the next state both depend on the current input and the current state. This formal similarity leads one to suspect that the tasks for which finite-state automata are appropriate would also be tasks for which networks of this form would be well suited. For example, we might expect them to be appropriate for the recognition of regular languages, and they have in fact met with some success in the domain of grammatical induction (Servan-Schreiber, Cleeremans, and McClelland 1988; Cleeremans 1993).

However, we can expect simple recurrent networks to be inappropriate for the task on which we are currently focusing, for at least two reasons. In the first place, there is no separate representation of the initial input, or the source in the terminology we are adopting here, so the network must learn to retain this information in its hidden-layer state representation whenever this is relevant— and it often is. This can add considerably to the difficulty of the learning task. In addition, in simple recurrent networks there is no straightforward representation of the fact that an event has occurred, independent of the time step during which it occurred. Therefore, if we had two movies of a trajector moving *through* a landmark, and in one movie it entered the landmark in the 7th frame whereas in the other it entered the landmark in the 16th frame, networks of this sort would have to learn to develop representations that ignored the time step during which the entering occurred. This could also significantly increase the difficulty of the learning process.

These are only expectations, however. Let us take a somewhat closer look at three separate training techniques for such networks, to see if the prospects for applying these methods to the task at hand seem better when viewed in greater detail. Figure 5.28 presents these methods. The original recurrent network, shown at the top, points to the three methods we shall be considering. The first is back-propagation through time, which we encountered in chapter 3. This method is illustrated here in (a). It amounts to unrolling the network during training, so as to convert the recurrent network into a feedforward one of equivalent functionality for sequences of a given length. The result is a network of depth equal to the length of the input sequence—this is done since back-propagation operates on feedforward networks only. As it happens, this more detailed consideration of back-propagation through time highlights a solid reason to avoid this approach. We can see from the figure that the network is fairly tall: in fact, it has as many layers as there are frames in the movie, and since the movies may be arbitrarily long, this would lead to extremely tall networks.

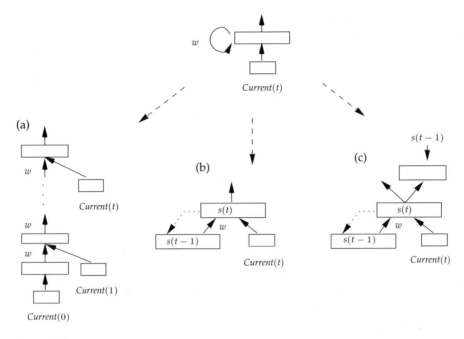

Figure 5.28
Three training methods for recurrent networks

Unfortunately, tall networks with tied weights between layers, such as would result when trying to learn long sequences, tend to be difficult to train (Mozer 1988; Pollack 1990a). This encourages us to look elsewhere for more appropriate sequence-learning methods.

The network labeled (b) in the figure is a simple recurrent network, or SRN, of the sort proposed by Elman (1988). We encountered this type as well in chapter 3. Here, the contents of the hidden layer at time step t, $s(t)$, are copied down to the state units, labeled $s(t - 1)$ in the figure. Thus, the recurrent connections are implemented by keeping a one-time-step-old copy of the hidden layer, treating it as we would input, and training the connections from it to the hidden layer itself. We saw in chapter 3 that one of the limitations of networks of this sort is their inability to handle long-range temporal dependencies, that is, their generally poor performance on sequences in which events in the distant past are relevant to current decisions. The particular example we examined there concerned a training set of two strings: PSSSP and TSSST. These are to be viewed as sequences of letters, and the network's task is, at each time step, to predict the next letter in the sequence. The point, of course, is that only the final letter of the sequence depends on the first letter: this is the kind of long-range temporal dependency that is difficult for these networks. In fact, networks of this type have been applied to this problem (Cleeremans 1993), but the difficulty of the learning process increases exponentially with the length of the intervening SSS...S sequence. We attributed this difficulty to the fact that at the final time step, back-propagation is not able to have its influence trickle back to the beginning of the sequence, as it would be able to—at least in principle—under back-propagation through time. Rather, its influence is cut short at the $t - 1$st time step.

This might not be a problem for some tasks, and indeed these networks are widely used in the connectionist community. For us, however, the fact that long-range temporal dependencies are problematic for such networks essentially rules them out as a viable temporal integration method. Why should this be? The problem is that the beginning of the movie, or the source in the terminology we have been using, is very often relevant to the categorization of the movie as a whole, as is the end of the movie, the destination. Since the destination is often significant, the network cannot output a classification until it has seen the final frame. But at that point the first frame may already lie in the relatively distant past. After all, there is no principled reason to place a limit on the allowable length of the movies. Thus, the long-range temporal dependency issue for these networks translates into an obvious inappropriateness for the task at hand.

This method is simple and elegant, however, so it is tempting to see if it can be salvaged. The architecture shown in (c) of the figure constitutes such an attempt. This is what Maskara and Noetzel (1992) refer to as a *forced simple recurrent network,* or FSRN. It is identical to the SRN in (b), except that here there are two outputs, indicated by the two arrows branching up and outward from the hidden layer. The leftmost output serves the same function as the output in (b): it delivers the network's categorization of the movie. The rightmost output, on the other hand, is an auxiliary output layer the sole purpose of which is to force the network to retain, in its state representation, information concerning earlier events. This is done in the hope that it will improve the network's performance on tasks that involve long-range temporal dependencies. How does this work? The system is trained, at every time step except the first and the last, to output the contents of the hidden layer at the previous time step on its auxiliary outputs. That is, at time t, when the contents of the hidden layer are $s(t)$ and the contents of the state units are $s(t - 1)$, the system must produce $s(t - 1)$ on its auxiliary outputs. Any deviation from this is corrected through back-propagation. The idea behind this approach is that if the system successfully performs this learning task, $s(t)$ will contain a representation of $s(t - 1)$, in the sense that the network will always be able to produce $s(t - 1)$ from $s(t)$—no information from $s(t - 1)$ has been lost. Similarly, it will be able to produce $s(t - 2)$ from $s(t - 1)$, meaning that no information is lost from $s(t - 2)$. As we apply this analysis recursively back through time, we reach the conclusion that all information from all states, starting with that of the very first time step, $s(0)$, is encoded in $s(t)$, in the sense that it can be recovered from $s(t)$. To see this, consider what would happen if we fixed the values of the hidden units to be $s(t)$: we would get $s(t-1)$ on the auxiliary outputs. We now take that auxiliary output vector and fix the hidden units of the network to those values, the values of our reconstructed $s(t-1)$—we will see a reconstruction of $s(t-2)$ on the auxiliary outputs this time. Continuing in this fashion, we will eventually be able to recover $s(0)$ from $s(t)$. Thus, we get a nesting of state representations, one inside the other. This is cute, but why is it relevant? It is relevant because if this technique causes all the information from the very beginning of the movie to be encoded in the state representation for the final step, it sounds like a reasonable means to overcome the problem of long-range dependencies—the model will not "forget" earlier events. On the last time step of the movie, we can ignore the outputs on the auxiliary output layer and train solely on the leftmost outputs—those that indicate whether the movie should be classified as *through* or *into* or some other spatial event or relation. If the method works as we hope, the hidden-layer representation at the last time step will contain all the information from the movie as a whole, so this categorization will have all the information that it needs available to it. The categorization outputs are trained only at the last time step, when a representation of the entire movie has been built up in the state representation. This method, similar in flavor to Pollack's *recursive autoassociative memory* (Pollack 1988, 1990b), has been used with some success for sequence learning in the domain of natural language sentence comprehension (Miikkulainen 1991) and in inducing finite-state machines (Maskara and Noetzel 1992).

This sounds good, but unfortunately there is a critical difference between having the movie as a whole encoded in the state vector and having it all there *in an appropriate format*. A simple experiment showed that this technique is also inadequate for our purposes. This pilot study used an architecture of the form shown in (c) as the temporal integration structure for the task of learning motion-based semantics for spatial terms.

Since this network learns to produce the previous state from its current state, there is a sense in which it nests the state representations one inside another, as we saw above. Given that the network uses this method to form a representation of the path, there is a concern one might have at the outset regarding the application of this technique here: one would expect the representations formed to be very sensitive to the exact frame in which a particular event occurred. Let us consider a specific example, the English preposition *through*. It is critical to *through* that the trajector be inside the landmark at some point along the path, but it is not critical exactly where along the path this happens, as we saw in figure 5.23. Now this sort of insensitivity to exact timing is just what the source-path-destination buffers are supposed to capture. The question is, Will an FSRN also be able to capture the general idea of inclusion somewhere along the path, or will the nested nature of the representations hinder the formation of such a generalization?

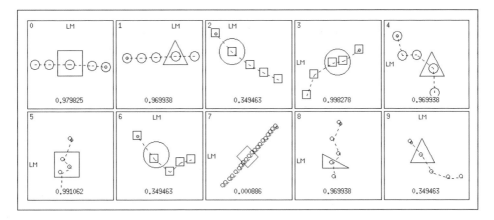

Figure 5.29
English *through* learned using an FSRN: a test set

To examine this issue, I trained two separate architectures to discriminate positive from negative examples of *through*. The first architecture to be tested used an FSRN as its temporal integration mechanism, and the second used the source-path-destination motion buffers described above.

Training the FSRN proceeded as follows. There were a total of 25 positive and 25 negative examples of *through* in the training set. The part of the network that outputs the Current buffer representation of the current input frame was first trained separately, to ensure that at least one node in the Current buffer responded to inclusion of the trajector within the landmark. The weights that learned to detect inclusion were then frozen. Next the Current buffer was hooked up to the FSRN mechanism, and the network as a whole was trained. This pretraining on inclusion makes the sequential learning task easier than it might be otherwise, since the network need not learn to detect inclusion and to handle sequences simultaneously—it learns inclusion first, the weights that detect inclusion are frozen, and the network is then trained on sequences. The best result obtained was convergence to 0.46 summed squared error after 2630 back-propagation epochs. The system was trained under standard back-propagation, rather than a second-derivative method such as quickprop (Fahlman 1988), because training in this fashion, without back-propagation through time or some other means of arriving at the true gradient, yields only an approximation to the gradient. Thus, a relatively cautious learning algorithm is called for. Training networks of this sort under quickprop has not generally been successful. The system's performance on a test set can be seen in figure 5.29. Here, the small number at the bottom of each box indicates how good an example of *through* the system has judged the movie as a whole to be. Clearly, the system appears

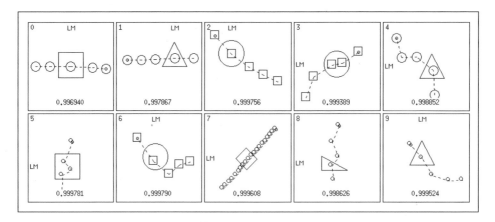

Figure 5.30
English *through* learned with source and path buffers: a test set

to be quite sensitive to the actual frame in which inclusion occurred. Notice that those movies in which inclusion occurred only in the fourth frame are not judged as good examples of *through*. This is in spite of the fact that the training set included such a movie. That movie in the training set was never learned correctly either. In addition, notice that movie number 7 here, a 20-frame movie that most English speakers would consider a perfectly good *through*, is judged as a very poor example. Recall, moreover, that this was an artificial training situation: the problem of learning to detect inclusion was separated from the problem of sequence learning. The fact that poor results were obtained even in this idealized situation indicates that the method as a whole is not well suited to the task at hand.

Given these disappointing results from the FSRN approach, we now turn our attention to the technique we are actually adopting, involving the use of source and path buffers to handle temporal integration over the movie. A network incorporating this structure was also trained to discriminate positive from negative examples of *through*. The two concepts *through* and *in* were learned together, and there was no pretraining for inclusion as there was in the case of the FSRN. Despite this, learning was extremely fast, converging to less than 0.01 summed squared error in 80 quickprop epochs. Figure 5.30 illustrates the system's performance, once trained, on the same test set for *through* that was used in testing the FSRN architecture. In addition, figure 5.31 presents the system's performance on a test set of negative examples of *through*. The performance is clearly much better than it was in the case of the FSRN. The system is no longer sensitive to the particular frame along the path in which an event occurred. The total summed squared error on these test sets of positive and negative examples of *through*, together with a similar pair for *in*, was under 0.01, over a total of 40

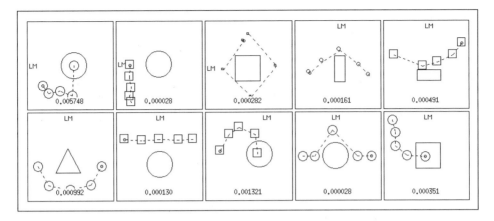

Figure 5.31
Negative examples of English *through*: a test set

test movies, indicating excellent generalization from the training set to the test set. It is particularly instructive to note that movie 7 in figure 5.30, which is 20 frames in length, is correctly classified, even though the training set contained only movies of 5 frames each. This indicates that the system is able to generalize to correctly classify movies of greater length than any in its training set. More generally, this experiment indicates that this method is potentially quite useful in the spatial sequence-learning task we are faced with here.

This underlines the point made earlier: different cognitive tasks call for different architectures. The basic temporal characteristics of the spatial semantics task, namely, the privileged status of source and destination, and the insensitivity to precisely when an event occurred along the path, made the more common connectionist sequence-learning methods inappropriate. An extension to one of those mechanisms, the FSRN approach, was also shown to be not as well suited to the task as the motion buffer approach finally adopted. The general lesson is that any structure built into a network will translate into constraints on its operation, and it therefore behooves the modeler to make sure that the structures selected are well chosen for the modeling task at hand.

In sum, then, the three architectural principles of orientation combination, map comparison, and source-path-destination structuring of motion trajectories form the scientific heart of our modeling endeavor. The structures in which these principles are embodied put the "constrained" in "constrained connectionism." The structures bias the learning process in ways that I postulate are appropriate, making some things particularly easy to learn, and others difficult. We have just seen an example of this in the pilot study comparing FSRNs with source-path-destination buffers: the kind of motion structuring we are after is much more easily learned in a network of the latter sort. In addition, whatever independent motivation the model's structure has is derived from motivation for the structures that are embedded within it. Although this motivation has a piecemeal character, in that there is no single neural or psychological structure that we can point to as the foundation for the model, it does reassure us that the structures we are incorporating into the model are at the very least similar in nature to known perceptual mechanisms. Finally, the simplicity of the structures lends an ease of analyzability to the model that will be particularly useful when we try to determine what the model can tell us about semantic acquisition generally.

Chapter 6

A Model of Spatial Semantics

6.1 Overview

This book began with a set of interrelated questions: What sort of model can adapt itself to the different structurings of space manifested in the world's languages? How can such a system learn without explicit negative evidence? What can such a model tell us about possible semantic universals? In sum, how can such a model help us in characterizing the human semantic potential for spatial events and relations?

Several more technically oriented questions suggest themselves as well: Where does constrained connectionism come in? How can it help us in this endeavor? Having seen some of the structures to be incorporated into the model, we can now ask just how they fit in, and how they constrain the model's operation. How analyzable and how well motivated is the resulting model, and how effective a learning mechanism is it?

We are still somewhat in the dark regarding much of this. Although we have seen the outline of a solution to the issue of learning without explicit negative evidence, the rest of these questions remain unanswered, and it will be the burden of this chapter to rectify that situation by pulling together the various parts of the model. We shall examine the model's architecture and the manner in which its design incorporates the structural devices we have just reviewed. We shall also consider the way in which the model is trained, and we shall see the results of training on a number of different languages.

The model's design is informed by three very general guiding principles. The first and most important of these is *adequacy:* the model must perform the task for which it was designed. To put it simply, it must work. For us, this means that the model must be able to acquire perceptually grounded semantics for spatial terms without using negative evidence. The structures to which we were introduced in the previous chapter perform computations that are clearly relevant to this task, in that they detect such semantically significant features as contact, general "aboveness," and the like. The point here is that these structures, along with the rest of the design, were arrived at in part because they facilitate the acquisition of spatial semantics. Again, simply put, they were chosen in part because they work. This is only the first part of the story, however. Another principle is *motivation:* these structures were chosen not only because they are computationally appropriate, but also because some form of independent motivation can be adduced for them. The idea here is that if we have independent evidence for particular computational structures, these will be preferred over other equally efficacious structures, since we are being asked to take less on faith—there is already good reason to believe that structures of this nature exist. All modeling involves a certain amount of conjuring into existence of novel entities, and therefore any modeling effort must beg the reader's indulgence to some extent. But there is less of a strain on the reader's credulity if the structures posited can be shown to serve some independent purpose as well. Finally, the design was also guided by the very general principle of *simplicity*, of preferring uncomplicated models over others that are more complex and correspondingly more abstruse and impenetrable. The overall goal, after all, is to arrive at a clear characterization of the human semantic potential, and the simpler the model, the clearer the resulting characterization will be.

These three general principles match up with the three benefits of constrained connectionism we saw earlier: improved generalization, motivation, and analyzability. Generalization from the training set to the test set is after all a form of adequacy, a measure of the degree to which the model has successfully performed the task of semantic acquisition. Motivation is both a general principle being advanced here and a strength of constrained connectionism. And analyzability, the third advantage we have seen cited for constrained connectionism, is precisely what one would expect of a simple model. Thus, a possible rephrasing of the above declaration of design principles could be that the model was designed to milk each of the benefits of constrained connectionism for all it is worth, in the belief that these truly are desirable features in any model, and well worth pursuing.

6.2   The Problem

The model's task is to acquire visually grounded semantics for spatial terms. What does this boil down to? Given simple movies of objects moving relative to one another, the model must learn to label the movies appropriately using spatial terms from some natural language. Let us make this as concrete as possible by taking a close look at the input that the model must learn to classify linguistically. Input movies are constructed as illustrated in figure 6.1. Using the movie editor shown here, one may put together movies such as this positive example of English *through*. Any of the objects shown in the middle section of the screen may be chosen as either trajector or landmark—each scene contains one trajector and one landmark, and no other objects. These are then arranged relative to one another in the scene. Note that the landmark remains stationary throughout the movie, whereas the trajector may move. The five-frame movie shown in the

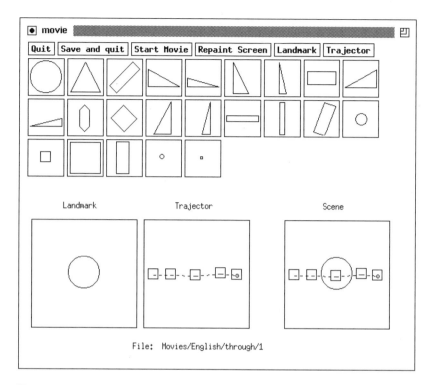

Figure 6.1
Constructing a positive example of English *through*

figure depicts a circular landmark and a small square trajector moving through it. The movie frames are superimposed on top of one another, with the dashed lines connecting successive positions of the trajector as it moves. The final frame of the movie is indicated by a tiny circle located inside the trajector.

In this manner, one can put together a training set. Let us consider a training set for English, bearing in mind that this is simply a convenient example: in actuality, we shall construct training sets for a variety of languages. Figure 6.2 presents a set of 13 positive examples of English *through*, which were put together in the manner described above. A similar set of movies is constructed for each of the other English terms to be learned. These movies, each one labeled as an instance of some English spatial term, make up the training set for English. The idea is that whenever the learner sees one of the movies, it also "hears" (receives as a training signal) the corresponding word, and eventually it comes to associate the linguistic form with some semantic generalization over the movies that were labeled with that form. It should then be able to produce the appropriate English word when presented with movies on which it has not been trained.

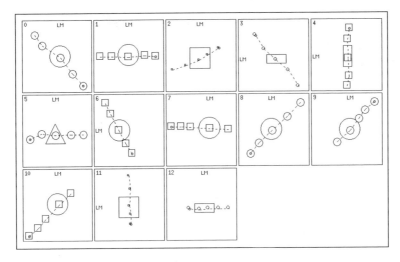

Figure 6.2
Positive examples of English *through*

6.3   The Model

The model is illustrated in figure 6.3. Although this is rather a busy diagram, only two aspects of it are important for the time being. The first is the model's input and output behavior; the second is its constrained connectionist architecture. Let us consider each of these in turn.

6.3.1   Movies as Input, Categorization as Output

The model accepts movies of spatial events as input and produces linguistic categorizations of the events as output. The current input   frame, with trajector and landmark labeled, is shown at the bottom of the figure. The outline of the trajector is copied into the *TR boundary map*, and the outline of the landmark is copied into the *LM boundary map*. These two boundary maps are kept in register such that if they were to be superimposed, the result would be identical to the input scene. The rest of the processing proceeds based on the contents of these two maps, eventually resulting in a response at the output layer. This is done on a frame-by-frame basis: for each frame, the trajector and landmark are copied into the boundary maps, and a response is given at the output layer. Once the network has been trained, each output node at the top will yield a value indicating how appropriate the corresponding spatial term would be as a description of the movie up to and including the current frame.

Movies may be of arbitrary length. Indeed, it seems artificial in the extreme to stipulate that movies be of a particular length in order to be considered good examples of some spatial event. For example, although the movies shown in

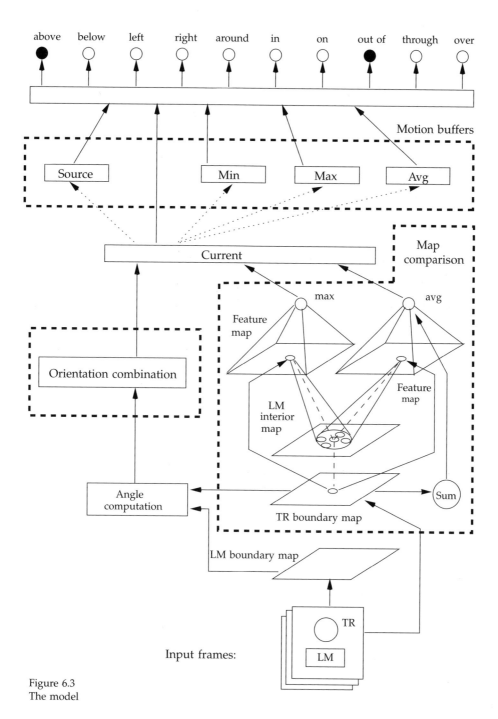

above below left right around in on out of through over

Motion buffers

Source   Min   Max   Avg

Current

Map comparison

max   avg

Feature map

Feature map

LM interior map

Orientation combination

Sum

Angle computation

TR boundary map

LM boundary map

TR

LM

Input frames:

Figure 6.3
The model

figure 6.2 all happen to be 5 frames in length, similar movies with more frames would be equally good examples of *through:* consider, for example, figure 5.30, in which movie 7 has 20 frames and is a perfectly good example of *through.* English speakers' own intuitive judgment of the appropriateness of using this or other spatial terms is unaffected by the number of frames it takes to represent the event; the model should similarly be insensitive to movie length. This may seem an obvious point and not worth belaboring, but it has consequences. As we saw in the discussion of sequence-learning mechanisms in chapter 5, this means that no mechanism that restricts us to sequences of a fixed length is acceptable, and this rules out such options as time-delay neural networks. As we shall see, there are other ramifications as well.

The model's response at the final time step of the movie, after viewing the final frame, is taken to be its response to the movie as a whole. This idea is also fairly commonsensical, since the model cannot reasonably be expected to produce a classification of the movie as a whole before it has seen the movie as a whole. What if the movie is a positive instance of *into* and the trajector enters the landmark only in the last frame? It is only at the final time step that the model is able to categorize the movie as a whole, and therefore it is at the final time step that we interpret its output as a classification of the entire movie. This is of course true of human language learners as well: one cannot classify an event prior to having seen it in its entirety. This observation and the one above, taken together, imply that once the model has been trained, it must respond at every time step, indicating the appropriateness of each spatial term for describing the portion of the movie viewed so far. Why is this? Following the first assumption, movies may be of arbitrary length; therefore, each frame could be the final one, that is, the one after which a judgment regarding the movie as a whole will be required. The system therefore has to give a running judgment of the movie so far, at each time step.

This characterization of the model's operation over time leads naturally to a training paradigm in which the system is trained only at the end of the movie. To see why this should be the case, let us start with the fact that the model learns by comparing its classification of the input movie with that supplied by a "teacher" and then reduces the discrepancy between the two by changing its output to match that of the teacher. In the case of a child learning his or her native language, the teacher would be any linguistically competent speaker who describes the events the child is seeing, using spatial terms from that language. In our case, this situation is modeled by prelabeling the movies as described above and then presenting the model with both the input movie and the desired linguistic form. The model then uses back-propagation to adjust its weights so that the output classifications match those in the training set. The critical point in all of this is that the training data only specify how the movie as a whole is labeled; they do not say anything about the individual frames that make up the movie. This is true for children as well as for the model. To follow up on the example we have been using, there is no evidence to my knowledge that children are told, when learning a word such as *through*, "Now it's outside—now it's inside—now it's outside: see? It went through." This may occur occasionally, but it would be a stretch to assume that such input is available to children on a regular basis. Similarly, in the case of the model, although each of the movies shown in figure 6.2 has been labeled as a positive example of *through*, that is all the information that has been supplied: we are not told what an appropriate response would be on a frame-by-frame basis. Moreover, it would be inappropriate to train the model to respond strongly for *through* at each frame of a movie labeled with this word. Why is this? At the beginning and in the middle of the movie, a strong response at the *through* output node would be entirely out of place: when viewed only in part, the movie would be a fine example of *toward* or *into*, but not of *through*. Given this, we cannot train the model frame by frame; instead, we must train it based only on its response to the entire movie. As we saw above, this response to the movie as a whole is given by the model's output at the last time step of the movie. This output then is compared with the desired output, and training is directed to reduce the difference between the two. It is for this reason that training occurs only on the final time step. Note that even though we expect the model to eventually respond appropriately at every time step, the point here is that we do not have training data available to actually train the model at every time step.

As we shall see, this notion of training on the final time step will be significant, so it is worth stressing that this aspect of the training paradigm follows in a straightforward manner from the rather reasonable assumption that each sequence as a whole is labeled, rather than its individual frames or subevents. It is also worth stressing that this is not simply a technical idiosyncrasy of the particular modeling approach being employed here. Rather, it follows logically from the nature of the data supplied to the language learner. Furthermore, these data are qualitatively similar in character to those encountered by the language-learning child. In the absence of any indication that children are regularly exposed to such linguistic blow-by-blow accounts as the "out-in-out" example for English *through*, I assume that they are not exposed to these data. In other words, I assume that children do not have reliable access to explicit labels for the subparts of events they are learning to name. This leaves our language-learning child in a situation very similar to the one that the model faces: a single word describes the event as a whole. And as in the case of the model, it is only after the event as a whole has been perceived that the child is in a position to compare his or her tentative classification of the event with that of the teacher.

6.3.2 A Constrained Connectionist Architecture

Having considered the input/output behavior of the model in some detail, we can now move on to the second point of interest for us: the model's constrained connectionist architecture. The design combines the detailed structures typical of structured connectionism with elements of the parallel distributed processing (PDP) approach to connectionism. In particular, the structures to which we were introduced in chapter 5 are shown in figure 6.3 in bold dashed outline, embedded in what would otherwise be a PDP network, a comparatively unstructured multilayer perceptron. Thus, in the lower left we see the orientation combination structure, responsible for determining the degree of alignment of various orientational features and combining evidence from these sources. In the lower right we see the map comparison structure, responsible for detecting such nondirectional, quasi-topological features as contact and inclusion. Near the top we see the motion trajectory structure, which implicitly parses events into source, path, and destination. These should look familiar, for these three structures and the principles they embody were the focus of our attention in chapter 5. In contrast, the two layers shown outside the structures, the Current layer and the top layer of the network, are homogeneous unstructured layers of nodes such as are commonly found in multilayer perceptrons. The network as a whole is trained under back-propagation. This results in the development of distributed representations in the unstructured layers, and the effects of training also penetrate into and through the structures, adjusting parameters associated with them.

What are the advantages of this approach to model building? We have seen these already, but a repetition cannot hurt, since we are about to see the ideas in action: principle will meet practice in the very near future. For our purposes, it is clear that a learning system is required, since we are concerned primarily with semantic *acquisition*. Given this, the many advantages of distributed representations make PDP an attractive choice as a connectionist modeling language: graceful degradation, graded responses, and the ready availability of a training algorithm. But the appeal of structured connectionism is also very real. As we saw in our discussion of constrained connectionism as a design philosophy, the incorporation of task-appropriate structure into a learning system tends to improve its generalization capacity. In addition, if the structures are motivated, that fact helps to motivate the model as a whole. Finally, models with built-in structures lend themselves to more straightforward analysis than do relatively unstructured networks. As we saw earlier, these three general advantages of constrained connectionism match up with the three guiding principles that inform this particular model's design. Enhanced generalization is a form of adequacy: if the model exhibits superior generalization from the training set to the test set, it is in that sense doing its job more completely. Independent motivation is both a guiding design principle here and an advantage of properly built constrained connectionist models generally. And clear analyzability, one of the most compelling reasons to choose a constrained connectionist methodology, should flow naturally from a model that is kept as simple as possible. This at any rate is the hope.

On this topic of simplicity, a few words are in order. It may seem at first that the tangle of maps, nodes, and links that we see in figure 6.3 is anything but simple. Nonetheless, it is the end result of an attempt to build an uncomplicated, clear model of the spatial semantic acquisition task. Although a simpler model may be possible, the task itself is demanding enough that no obvious trimmed-down alternative suggested itself. In fact, we have seen this diagram before, but this time we come to it equipped with a solid grounding in the structural devices that form its core. As we saw, these structures are fairly straightforward. Since the model as a whole really amounts to the structures plus a minimal amount of additional machinery, it is not as complex as one might imagine at first.

Let us run through the model from input to output, to see exactly how the structures are used, and how they fit into the larger picture of semantic acquisition for spatial terms. An understanding of just why the model works as it does will then give us a solid basis upon which to discuss the model's ramifications.

6.4   A Run through the Model

Referring back to figure 6.3, note that as each movie frame is presented to the model, the trajector outline is copied into the trajector boundary map, and the landmark outline is similarly copied into the landmark boundary map. These two maps are kept in register such that if they were superimposed, the result would be the scene shown in the input frame. It is from this original separation of the two objects into separate maps that all other processing proceeds. Of course, object segmentation in a more realistic environment is a significant task in and of itself; this simplified version is used here because our real focus is on the linguistic categorization of spatial relations, rather than on object segmentation.

Given these beginnings, we are already prepared to see how the structures fit in. Consider first the structure responsible for orientation combination, shown in the lower left of the figure. Recall that the basic idea behind orientation combination is that even such simple words as English *above* involve a combination of evidence from a number of sources. In particular, they involve determining the degree of alignment of several relational orientations with several reference orientations. In the structure we reviewed, orientational alignment was computed using units called θ-nodes. Each such node determines the alignment of a single relational orientation (e.g., the proximal orientation) with a single reference orientation (e.g., upright vertical). The evidence from a number of such θ-nodes is then combined. The structure shown in the figure is simply a layer of θ-nodes, each one calculating the alignment of one relational orientation with one reference orientation. These relational and reference orientations are extracted from the input frame through processes that are described in the appendix and that are indicated in the figure by the small box marked *angle computation*. Since θ-nodes yield only the alignment of two orientations, the combination of evidence from the various θ-nodes actually occurs in the unstructured layer above the θ-node layer. This layer is referred to as the *Current* layer since, as we shall see, it contains a representation of the current input frame. For our purposes now, the important point is that the units in the Current layer combine evidence from the θ-nodes in the layer below by taking the summed weighted output over a set of θ-nodes and passing this sum through the usual sigmoidal squashing function $f(x) = 1/(1 + e^{-x})$. This is the activation function commonly used in networks trained under back-propagation, and in fact the weights connecting the θ-node layer to the Current layer are trained under back-propagation just as any other weights might be. Thus, although the structure dictates that the relevant operation is one of orientation combination, the weighting given to the various sources of evidence is determined by the learning algorithm. The back-propagation error term also penetrates back into the θ-nodes themselves and can adjust the sensitivity of these nodes.

Let us now turn to the map comparison structure. While orientations are being extracted and compared with one another, this structure detects such semantically significant quasi-topological features as contact, amount of contact, and inclusion. This is done in the manner reviewed in chapter 5. To see how this structure is plugged into the rest of the network, let us start with the trajector and landmark boundary maps. As we have seen, these maps receive their input directly from the current input frame. The trajector boundary map is in fact a part of the map comparison structure—this is the map that gates the responses of units in the feature maps. The next map up in the structure, the landmark interior map, is derived from the landmark boundary map through the straightforward flood-fill routine that we saw earlier. These lower two maps in the structure, marking the trajector boundary and the landmark interior, are all that is required by way of input for the map comparison mechanism to operate. This structure then produces its output at the feature map head nodes. These are the two nodes shown at the top of the structure, which commonly come, through training, to detect contact or inclusion. These nodes project to the Current layer just as the θ-nodes in the orientation combination structure do, and the weights on these links are trained under back-propagation. The weights inside the structure, dictating exactly which topological features are to be detected, are similarly trained along with the rest of the network.

We can now see why the Current layer is said to contain a representation of the current input frame. Any information from the current input frame that reaches the higher regions of the network must pass through the Current layer, either through the orientation combination structure or through the map comparison structure. It is a bottleneck of sorts, a single hidden layer in which some representation of the current frame is formed, based on the features detected by the structures that project to it. Note that there is no memory for previous frames in any of the network elements we have viewed so far, so we can be sure that the representation formed in the Current layer contains information only from the current input frame, and not from any earlier ones.

We can now move up to the motion buffers, which implement the source-path-destination structuring of the trajectory. At each time step the Current buffer supplies some representation of the current input frame to this structure, which integrates the information over time in the manner we reviewed. In short, the contents of the Current buffer at the first time step are copied to the Source buffer and remain there throughout the rest of the movie, providing an unchanging representation of the beginning of the movie. The buffers labeled *Min, Max,* and *Avg* track the minimum, maximum, and average values attained by the nodes in the Current buffer and in this way build up a simple static representation of the path as a whole. At the last time step of the movie, the Current buffer itself contains a representation of the final frame, so this is taken as our representation of the destination. All of these buffers then project to the top hidden layer, an unstructured layer of the more or less classic PDP variety, and this then projects to the output nodes.

There is one aspect of this network that calls for particular emphasis, since it has a profound effect on the kinds of events the network can learn to recognize. To see this, let us begin by defining a *static feature* as any perceptual feature of a single input frame. For example, contact between trajector and landmark is a static feature, as are inclusion, location of the trajector above the landmark, and so on. There is an important constraint on just which static features will be learned, and under which conditions: the network will learn to extract those static features that are present in the *final frame* of movies in its training set. Thus, if the training set includes movies that *end* in contact between the two objects, the network will be able to learn to pick up on contact whenever it occurs in a movie. On the other hand, if the training set does not include movies that end in contact, the network will most probably not learn to detect contact. This is rather a strong constraint on the network's operation, so let us consider why it holds.

As we have seen, the Current layer holds a representation of the current input frame. This representation is learned through back-propagation, combining evidence from the structures immediately below the layer. So far, this could be a description of learning in any of a wide variety of connectionist networks. Recall, however, that the network receives a training signal only on the last time step of the movie. This is the source of the constraint. Because of this, error is back-propagated only on the last time step. At that point the Current layer and the structures that feed into it contain information only from the final frame of the movie—information regarding the movie as a whole is restricted to the motion buffers and the layer above them. Why is it significant that the information in the lower structures concerns the final frame alone? Because the learning algorithm updates weights in this lower section of the network based on the activation values it finds there—and these are the result of the final frame only. Thus, the network is trained to pick up only on those static features that are present in the final frame of movies on which it has been trained. Other static features may be learned more or less fortuitously, if the weights in the

into   through

Figure 6.4
Endpoint configuration: the cases of English *into* and *through*

network happen to be initialized in a manner that allows that. But there is no external force pushing the network to pick up on static features other than the ones that appear at the end of movies. This means that the network learns to detect those static features that appear at the end of movies and is much less likely to detect those that do not. I shall refer to this as the *endpoint configuration constraint*.

To see just how tight a constraint this is, consider figure 6.4. Learning English *into* should be straightforward, since the relevant static feature, inclusion, will be present in the last frame of all the positive instances. Once the static feature of inclusion has been learned, the system can learn to track it over time using the source and path buffers, to arrive at a classification for each movie. Now consider the case of English *through,* also shown in the figure. Here, the static feature of inclusion is again relevant, but it appears only in midevent, never at the final frame. This situation is clearly more problematic than the one regarding *into:* we cannot expect the error feedback to cause the network to detect the feature of inclusion, because it is simply not there to be detected at the last time step. It looks as if something has gone wrong—if the model cannot learn even a fairly simple term such as *through,* of what use is it? Luckily, this is not a serious problem: we can easily get around it by training for several spatial terms simultaneously. In particular, if the model learns *into* and *through* together, then in the process of learning *into,* the network will learn to detect inclusion, and that can then be used in learning *through.* In chapter 4, learning concepts together as a set was critical for the purpose of learning without explicit negative evidence. There is now another reason to have the model learn them as a set: the static features that are learned for one term can be used in learning others, which might not have been learnable if the network had not been forced to detect the relevant static features. Of course, children are also exposed to "training data" for a large set of words in parallel, rather than learning one at a time, so it is reasonable for a cognitive model to do the same. It is also possibly significant that recent work in developmental psycholinguistics has determined that children have a tendency to linguistically categorize actions based on their *results*, as opposed to other aspects such as the means by which the actions were effected (Behrend 1989, 1990; Smiley and Huttenlocher 1994). This can be seen as a form of focus on the endpoint of the action, the idea being that children are biased to attend primarily to the results of actions. This is similar to the endpoint configuration constraint we are considering here, and it can be taken as a form of reassurance that the techniques we are positing are at least not grossly incompatible with available psycholinguistic data on semantic acquisition.

This constraint arises directly from the structure and training regimen of the model. In that sense, it arises in part from the desire to build a simple model—as we saw, the model's design was guided by the general criterion of simplicity. After all, it is not necessarily the case that any model trained only at the final time step would give rise to the behavior we see here. In particular, had we overcome the practical limitations of back-propagation through time and used it to adjust the weights in these lower structures, the weight modifications could have been based on their behavior at all time steps of the movie, not just the last one. However, this would have required that we save the state of the map comparison and orientation combination structures at each time step of each training movie; and this in turn would have meant a significantly more complex model. Thus, the endpoint configuration constraint can be at least partially traced back to the simplicity criterion that we considered at the outset. This is an example, then, of a nonobvious constraint on learning arising from a modeling effort.

This run through the model is meant to serve two purposes. On the one hand, it is meant to acquaint the reader with some of the details of the particular model with which we are concerned here. On the other hand, it can also serve as an illustration of constrained connectionism in practice. The hope is that through example this exposition makes the overall philosophy somewhat clearer. Constrained connectionism advocates a division of labor between structured and unstructured portions of the network, so that the resulting model is computationally appropriate, motivated, and analyzable. What we have examined is a very specific instantiation of this general philosophy. We have also seen the kind of analysis to which such networks lend themselves, in our discussion of the endpoint configuration constraint. The network structures are fairly easily understood, and this analyzability trickles out to the rest of the network, enabling us to articulate clear constraints on what the network as a whole is and is not capable of learning.

6.5   Results

Recall that we began this chapter by highlighting three very general principles that guided the model's design: adequacy, motivation, and simplicity. We have spent some time motivating the model's structures and arguing for the relative simplicity of its design. However, its adequacy has not yet been thoroughly demonstrated. In particular, we have no evidence so far that the model is capable of acquiring spatial semantic systems from a range of natural languages. This is critical because after all, the whole point of the model is to provide a characterization of the human semantic potential in the domain of spatial relations.

With this in mind, let us examine the model's performance on a number of languages. In doing so, we shall substantiate the claim that the network can learn terms from a range of languages, and in the process, we shall highlight some interesting crosslinguistic differences in spatial structure. The model was trained on spatial terms from Mixtec, German, Japanese, Russian, and English. In the case of English, training took place without explicit negatives, using implicit negatives through the heuristic of mutual exclusivity. However, I did not have full contrast sets for the other languages, so the model learned using explicit negatives in those cases. As we shall see, training through mutual exclusivity was successful for English, and I expect similar performance on other languages, once full sets of spatial terms are collected. Let us examine each of these languages in turn.

The spatial system of Mixtec differs significantly from that of English. As we saw in chapter 2, Mixtec has no words corresponding to English *above* or *on*. Instead, it uses the terms *šini* and *siki*, which translate literally as "head" and "animal back," respectively, but which are used to denote spatial relations as well as body parts. Both are used only in situations in which the trajector is either above or on top of the landmark, but the choice of which Mixtec term to use also depends on the orientation of the major axis of the landmark. If the landmark is vertically extended, the term *šini* ("head") is used. The motivation behind this is that if one were to view the landmark as an erect biped (e.g., a human being), the trajector would be located at or near the landmark's head; and it is of course easiest to view the landmark as such when it is vertically rather than horizontally extended. On the other hand, if the landmark is horizontally extended, the term *siki* ("animal back") is used. The motivation in this case is that if one were to view the landmark as a quadruped on all fours, the trajector would be located at or near the animal's back. It is critical to note that although the motivation for the terms springs from the anatomy of bipeds and quadrupeds, knowledge of this anatomy is not required in learning the perceptually grounded semantics for the terms; indeed, the model being presented is able to learn these Mixtec terms without any specialized knowledge of anatomy.

The model was trained on *šini* and *siki* together under quickprop, a variant of back-propagation that exhibits fast convergence. There were 9 positive and 15 negative examples of each spatial term in the training set. Training was quite fast, requiring only 40 epochs to bring the summed squared error lower than 0.01. Once the model had learned these two terms, it was tested on data to which it had not been exposed. Its generalization to a training set of 9 positive and 10 negative examples of each term was excellent: the summed squared error over the test set was also under 0.01. This is surprisingly good generalization given such a small training set. It becomes somewhat less surprising when we consider the nature of the architecture, however. As we saw earlier, the built-in structures could be expected to enhance generalization, since their inclusion

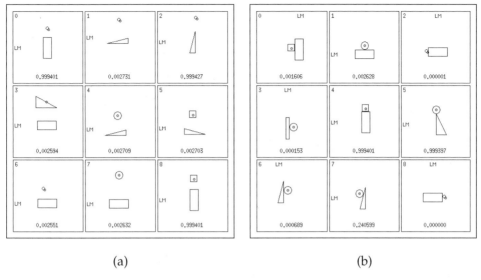

(a)   (b)

Figure 6.5
Mixtec *šini* tested on positive examples of English *above* and *on*

reduces the dimensionality of the search space and restricts the learning process to dimensions strongly suspected to be of significance. This, then, demonstrates that a constrained architecture can yield superior generalization. We shall see this in the results from other languages as well.

Figure 6.5 shows the model's *šini* responses to two other test sets consisting of positive examples of English *above* and *on*. The model had not seen any of these movies during training either. The number at the bottom of each scene indicates how good an example of *šini* the system has judged the scene to be. Here, 0 means poor and 1 means excellent. As the figure shows, the model accurately picks out the good examples of *šini* from among the various examples of *above* and *on*, and in doing so highlights differences between the Mixtec and English spatial systems. For example, notice that the only scenes considered to be strong examples of *šini* are those in which the trajector is located above or on a vertically extended landmark—in its "head" region. English does not make any analogous discrimination with respect to *above* or *on*. However, English does distinguish on the basis of contact between trajector and landmark. If a trajector above a landmark comes down to rest on it, the classification changes from *above* to *on*. This does not happen in Mixtec, as the figure shows: there are strong responses both to scenes that exhibit contact and to scenes that do not.

Figure 6.6 shows the model's *siki* responses to the same two test sets. Again, we see that Mixtec is sensitive to the major axis orientation of the landmark— whether it is horizontally or vertically extended—whereas English is not. And

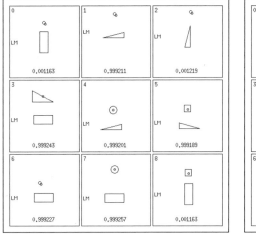 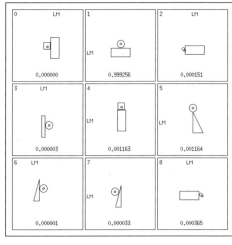

(a)   (b)

Figure 6.6
Mixtec *siki* tested on positive examples of English *above* and *on*

again we see that English is sensitive to contact between the trajector and landmark whereas Mixtec is not.

Although German is closely related to English, there are differences in the ways
in which the two languages structure space. The particular difference that we
shall examine concerns the German words *auf* and *an*. Although clearly distinct
in meaning, both are used in situations that would be described, in English,
using the single preposition *on*. In particular, *auf* denotes spatial relations in
which the trajector is located on a horizontal surface of the landmark, such as
its top, whereas *an* denotes relations in which the trajector is located on the side
of the landmark. Thus, one would use *auf* to describe a book on a table, but *an*
to describe a picture on a wall.

The model was trained on *auf* and *an* together. The training set for *an* contained 9 positive and 25 negative examples; the one for *auf* contained 25 positive
and 25 negative examples. Training was again quite fast: only 130 quickprop
epochs were required to bring the summed squared error lower than 0.01. Testing revealed excellent generalization in this case as well. The test set contained
9 positive and 9 negative examples of each of the two terms, and the summed
squared error over this test set was under 0.01. Figure 6.7 presents the model's
responses to positive examples of English *on*. The responses in box (a) indicate
how appropriate the model judges *auf* to be as a description of each spatial configuration shown; the responses in box (b) are appropriateness judgments for *an*.
As the scenes shown here illustrate, only those instances of English *on* in which

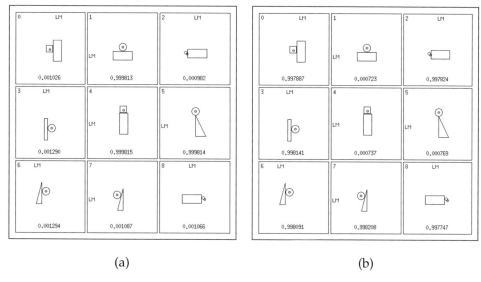

(a)   (b)

Figure 6.7
German *auf* and *an* tested on positive examples of English *on*

the trajector is on the top of the landmark are considered to be good examples of German *auf*. In contrast, those scenes in which the trajector is on the side of the landmark are taken as good examples of *an*. German *auf* and *an* thus have an orientational component that is missing from English *on*: the critical feature distinguishing the two German spatial terms appears to be the orientation of the landmark surface that the trajector touches. In fact, it is probably more accurate to cast the distinction in terms of the trajector being *supported* by the landmark from below, in the case of *auf*, or hanging from it, in the case of *an*. But force-related features such as support and hanging are not present in the model as it stands, and indeed are not directly visually perceptible, so language-learning children and models thereof must make do with the visual correlates of these features, namely, contact and the orientation of the contacted surface.

Japanese differs from Mixtec, German, and English in that it has a single spatial term, *ue ni*, that can be used to describe the location of a trajector either on top of the landmark or above it. This spatial term thus seems to convey the rather abstract meaning of being located higher than the landmark, without being sensitive to contact or support relationships between the two objects. The insensitivity to contact is reminiscent of Mixtec, but unlike Mixtec, Japanese is in addition insensitive to the horizontal or vertical extension of the landmark.

The model was trained on 13 positive and 10 negative examples of *ue ni*, and it converged to under 0.01 summed squared error in 100 quickprop epochs. Generalization to a test set was again extremely good: the summed squared error

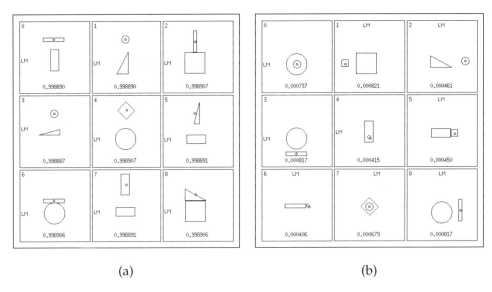

Figure 6.8
Japanese *ue ni:* positive and negative test sets

over 9 positive and 9 negative test examples was also under 0.01. The model's performance on this test set is illustrated in figure 6.8. In this figure we can see *ue ni*'s insensitivity to contact, for the model responds equally strongly to scenes in which the trajector and landmark touch and to those in which they do not. One way of thinking about this spatial term, then, is as an abstraction covering both English *above* and *on top of.*

Although these examples do indicate that the model can learn a variety of linguistic spatial systems, the examples so far concern static spatial relations only, rather than spatial events involving motion. As an example of the model's ability to learn motion-based semantics for spatial terms from a language other than English, let us focus on Russian. As we shall see, Russian is an appropriate choice when we shift our attention to motion. Although its static terms tend to be fairly similar to those of English, it exhibits some interesting differences from English in the linguistic categorization of spatial events. In particular, consider the two Russian prepositions *pod* and *iz-pod*. Whereas *pod* translates as "below" or "under" in English, there is no single English preposition corresponding to Russian *iz-pod*, which is best translated as "out from underneath" (Taube et al. 1987). The single word *iz-pod* is in fact morphologically derived from the words *iz* ("from") and *pod* ("under"), much the way English *into* is derived from *in* and *to.*

The system was supplied with 16 positive and 16 negative examples of *pod*, and 16 positive and 16 negative examples of *iz-pod*. Learning was again extremely

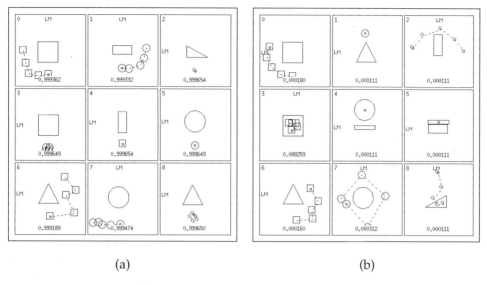

Figure 6.9
Russian *pod:* positive and negative test sets

fast, requiring only 40 quickprop epochs to converge to summed squared error under 0.01. Once trained, the model was given a test set made up of 10 positive and 10 negative examples of each of the two prepositions. The summed squared error over all 40 movies in the test set was equal to 0.01, indicating that the model generalized well for this experiment also. The model's performance on these test sets is shown in figure 6.9 and figure 6.10. This experiment once again makes the point that a constrained model of this sort can exhibit excellent generalization from the training set to the test set, and it also gives us an example of non-English spatial structuring that involves motion.

It gives us an example of something else as well. Recall that the behavior of this model is characterized by what we have been calling the endpoint configuration constraint. This constraint states that the model is biased to pick up on only those static features that are present in the final frame of movies in its training set. This is relevant here since the static feature of location underneath the landmark is critical to *iz-pod*—after all, the term means "out from underneath," so the source of the trajectory must be under the landmark. Thus, acquiring the semantics of *iz-pod* requires that the model pick up on the static feature "trajector underneath landmark." However, this will happen only if training movies have the trajector under the landmark in the final frame—and this will never be the case for positive instances of *iz-pod*. We can see this by considering the examples in figure 6.10(a). This in turn means that we can expect the model to have difficulty in learning *iz-pod* by itself, since the model will be biased

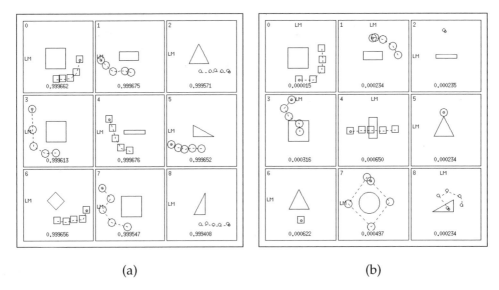

(a)   (b)

Figure 6.10
Russian *iz-pod:* positive and negative test sets

against learning the static feature "trajector underneath landmark," given only an *iz-pod* training set. (Three of the 16 movies that were negative instances of *iz-pod* in the training set did have the trajector located underneath the landmark in the final frame, but this is a small fraction of the training set as a whole.) As it happens, the model does have difficulty in these circumstances. When learning *iz-pod* in isolation, the network does not always converge on a solution, and when it does, the generalization to the test set tends to be substantially poorer than when *iz-pod* and *pod* are learned together. Out of five training sessions on *iz-pod* alone, two never converged to under 0.01 error within 400 quickprop epochs, and they showed no signs of converging at any point in the foreseeable future. The remaining three required an average of 320 quickprop epochs each. When the network did converge, generalization to the test set was only fair: a typical training session yielded 2.40 summed squared error over 40 test movies. This translates into approximately 0.24 error per test movie, indicating that the solution reached is not very close to that desired. In contrast, when *iz-pod* and *pod* were trained together, each of five training sessions converged to under 0.01 error in under 90 quickprop epochs, and they exhibited summed squared test set error of approximately 0.01, or around 0.04 error per movie. Thus, accurate acquisition of *iz-pod* is enabled by learning *pod* ("under") together with it.

Let us now move on to more familiar ground: English. The model was trained on movies corresponding to 10 English spatial terms, and in a significant de-parture from earlier practice, training took place without the benefit of explicit negative evidence. This was done through the technique of mutual exclusivity with deliberately attenuated negative evidence. Thus, this experiment brings together the issues of learning without explicit negative evidence, learning static features in individual frames, and recognizing events over time. In a sense, this is what we have been leading up to all along: a demonstration that the disparate elements of this model are effective when integrated into a coherent whole. Prior to this we have only considered these elements in isolation from one another.

The 10 English spatial terms are *above, below, left, right, around, in, on, out of, through,* and *over.* (The English preposition *over* is highly polysemous (Brugman 1981); for the time being we are considering only the sense of *over* that denotes motion over and across the landmark.) The network we saw in figure 6.3 had output nodes labeled for this training set. The model was supplied with 126 training movies, each composed of between five and nine frames. There were 25 examples of *in,* 16 examples each of *above* and *below,* 13 examples of *through,* 10 examples each of *around, on, out of,* and *over,* and 8 examples each of *left* and *right.* Training required 3000 epochs under back-propagation, with the attenuation factor B set to 0.067, eventually converging to 0.54 summed squared error. At that point, performance on a test set of positive and negative examples of each of the prepositions showed 0.59 summed squared error, over a total of 180 test movies. Once again, this is extremely good generalization to the test set.

Let us take a closer look at the model's performance on these test sets. Figure 6.11 presents the system's performance on the test sets for *above;* figure 6.12 presents *below;* figure 6.13 presents *left;* figure 6.14 presents *right;* figure 6.15 presents *around;* figure 6.16 presents *in;* figure 6.17 presents *on;* and figure 6.18 presents *out of.* The model's performance on *through* and *over* will be presented below. Most responses are within 0.1 of the desired output, and none is more than 0.34 from the desired output.

There are dependencies among the spatial terms learned here, just as there was in the case of Russian *iz-pod* and *pod.* Specifically, *through* is dependent on *in.* No positive example of *through* ends with the trajector included in the landmark. This means that if the model were to be trained on *through* alone, it should have difficulty detecting the static feature of inclusion; and since inclusion is critical to *through,* it should therefore have difficulty learning *through.* However, if it is trained on *in* and *through* at the same time, this problem is solved. Since movies described by *in* always end with the trajector included in the landmark, the model will be able to learn to detect inclusion and will then be able to use this feature in learning the semantics for *through.*

The responses shown in these figures were obtained at the last time step of each movie. However, recall from the earlier discussion that we can expect the training regimen used here to cause the system to respond appropriately *at each time step* to the portion of the movie viewed so far. For example, we can expect the output node for *in* to respond strongly in midevent for movies that correspond to *through;* similarly, we can expect the output node for *above* to

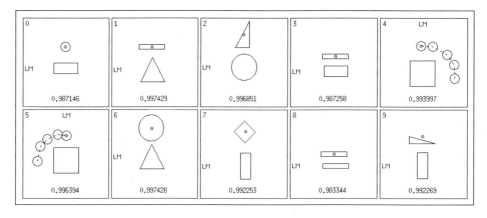

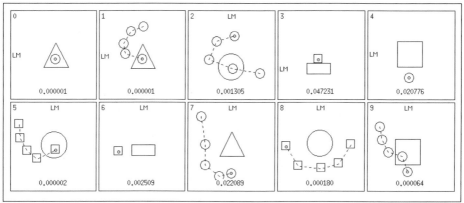

Figure 6.11
Positive and negative examples of English *above:* a test set

exhibit a strong response in midevent for movies corresponding to *over,* since we are restricting our attention here to the over-and-across sense of *over.* Let us now look at examples of the system doing just that.

Figure 6.19 presents the system's performance on a test set of positive examples of *through,* and figure 6.20 shows the model's response over time at the output node for *in* while viewing the positive examples of *through* shown in figure 6.19. (In addition, figure 6.21 presents the model's performance on a test set of negative examples of *through.*) Each box in figure 6.20 stands for the corresponding movie in figure 6.19. Within each box the horizontal dimension represents time, such that each tick is a single frame; while the vertical dimension represents the activation value of the output unit for *in.* Comparing these two figures movie by movie reveals that the output node for *in* is strongly activated whenever the movie up to and including the current frame is a good example of *in.* For

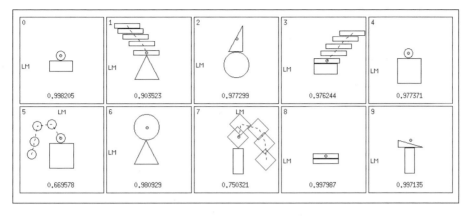

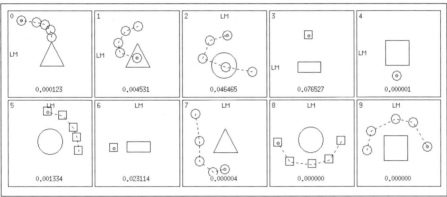

Figure 6.17
Positive and negative examples of English *on:* a test set

not dictate that the results be of this form; it merely allows it. In fact, other training runs on *in* have yielded responses that were far more discrete than this. Both types of results are valid given the training set, and importantly, both are sanctioned by the design. The fact that these graded results are not imposed by the structure tells us something, when we take this as a model of human spatial semantics. It suggests that we look for this graded structure in the input rather than in the perceptual mechanisms that process that input. After all, unlike the model, humans *reliably* pick up on the degree of inclusion and find that linguistically significant. The model only *sometimes* does this, given the binary nature of its training set. This means that forcing the model to be sensitive to this gradation—as humans appear to be—would require graded items in the training set. Translating this into psychological terms, it suggests that children not only are sensitive to simple binary all-or-nothing categorizations but also understand

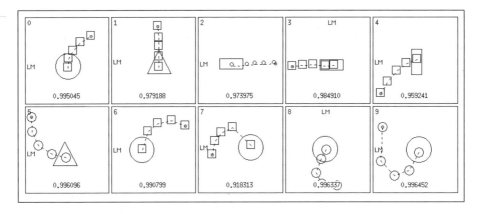

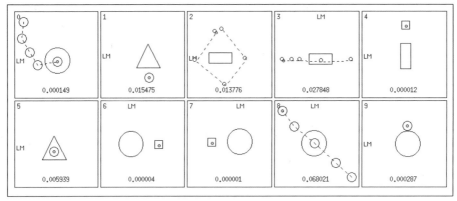

Figure 6.18
Positive and negative examples of English *out of:* a test set

and make use of hedges, qualifiers, prosody, and other means of indicating that a particular configuration is a less-than-perfect example of some spatial term.

In the case of *in*, the graded membership is attributable to the strength of a single feature, inclusion, and the manner in which the model's structures compute that single feature. It will not always be the case that prototype effects are so handily accounted for, however. We saw earlier that another possible form of explanation for prototype effects, both in general and specifically here in the domain of spatial categorization, is that prototypical instances of categories are instances in which there is strong evidence for the category from a number of different factors, each of which provides partial support for category membership. More concretely, one could imagine a prototypical *above* as being one in which both the proximal and center-of-mass orientations are perfectly aligned with upright vertical. Figure 6.26 presents a case of graded category membership

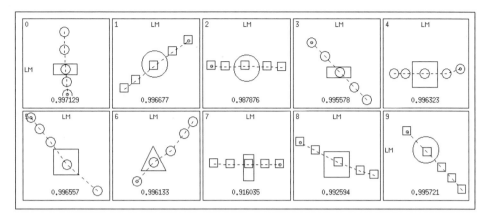

Figure 6.19
Positive examples of English *through:* a test set

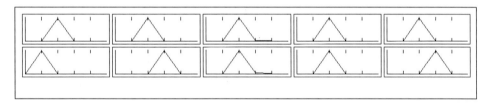

Figure 6.20
Response over time to *in* while viewing positive examples of *through*

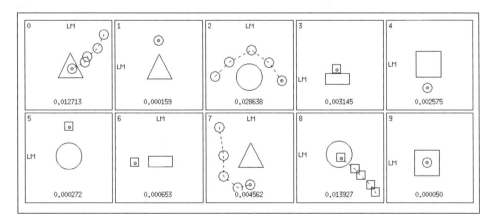

Figure 6.21
Negative examples of English *through:* a test set

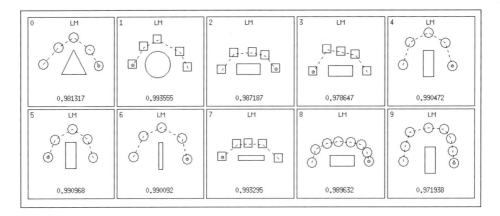

Figure 6.22
Positive examples of English *over:* a test set

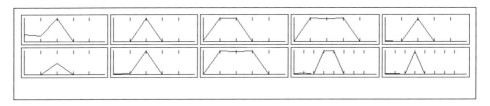

Figure 6.23
Response over time to *above* while viewing positive examples of *over*

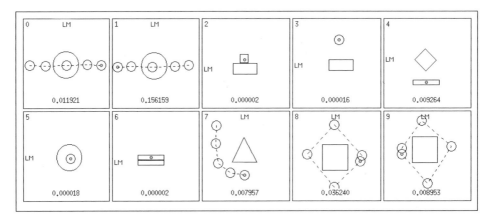

Figure 6.24
Negative examples of English *over:* a test set

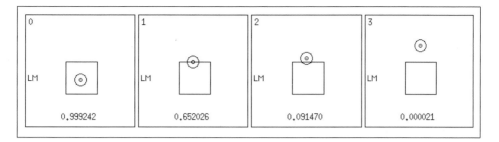

Figure 6.25
Graded responses to English *in*

in which the overall response appears to depend on a combination of factors. In English *above*, I have been postulating that two of the contributing factors are the proximal and center-of-mass orientations.

The first row of scenes in figure 6.26 shows a small circular trajector located relative to a triangle. In the three scenes, the proximal orientation is kept constant, but the trajector slides up the hypotenuse of the triangle, so that the center-of-mass orientation gets closer and closer to upright vertical. At the same time, the scenes become increasingly prototypical cases of *above*, as reflected in the responses given by the model to these three scenes. This, then, shows the role played by the center-of-mass orientation in classifications of English *above*. The second row of scenes shows that the proximal orientation plays a role in these classifications as well. The center-of-mass orientation is roughly the same in the three scenes of this row, but the proximal orientation varies, getting closer and closer to upright vertical. Correspondingly, the model's response differs from scene to scene, more or less in accord with our intuition as to how good an example of *above* the particular scene is. Finally, the scenes of the third row illustrate the notion of prototypicality as the co-occurrence of strong evidence from several sources. In the first scene, both proximal and center-of-mass orientations are aligned with upright vertical, and the system's response is correspondingly strong. In the second scene, the proximal orientation is still perfectly aligned with upright vertical, but the center-of-mass orientation is not; the response for this somewhat less prototypical instance of *above* is slightly weaker. Finally, in the third scene, neither of the two orientations is perfectly aligned with upright vertical. Here, the response is significantly weaker, corresponding to our intuition that although this scene is an instance of *above*, it is a rather weak one.

Significantly, these results were not obtained from the same training run whose results we viewed in detail above. The output for *above* on that run was far more discrete than the one shown here and did not at all match my intuitions regarding prototypical and nonprototypical instances of *above*. This is of course another

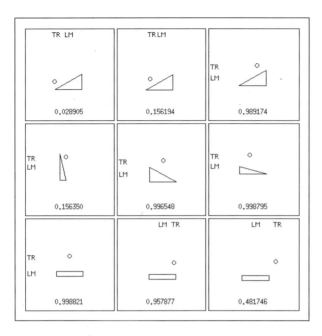

Figure 6.26
English *above:* prototype effects

illustration of the point raised earlier in connection with *in:* the structure of the model allows, but does not dictate, graded responses consonant with human prototypicality judgments. Again, this suggests that the reliably graded nature of the output may instead be present in the input.

6.7   Discussion

Let us try to take stock of what we have learned. Specifically, let us view the model in terms of what it may suggest regarding the human semantic potential for spatial terms. Our primary goal, after all, is to characterize that semantic potential. In particular, we have been wondering (1) what sort of mechanism could adapt itself to the different structurings of space found in the world's natural languages, (2) how such a system could learn without explicit negative evidence, and (3) what such a model might tell us about possible semantic universals.

The examples above clearly indicate that the model can adapt itself to a range of quite dissimilar spatial systems, and the technique of mutual exclusivity with attenuated error provides a means of learning without negative evidence. So the first two points are answered, at least preliminarily. But does the model tell us anything further? Does it suggest any semantic universals in the domain of space?

A rather jaundiced view might hold that we have learned nothing new and that the model suggests nothing new. After all, the argument would run, there really are only two additional things we can take away from the model. One is the general idea that the acquisition of spatial semantics is perceptually grounded. The other is the idea that it is neurally implemented. Neither of these is news. We knew and subscribed to these notions well before we started. The modeling effort therefore has yielded no new insight. It is scientifically empty.

Fortunately, this uncharitable appraisal is demonstrably incorrect. As it happens, there *are* things the model can tell us beyond the two vague and unhelpful generalities outlined above. This is where constrained connectionism comes in. The structures built into the model place easily articulable constraints on the model's operation, and these constraints can then be translated into predictions regarding the human acquisition of spatial semantics. Let us consider three specific examples.

Graded response prediction

Children receive and are sensitive to linguistic input that indicates how central a member of a spatial category a particular spatial configuration is.

We have already seen the basis for this prediction, in our discussion of prototypes. Although the model *allows* graded responses of the sort that match human prototypicality judgments, it does not *dictate* that such responses be exhibited. Each movie in the training set is labeled as a perfect example of some spatial term. Given this information, some training runs result in graded responses, such that mediocre examples of some category receive a rating somewhere between that for good examples and that for poor ones. Other training runs result in fairly discrete responses, such that mediocre examples of a category are classified either as good examples or as poor ones—there is no interpolation in this case. This tells us that if we want the model to reliably produce graded responses, as humans do, we will have to supply it with graded judgments in its input. It will then be explicitly trained to match those graded judgments. For example, when shown a fair-to-middling example of *in* or *above*, the model should be told that this is only a fair example, and it should be trained to output a value somewhere between that appropriate for a good example and that appropriate for a poor one. In short, if the interpolation does not consistently arise from the model's structures, then graded judgments must actually be present in the input. Translating this into human terms, this suggests that children also receive and attend to graded judgments in their input. These could take the form of utterances such as "partway in" or could be conveyed through prosody.

Intermediate sequentiality prediction

The only sequentiality that is relevant in closed-class forms for spatial events is the tripartite structure of beginning configuration, path taken, and ending

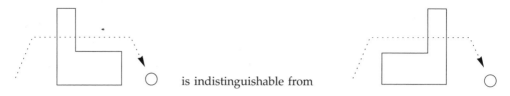

Figure 6.27
Intermediate sequentiality prediction: Sequentiality within the path is irrelevant

configuration, or source-path-destination. In particular, no language will distinguish two events that differ only in the sequence in which configurations *within the path* occur.

Consider, for example, the two events illustrated in figure 6.27. The model predicts that these two events will not be distinguished on the basis of sequentiality by closed-class terms in any language. This is because the two events are identical in their source-path-destination structure except for the order in which passing through the landmark and passing over a region of the landmark in midpath occur. Note that beginning and end configurations are essentially identical in the two cases: in both cases the trajector begins its path to the left of the landmark and ends its path to the right of it. Moreover, in both cases the path includes a segment during which the trajector is *inside* the landmark and one during which it is *above* the landmark. In fact, these two overall trajectories are distinguished only by the order in which these path-internal *above* and *inside* segments occur: in the first case *inside* occurs before *above*, and in the second case the order is reversed. Since it is only path-internal sequentiality that distinguishes the source-path-destination structure of these two events, the prediction asserts that no language will distinguish these events on the basis of sequentiality using a closed-class form.

How does the model give rise to this prediction? It follows directly from the tripartite trajectory representation discussed in chapter 5. Recall that because of this structure, source-path-destination sequentiality is preserved, since there are separate representations for the source (first frame), destination (final frame), and path (intervening frames). However, the path representation for the intervening frames simply records what has occurred over the path as a whole; it is not sensitive to exactly when particular events occurred. In particular, it simply records the maximum, minimum, and average values attained by nodes in the layer below it over the course of the movie. This idea of insensitivity to exactly when something happened is clearly a good idea for such spatial terms as *through:* it is critical that the trajector be inside the landmark at some point after the source and before the destination, but it is not critical just when. The representation used captures this idea of recording the occurrence of spatial events over the path independent of their timing. In the process, though, it ignores all sequentiality within the path, and it would therefore be unable to distinguish the two events shown in the figure. We saw that this structure is appropriate for words such as *through*; now we are considering other ramifications of choosing a structure of this nature. This is an example of a prediction resulting from structures built into the model—the correlate in the model of either innate or universally acquired human perceptual structures. In this regard, it is important to indicate that my primary theoretical commitment here is to the idea of a motion perception mechanism that is insensitive to precisely when an event occurs, rather than to the particular implementation of this general idea that was used in the model. Given this, one obvious question that arises is whether the intermediate sequentiality prediction necessarily results directly from this abstract idea of timing-insensitivity. That is, does the prediction flow directly from the idea to which I am theoretically committed? The answer is, not necessarily. One might discard exact timing but retain order information, keeping a list of significant events in order without any indication of the exact time of their occurrence. If this is the case, doesn't the prediction flow from an implementation detail to which I am not theoretically bound, rather than from a general principle to which I am? In other words, is it the case that the model exhibits order-insensitivity for theoretically uninteresting reasons?

The answer is that the prediction results from the confluence of two commitments: my commitment to the idea of timing-insensitivity, and my commitment to building a simple model. Although an order-sensitive model of the sort sketched above could in principle be built, the simplest architecture considered in the design process was the order-insensitive one we have been viewing. Thus, the prediction flows not just from the theoretical notion of timing-insensitivity, but also from the more general desideratum of model simplicity.

This prediction is of course open to empirical falsification. It is interesting to note, however, that there are languages with particularly rich systems of path specification that seem to conform to it. Atsugewi, for example, has a system of closed-class verbal suffixes indicating such intricate notions as "down into a gravitic container (e.g., a basket, a cupped hand, a pocket, a lake basin)" and "over the rim into a volume enclosure (e.g., a gopher hole, a mouth)" (Talmy 1983, 15). These suffixes, although semantically quite elaborate, do not express path-internal sequentiality, but rather specify the nature of the landmark. Notice that even in the case of "over the rim into a volume enclosure" only one event is specified as taking place during the path, namely, going over the rim; this suffix is therefore also consistent with the intermediate sequentiality prediction.

One ramification of this prediction is that it implies that the description of complex paths in which path-internal sequentiality is significant will require the *composition* of closed-class forms, resulting in such constructions as "go over and then through." Here, the individual closed-class forms *over* and *through* serve as building blocks for the description as a whole, and although they do not express path-internal sequentiality themselves, the expression as a whole does.

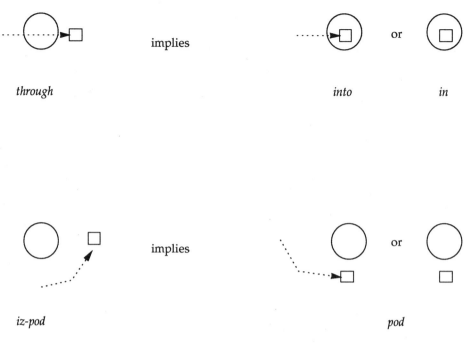

Figure 6.28
Endpoint configuration prediction: Any language that has a closed-class form denoting motion out of or motion through some configuration will also have a closed-class form denoting either motion into that configuration or static location in it

Endpoint configuration prediction
Any language that has a closed-class form denoting motion out of or motion through some configuration will also have a closed-class form denoting either motion into that configuration or static location in it.

Consider, for example, the English lexeme *through*, shown in the upper left of figure 6.28. Here we see a small square trajector moving through a circular landmark object. We can view the lexeme *through* as denoting motion through a configuration of inclusion, in that inclusion of the trajector within the landmark occurs in midevent for *through*. This leads us to predict, by our posited universal, that English will have a closed-class form denoting either motion into a configuration of inclusion (*into*) or static location in the configuration of inclusion (*in*).

Consider the lower example, from Russian. The fact that Russian has a closed-class lexeme *iz-pod*, denoting motion of a trajector out from underneath a landmark, leads us to predict that it will also have a closed-class form denoting either motion into the region under the landmark or static location under the landmark. In fact, Russian *pod* can be used in either of these two senses.

The model gives rise to this prediction because the attempt to build as structurally simple a model as possible resulted in a model with a particular constraint on its operation: the endpoint configuration constraint. The model learns to categorize based on only those spatial features that occur at the end of some event it has seen. In this sense, the model exhibits a form of endpoint emphasis, a phenomenon that has been noted in children when learning words for events (Behrend 1989, 1990; Smiley and Huttenlocher 1994). Thus, if it is never exposed to an event ending in the inclusion of the trajector in the landmark, it will be biased against detecting the static spatial feature of inclusion and making use of it in the categorization of other events. This means it will not be able to learn *through*, since inclusion in midpath is a critical element of *through*. And since the use of mutual exclusivity here means that the model is exposed to only positive instances of spatial terms from the language being learned, it will only see examples of events ending in inclusion if the language in fact has closed-class forms denoting such events. Thus, the existence of a form denoting *through* in a language implies the existence of forms like *in* or *into*, since the model predicts that *through* would be unlearnable otherwise.

The essential idea behind this prediction, then, is that closed-class linguistic expression of motion out of or through some configuration depends on the prior recognition that location in that configuration is linguistically relevant; in turn, this recognition depends on the existence in the language of terms denoting either location in that configuration or motion into it. The prediction is clearly falsifiable: any language containing a closed-class form for motion out of or through some configuration that did not also contain forms for motion into or location in that configuration would falsify it. Moreover, since the prediction arises from the perceptually based endpoint emphasis of the model together with the principle of mutual exclusivity, it illustrates determination of semantic structure by a combination of nonlinguistic cognitive constraints and a universally posited naming heuristic.

One possible response to this last prediction would be that it could have been arrived at without going through the trouble of building a model. The prediction might depend only on the very abstract notion of endpoint emphasis, independent of architectural details. That is, one might argue that the psychological and linguistic data themselves clearly embody some form of endpoint emphasis and that this is enough to warrant this prediction. For example, the same word is often used to denote location in some configuration and motion into that configuration: "The dog is hiding *under* the bed" (location) and "The dog crawled *under* the bed" (motion to location). This could be taken as evidence that language emphasizes the endpoint of motion, since the word used to denote the spatial event of the dog crawling under the bed (*under*) is the same as the word that would be used to describe the configuration at the *end* of that motion— the description of the event as a whole is the same as the description of the endpoint. The endpoint configuration prediction then follows directly from the general idea of endpoint emphasis, and *any* model that embodies this abstract notion will of necessity give rise to this prediction. Under this view, the prediction is not so much a product of the particular architecture and training regimen used here as it is a product of this very general feature that characterizes this system among many other possible ones. It could perhaps be arrived at, then, simply by noting the existence of endpoint emphasis in language and by working out the ramifications of such a phenomenon—without having to build a model at all.

There is a serious problem with this line of argument, however: the prediction does not strictly *follow* from the abstract notion of endpoint emphasis; it is only made to seem *plausible*. Although it does seem reasonable, given the general idea of endpoint emphasis, that static features would be learned only if they appeared at the end of some training movie, the general concept of endpoint emphasis is too imprecisely formulated for us to say that this prediction actually follows from it. Notice that the same abstract notion of endpoint emphasis also makes it seem plausible that terms that in some way highlight the beginning of the event, rather than the end, could not be learned. But this is not the case at all, Russian *iz-pod* ("out from under") being a counterexample. This spatial term, which highlights the beginning of the event in that it focuses attention on where the landmark was *before* it started moving, has been learned by the system described here. This then illustrates the importance, in this instance, of working out the details of a model, rather than dealing with these notions at a more abstract level.

There is another point that cannot be so easily dismissed, however. This concerns the status of the model itself and the degree to which we are justified in drawing predictions from it. The model we have been examining cannot be taken as a fully explanatory account, since there is at least one very significant influence on spatial semantics that has not been taken into consideration here at all. In particular, there is no account of nonlinguistic spatial conceptual development and the manner in which this might affect the linguistic categorization of space (Piaget and Inhelder 1967; Clark 1977; Huttenlocher, Smiley, and Ratner 1983; Johnston 1985; Mandler 1992). All spatial learning in the model is driven by language, and this is certainly not the case for children. This is a major shortcoming, and it highlights the fact that what we have on our hands is a *partial* model of the acquisition of spatial semantics, a model of only certain aspects of the process as a whole. The primary issue associated with this point is the explanatory force of the model: for if it is only a partial model, it could well be the case that parts of the acquisition process not modeled here will interact with those parts that are modeled and will affect the validity of the predictions made. Let us consider a concrete example, the endpoint configuration prediction. As we have seen, this prediction posits that *through* will be extremely difficult to learn unless the network is also learning some term denoting an event or relation ending in inclusion, such as *in* or *into*. This is so because otherwise the model's structure and training regimen will make it difficult for it to pick up on inclusion, and *through* will therefore be hard to learn. The incompleteness of the model is problematic for us here. What if prelinguistic spatial conceptual development had already equipped the language-learning child with a notion of inclusion? Why should the child not bring that to bear on the learning of words such as *through*, independent of the presence or absence in the language of such words as *in* or *into*? Clearly, this is a possibility, and in this case we would not be justified in stating that the model gives rise to the endpoint configuration prediction; this state of affairs would invalidate our derivation of the prediction from the model. However, there is another possibility. It may be the case that prelinguistic spatial conceptual development does *not* supply the child with the concepts required by language at all. In the case of a concept as foundational as inclusion, this is unlikely. Therefore, the endpoint configuration prediction is probably not applicable in this case, despite its being used as an example above. But not all spatial terms denote such primitive spatial concepts. For instance, recall that the Mixtec term *šini* ("head") is applicable whenever a landmark is above or on top of a vertically extended landmark. Such a comparatively complex concept is far less likely to be acquired through prelinguistic conceptual development than is a fairly primitive one such as inclusion. Its acquisition is therefore more likely to be language-driven. If this is the case, the endpoint configuration prediction is valid when applied to such a concept, even if it is not necessarily valid in the case of inclusion.

Where does all of this leave us? Since prelinguistic spatial conceptual development was not modeled, the validity of the endpoint configuration prediction depends on the concepts in question and on whether those concepts have in fact been prelinguistically acquired. Thus, the prediction is applicable in at least some cases. The general point here is that the unmodeled aspects of semantic acquisition can make the derivation of predictions from the model a less than straightforward matter, since the interaction of the modeled and unmodeled aspects of acquisition is not specified. The incompleteness of the model therefore damages our ability to translate constraints on the model's operation into clear behavioral predictions. It is probably best under the circumstances to take the three predictions listed above quite tentatively and to view them as suggestions from a partial model rather than predictions from a fully specified one.

Recall that one of the central themes of this book is that a focused computational modeling effort in a subfield of linguistic inquiry can both give rise to general techniques that may find applicability outside the original domain for which they were invented and provide explanations concerning the nature of language. Earlier we saw that the technique of using weak implicit negative instances is a very general method that resulted from the work described here; that is, it is an example of the way in which such a modeling effort can give rise to computational techniques of general applicability. Here, we see the other side of the coin. The predictions, or suggestions, outlined above arise from the particular architecture and training regimen used and thus provide an example of a modeling effort giving rise not just to techniques but also to concrete, if tentative, predictions regarding linguistic phenomena.

Chapter 7
Extensions

This chapter presents several extensions to the model that we have just seen. A good number of directions for extension suggest themselves—so many, in fact, that the work actually done to date seems, in retrospect, to be more a foundation-laying than anything approaching the final word. Some of the most linguistically interesting issues related to the acquisition of perceptually grounded semantics, such as polysemy and deixis, are in fact addressed by various extensions, rather than by the core model. Under this view, the model itself has served primarily to provide a framework within which to think about these issues and a software environment within which to investigate them. This chapter is devoted to outlining some of these issues. In some cases preliminary modeling efforts have already been made; in others this has not yet happened. Let us begin by examining two issues that have been modeled at least initially; we shall then move on to some others that have not. These first two issues are polysemy and deixis.

7.1 Polysemy

Polysemy is the phenomenon whereby a single word has a number of distinct but related senses. In some cases it is possible to find a single abstract meaning covering the various senses, but in others this is demonstrably impossible. Let us consider one example of each sort.

Figure 7.1 presents the model's performance on a test set for English *in*, after it was trained on this spatial term alone. A form of polysemy is manifested here, since movies of two distinct sorts appear: movies depicting the trajector remaining within the landmark (movies 1, 3, 7, and 9), and movies depicting motion of the trajector *into* the landmark (movies 0, 2, 4, 5, 6, and 8). There is in fact a single abstraction over these two cases: the trajector is inside the landmark at the last time step of the movie. This single, simple criterion serves to distinguish positive from negative examples of *in*, leaving no need for more intricate semantic theorizing—or at least not within this limited domain. In actuality, the full semantics of *in* are a good deal more subtle than I make them out to be here. Compare, for instance, "He walked *in* the room," which seems a perfectly normal usage of the word *in* in its motion-into sense, with "He drove

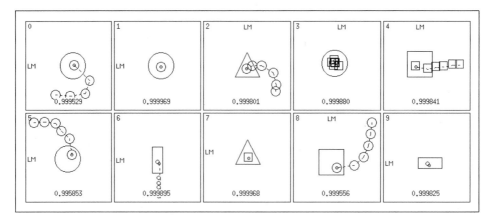

Figure 7.1
A test set for English *in*, learned by itself

in the city," which does not admit a motion-into interpretation. (I am indebted to George Lakoff for this example.) In any event, even if there are fairly delicate constraints governing exactly when this word may be used in which sense, the central point remains: there are two senses for *in*, which may be collapsed into a single abstraction. Given the existence of such an abstraction, it is not clear on what basis one might say that these two senses are distinct, without starting down a slippery slope that would lead us to assert that each and every movie in the set is an instantiation of a "distinct" sense. After all, in some motion-into movies the trajector approaches the landmark from above, and in others it approaches from below—why should these not count as separate senses? Yet we do have the persistent intuition that the movies in the figure break down into the two senses just outlined. It is this intuition of sense-distinctness in the face of a simple abstraction that will be our immediate concern. One possibility is to make recourse to the perceptual salience of motion itself and to assert that it is because of this salience that the distinctness of the two senses seems so natural. Notice, however, that movie 3, in which the trajector moves but remains within the landmark, is an instance of the inclusion rather than the motion-into sense, so simple motion cannot be the answer either. Let us try to determine under what conditions the model will make this inclusion/motion-into distinction, to see if it can shed any light on this issue.

Figure 7.2 presents the activation vectors for the top hidden layer of the model at the last time step of each movie, for the movies shown in figure 7.1. In other words, each rectangle shows the strength of activation of each of the units in the top hidden layer of the model at the end of one of the movies viewed. Ten activation vectors are shown, one for each movie in the figure; the position of the activation vector within figure 7.2 corresponds to the position of the movie it

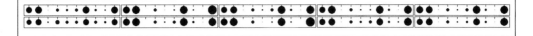

Figure 7.2
Contents of the top hidden layer for English *in*, learned by itself

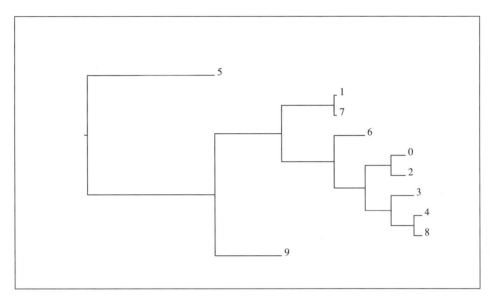

Figure 7.3
Cluster diagram for *in*, learned by itself

represents in figure 7.1, and the size of the black circles indicates how strongly a particular unit in the hidden layer is activated. It should be apparent that these activation vectors do not differ much from movie to movie; in particular, there is no obvious division into two types of activation signature, which could be interpreted as corresponding to the two senses outlined above. Similarly, when we examine figure 7.3, which presents the results of hierarchical clustering on the activation vectors shown in figure 7.2, we find that the clustering does not correspond to the two-way breakdown that seems so intuitively obvious. Here, the horizontal spacing between nodes in the tree is proportional to the Euclidean distances between clusters. (The clustering algorithm takes the distance between two clusters to be the distance between their nearest two points.) The primary distinction made here is between movie 5 and all others, rather than between "remaining-in" and "moving-in." This, together with the fact that the activation vectors do not differ much across movies, leads us to conclude that the distinction between being in and moving into was not captured by the network.

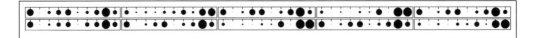

Figure 7.4
Contents of the top hidden layer for *in*, learned together with *through*

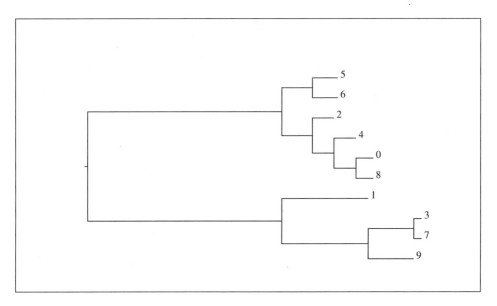

Figure 7.5
Cluster diagram for *in*, learned together with *through*

On the other hand, when *in* is learned in conjunction with *through*, an entirely different picture emerges. Figure 7.4 presents the top-hidden-layer activation vectors at the last time step, for the movies we saw earlier, and figure 7.5 presents the results of hierarchical cluster analysis performed on those vectors. The activation patterns in figure 7.4 are of two general forms, one of which appears for movies 0, 2, 4, 5, 6, and 8, and the other of which appears for movies 1, 3, 7, and 9. Thus, these two forms can be seen as corresponding to the two senses outlined above, since they represent movies of these two types. Similarly, figure 7.5 reflects the fact that the primary distinction made here is between these two sets of movies, corresponding to the distinction between the static inclusion and motion-into senses of English *in*.

When *in* is learned in conjunction with *through*, then, the activation patterns of the top hidden layer of the system reflect the polysemous structure of *in*— or, perhaps more accurately, reflect our intuition that the two senses outlined above should be considered distinct even though there is an abstraction that covers the two. And this separation does not occur when *in* is learned alone. Although it might not be obvious ahead of time that this would be the case, it makes perfect sense: learning *through* forces the system to bring information concerning inclusion (or lack thereof) from earlier parts of the movie into its top-hidden-layer representation, since inclusion occurs in midmovie for *through*. That would serve to differentiate the two senses of *in*.

This experiment, then, has shown how the *paradigmatic context* of a linguistic form—the contrast set of linguistic forms that might grammatically be used in its place—can affect the way in which the polysemy of a single word is learned. It suggests that the basis of our intuition that the two senses of *in* are distinct may be found in the nature of the representations that are formed when we learn *in* together with other words. Although a perfectly serviceable abstraction over the two senses can be found, we are left with the notion that they are distinct primarily because of the influence of other words in our vocabulary.

This sounds plausible, but it cannot be the whole story. The obvious question that arises is, What happens when *in* is learned not just with *through* but with a full contrast set? As we saw, it makes good sense that *through* would affect the representations in the manner seen here—but wouldn't *above, below, around, over*, and other words affect these representations in a manner that would not highlight the distinction between the two senses we are considering? It seems reasonable to assume, for example, that learning *in* together with *above* and *below* would cause the representations formed to reflect the distinction between motion from above and motion from below, a straw-man semantic distinction that we entertained and quickly discarded earlier, since it is intuitively much less salient than the inclusion/into distinction. In fact, figure 7.6 demonstrates that these misgivings are well founded. This shows the clustering that results when *in* is learned together with *above, below, left, right, around, on, out of, through*, and *over*—the same contrast set that we saw in chapter 6. Clearly, the movies do not cluster neatly into the two senses as they did when *in* was learned with *through* only. This tells us that the simple account given above, under which the intuitive separateness of the two senses of *in* can be traced to the contrast set learned along with *in*, is at best incomplete. In order for the distinctness of the senses to be explained in this fashion, we would need something in addition to the model as we know it. In particular, we would need some means by which words are grouped together in sets such that only words in the same set can affect the nature of each others' representations. For example, consider the set of spatial terms involving inclusion: *in, out of*, and *through*. If some as yet unspecified mechanism arranged things so that terms in this set could influence the formation of representations for other terms in the set, and no other words could exert such an influence, then *through* and *out of* would be the only words in the contrast set that would influence the formation of polysemous representations for *in*. Under these circumstances, one would expect a situation similar to the

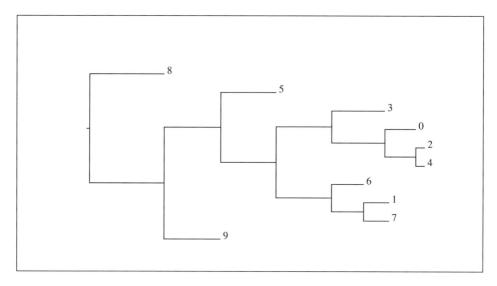

Figure 7.6
Cluster diagram for *in*, learned with a full contrast set

one that obtained when only *in* and *through* were learned together: one would expect the two senses of *in* to cluster tightly. But this assumes a currently nonexistent aspect of the model, the postulated grouping mechanism. Moreover, there is no obvious independent reason to posit such a mechanism, so the intuition of separateness is not explained by recourse to independently motivated mechanisms and processes. Should such a grouping mechanism for words prove to be useful for unrelated reasons, we would then have an explanation for the intuitive distinctness of the two senses of *in*. Until then, all we have is an intriguing possibility.

Let us next consider a case of "true" polysemy, polysemy for which it is demonstrable that no abstraction over the various senses exists: namely, the English preposition *over*. Figure 7.7 shows a test set for *over*, after the model was trained on this polysemous spatial term in isolation. Note that the three rows of movies correspond to three senses of *over*. The first row exhibits motion over and across the landmark without contact between trajector and landmark, as in the sentence "The bird flew *over* the house." The second row exhibits static location over the landmark, as in the sentence "The lamp is hanging *over* the table." The third row exhibits motion over and across, with the trajector touching the landmark en route, as in the sentences "I walked *over* the bridge" and "I climbed *over* the wall." It can easily be shown that no abstraction covers these three senses. Any abstract meaning for *over* would have to either allow or disallow contact between the trajector and landmark. Clearly, in some cases it

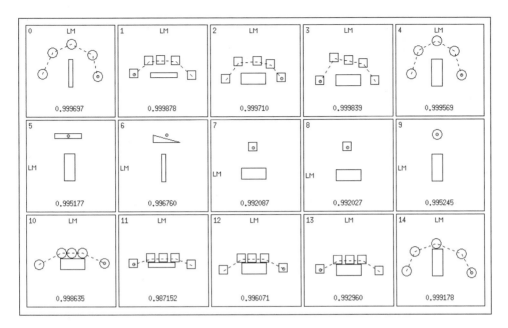

Figure 7.7
A test set for English *over*, learned by itself

should be allowed, since the movies in the bottom row are all positive examples of *over* and all exhibit contact. And clearly, it is not necessary, since the movies in the first row do not exhibit contact but are also acceptable examples of *over*. We might be tempted to say, then, that the abstract schema for *over* is neutral or unspecified as regards contact. But this will not work: consider the second row, in which the trajector never moves. If the trajector were to come down to rest on the landmark in any of these cases, the movie (or scene) would cease to be a positive example of *over* and instead would become a positive example of *on*. Thus, contact is apparently allowed when the trajector is in motion, but not when it is static. Any single abstraction would have to either permit or disallow contact between trajector and landmark; the fact that it is allowed in some circumstances but not in others indicates that there can be no single abstraction over these senses. Actually, things are even further complicated by the fact that static contact between trajector and landmark is allowed for *over* in the subcase of covering. Note that the sentence "Put the tablecloth *over* the table" is most easily interpreted as a command to cover the table with the tablecloth, a spatial relation clearly involving contact, whereas "Put the lamp *over* the table" does not allow any interpretation in which the two objects are brought in contact. The critical point remains: since contact is neither always allowed nor always disallowed, there can be no single abstract meaning for *over*.

Figure 7.8
Contents of the top hidden layer for *over*, learned by itself

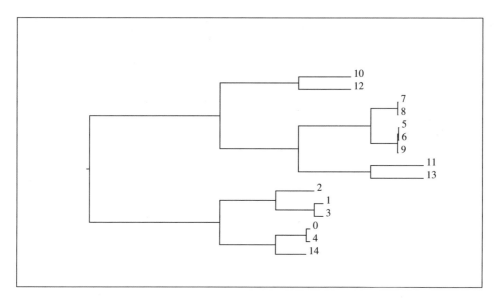

Figure 7.9
Cluster diagram for *over*, learned by itself

When the model is trained on *over* by itself, the activation vectors for the top hidden layer do not reflect this division into three distinct senses. Figure 7.8 in fact shows almost no difference whatsoever among the representations obtained at the final time step for the movies in the test set we saw earlier. This is echoed in the results of hierarchical cluster analysis on these activation vectors, shown in figure 7.9. Here, although some clustering can be seen, it does not correspond cleanly to the senses that we have identified. Although clusters can be found for static location over (movies 5–9) and for motion over without contact (movies 0–4), the sense of motion over with contact does not have its own cluster, but rather is split up, movie 14 appearing in the motion-without-contact cluster, and the others (movies 10–13) appearing nearer the static location cluster, and not all together.

When polysemous *over* is learned with the full contrast set we have been using (*above, below, left, right, around, on, out of, through,* and *in*), the picture clarifies itself

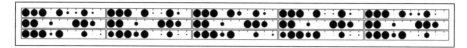

Figure 7.10
Contents of the top hidden layer for *over*, learned with a full contrast set

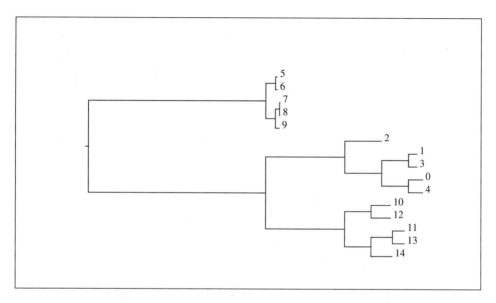

Figure 7.11
Cluster diagram for *over*, learned with a full contrast set

considerably. Figure 7.10 presents the activation vectors for these movies, taken from the model after it had been trained on the full contrast set. The activation vectors break down much more clearly into three basic types, corresponding to the senses we have been discussing. Here, the activation vectors of each row in the figure are all of the same general type, just as each row of movies in figure 7.7 corresponds to a single sense of *over*. Figure 7.11 shows the results of hierarchical clustering on these activation vectors. The three senses are clearly shown here. The top cluster (movies 5–9) is the static location sense, and the rest of the movies constitute a large cluster (the motion-over cluster), which is itself divided into two subclusters. One of these contains the movies portraying motion over the landmark without contact (movies 0–4), and the other contains the movies portraying motion over the landmark with contact (movies 10–14). Thus, the clusters reflect the three senses we have identified for *over*. This makes sense: since *above* is a word in the contrast set, we might expect static *over*, which is essentially synonymous with static *above*, to be clustered tightly; and since *on* is also in the contrast set, we might expect the contact/no-contact distinction to also be apparent, as it is here. This, then, again indicates how the contrast set can affect the polysemous representations formed for a single word.

What can we take away from all this? In the cases of both *in* and *over*, the set of words learned along with the spatial term in question affected the polysemous representations formed, causing the representations to cluster in a manner reflective of intuitively natural-seeming sense boundaries. Thus, in both cases, clustered representations result from learning spatial terms in consort, and it has been suggested that the intuitive distinctness of the various senses may be a result of the distinctness of the clusters in the representations. In both cases, learning the polysemous term in isolation yielded essentially monotone representations, that is, representations that do not reflect sense differences. Learning *in* along with *through*, and learning *over* with a full contrast set, brought these distinctions out quite clearly in the representations. The fact that learning *in* with a full contrast set obscured rather than highlighted the distinctions may indicate an overly simplistic approach here. It may be the case that only a subset of the terms being learned should be allowed to influence the representations of a given spatial term. For the time being, no independent reason has been found to posit such a state of affairs, but it remains a possibility. Should a principled basis be found for incorporating such a mechanism, this may be the direction in which a fuller account of polysemy will be found.

We have focused here on the effect of paradigmatic context on polysemy, that is, the effect of other words in the lexicon that could be used in place of the spatial term under study. Another source of influence is the *syntagmatic* context—those other words that appear together with a given word in an utterance. Zlatev (1992) has investigated this issue using an extension to the model described here, examining in particular the polysemous representations that are formed when the model learns to classify movies into the categories described by a verb together with a preposition. For example, the phrases *be over*, *go over*, and *fly over* can denote different senses of *over*: *be over* expresses the sense of static location above the landmark, *go over* can express motion over the landmark either with or without contact, and *fly over* expresses motion over the landmark without contact between the two objects. Zlatev examined the representations formed when the verbs *be*, *go*, and *fly* were used with the prepositions *over* and *under* to describe movies. As it happens, there is an interesting asymmetry in the meanings expressed by *go over* and *go under*, illustrated in figure 7.12. *Go over* denotes motion over to the other side of the landmark, as in "They *went over* the bridge," whereas *go under* may mean either motion under the landmark to the other side, as in "The dog *went under* the fence," or motion to the region underneath, as in "The dog *went under* the bed." The point here is that whereas *go under* admits both the sense of motion *into* the region underneath and the sense of motion *through* the region underneath, *go over* admits only the sense of

go over   go under

Figure 7.12
Meanings for *go over* and *go under*

motion *through* the region over the landmark. Zlatev found that this distinction, essentially a form of polysemy for the word *go*, was clearly manifested in the representations formed: the two main clusters indicated motion into a region and motion through a region. In addition, the polysemy of *over* and *under* themselves was clearly represented, matching the meanings conveyed by *be over, go over, fly over*, and so on. These results suggest that syntagmatic context may also play a role in the structure of polysemous representations. At the very least, they indicate that (1) syntagmatic context does not hinder the formation of such representations, and (2) the clusters formed correspond directly to the senses expressed by particular verb-preposition pairs. Other computational work also stresses the role that syntagmatic context plays in polysemy (Harris 1989; Munro, Cosic, and Tabasko 1991). This set of experiments as a whole then illustrates the importance of both syntagmatic and paradigmatic context in the development of polysemous representations.

7.2   Deixis

Much of spatial language is *deictically* anchored: it makes implicit reference to the physical position of either the speaker or some other agent involved in the utterance. For example, if I am facing a tree, and a dog is standing between me and the tree, I may describe the dog's position by saying "The dog is *in front of* the tree." The appropriateness of this statement clearly depends on my position vis-à-vis both dog and tree. Were I to move to the other side of the tree, the statement would no longer apply, even though I never explicitly mention my own position in the sentence. This is an example of deixis in spatial language, and my location is referred to as the *deictic center*.

The model we have been considering has no representation of the deictic center and therefore is unable to model deictic language use. However, Adam Jacobs and Sarah Taub, two students at the University of California at Berkeley, have extended the model, incorporating this additional feature. The extended model is able to learn deictically anchored senses of such words as *in front of* and *behind*. Figure 7.13 presents examples of the sort of input the extended model learns

(a)   (b)

Figure 7.13
Positive and negative examples of English *behind*

to classify: specifically, one positive and one negative example of the English spatial term *behind*. Each of these is a movie of length one, that is, a static scene. Jacobs and Taub chose to assume a bird's-eye view of the world, so the scenes shown here are to be viewed as if one were looking down upon a set of objects on a surface. Notice that in addition to the landmark and trajector, each scene contains a deictic center with an inherent front. This deictic center is marked by two lines, labeled *F* ("front") and *R*, ("right"), which indicate the orientation of the deictic center. In (a), the positive example of *behind*, the deictic center is facing toward the landmark; in (b), the negative example, it is facing away from the landmark and toward the trajector. In general, Jacobs and Taub constructed their training set such that the trajector was considered to be *behind* the landmark only if the deictic center was facing the landmark, and the trajector lay beyond the landmark from the deictic center.

What is the nature of this extended model? Perhaps the most important point regarding its design is that it is constructed entirely out of building blocks with which we are already familiar. Thus, extending the model to learn deictically anchored spatial terms did not require the incorporation of any novel structures. All that was required was to extract a number of new relational and reference orientations, and to add a number of θ-nodes to measure their alignment. In particular, the following relational orientations, similar in flavor to the proximal and center-of-mass orientations, were added: the orientation of the directed line segment from the deictic center to the closest point on the landmark; the orientation of the directed line segment from the deictic center to the closest point on the trajector; the orientation of the directed line segment from the deictic center to the center of mass of the landmark; the orientation of the directed line segment from the deictic center to the center of mass of the trajector. In addition to these, the inherent orientation of the deictic center was required as a reference orientation. θ-nodes were then added to the architecture so that each relational orientation was compared to each reference orientation. The resulting architecture was trained under quickprop, which yielded convergence to under 0.01 total summed squared error within 40 epochs. Figure 7.14 shows the model's performance on a test set for *behind*. Notice that the deictic center must be facing the

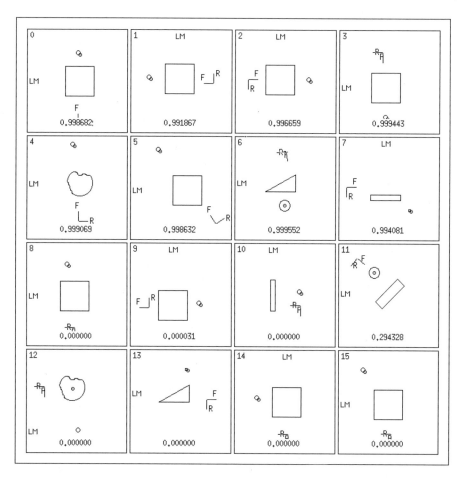

Figure 7.14
A test set: *behind*

landmark and trajector for the scene to be classified as *behind*. Consider scenes 8 and 9, for example; here, the trajector is on the other side of the landmark from the deictic center, but the deictic center is facing the wrong way, so the scene is considered an extremely poor example of *behind*.

The primary message these experiments convey is that no extra machinery of a novel variety is required for deixis. Deictically anchored language use can be modeled using essentially the same mechanisms employed for modeling nondeictic language use. This is an indication that although there is clearly an in-principle difference between these two sorts of spatial language, the difference is not so profound as to require entirely separate and dissimilar processing mechanisms.

It may seem that this modeling effort has gotten things completely backward. There is evidence that children begin with an ego-centered concept of space and only later learn to conceive of space in other than purely egocentric terms (Piaget and Inhelder 1967). Since an egocentric view of the world is precisely what is evidenced in deictic language use, one might expect that the egocentric concepts of space expressed by deixis would be the foundation upon which nondeictic expressions of spatial relations are based. Instead, in this model the egocentric mechanisms subserving deixis are an extension of those subserving nondeictic language. It is in this sense that the model has apparently gotten things backward. However, there is no real inconsistency, for deictic language often involves not only an egocentric conception of space, but an allocentric (object-centered) one as well. For example, the semantics of the word *behind* take into account not only the location of the trajector with respect to the deictic center but also its location with respect to the landmark, and in this sense rely on both egocentric and allocentric conceptions of space. (This is not true for all deictically anchored expressions, of course. The semantics of the phrase *over there* appear to have no allocentric component. Clearly, though, this sort of pure egocentricity does not hold universally of deictic terms.) If it is the case, then, that deictic expressions may involve both egocentric and allocentric notions of spatial location, whereas nondeictic language involves only allocentric ones, it should be no surprise that the mechanisms required for deictic language are a superset of those required for nondeictic language. It is also interesting to note that despite the temporal priority of egocentric spatial conceptualizations, deictic language use is not manifested earlier than nondeictic use in children. In fact, it appears somewhat later (Miller and Johnson-Laird 1976; Johnston and Slobin 1979; Johnston 1985), at least in the case of the terms *in front of* and *in back of*. One possible reason for this is that these deictic terms require both egocentric and allocentric notions of space, whereas nondeictic language requires only an allocentric one. Now admittedly the egocentric conception is what children begin with, so one might imagine that once a child has grasped the notion of allocentric space, deictic and nondeictic language would appear together. Why does this not happen? One possible reason is that the concepts conveyed by deictic terms are intrinsically more complex than their nondeictic counterparts, in that they involve a cluster of egocentric and allocentric features. After all, returning to our original example, for me to be able to say that the dog is in front of the tree, I must be facing the tree, and the dog must be between me and the tree. In contrast, if I want to nondeictically characterize the dog's position simply as *near* the tree, my position is irrelevant, and the concept denoted is in that sense simpler. Under this view, nondeictic terms are acquired first because of their comparative conceptual simplicity. In a similar vein, Johnston and Slobin (1979) note that crosslinguistically, children tend to acquire the nondeictic senses of *back* and *front* before the deictic senses, and they argue that this is at least partly explicable in terms of the conceptual simplicity of the nondeictic sense when compared to the deictic one.

7.3   Prelinguistic Conceptual Development

One shortcoming of the model is that it gives no account of prelinguistic conceptual development and the manner in which that process may affect the acquisition of spatial semantics. Since the acquisition of spatial semantics is almost certainly largely dependent on such prelinguistic spatial conceptual development (H. Clark 1973; Clark 1977; Huttenlocher, Smiley, and Ratner 1983; Johnston 1985), this shortcoming is indeed serious, and possible extension in this direction therefore suggests itself with some urgency.

This is clearly illustrated when we consider the acquisition order of various spatial terms. It is a well-established fact, confirmed crosslinguistically by Johnston and Slobin (1979), that children first learn *in, on, under,* and *beside;* then *between,* and *back* and *front* for featured objects (objects with inherent fronts and backs, such as persons and cars); and then *back* and *front* for nonfeatured objects. The authors attribute this order to a number of factors, including the conceptual complexity of the various spatial notions, as we saw above. The idea is that a child will not be able to learn a particular word until he or she has nonlinguistically acquired the corresponding spatial concept. Although this set of terms has not yet been tested on the model, there is no reason to believe that the model will exhibit exactly this order. In particular, *front* and *back* for featured objects would not be conceptually more complex in the model than a term such as *under:* the semantics would in both cases be based primarily upon orientation combination and would in neither case involve the proliferation of orientation-sensitive θ-nodes that we saw in the case of deixis. In addition, the model will have received no prelinguistic training, so no bias can be expected in favor of one set of terms over another. It is perhaps significant that a model with no account of prelinguistic conceptual development predicts that the acquisition order will be other than that observed empirically. This implicates such prelinguistic conceptual development even more strongly—if modeled aspects of the acquisition process offer no reason for the observed order to arise, it is likely to be due to that aspect of the process that was not modeled: the prelinguistic development of a conception of space.

In all fairness, there is one aspect of the empirically observed acquisition sequence that one would expect the model to exhibit: the acquisition of *front* and *back* for featured objects earlier than for nonfeatured objects. As we saw in the discussion of deixis, deictically anchored terms such as the nonfeatured senses of *front* and *back* rely on significantly more model machinery than their nondeictic counterparts and are in that sense more complex. This may translate into the acquisition order observed for children, although the idea has not yet been put to the test.

The main problem with the model as regards prelinguistic development is that its learning environment is extremely artificial. It is artificial in a number of ways, but the one that is most relevant here is perhaps the most theoretically damaging: the model is not embedded in a world of desire, action, and reaction.

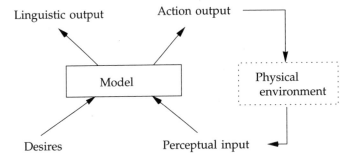

Figure 7.15
Acquiring both linguistic and nonlinguistic spatial knowledge

It does not have goals and therefore does not manipulate its environment in any way to achieve goals. All it does is passively note its perceptual input and learn to categorize it. This is clearly an inaccurate characterization of children's interaction with their environment. Language-learning children are surrounded by a complex physical environment that they are constantly physically manipulating and that they have been manipulating for years, in order to fulfill desires and in order to play. In this manner, children learn a considerable amount about the physical world before even beginning to speak.

How can we extend the model so as to make somewhat more realistic assumptions about the language learner's environment, and the learner's interaction with that environment? An outline of an answer can be seen in figure 7.15. This figure depicts an extension to the model that addresses some of these concerns. Part of this figure is the model as we know it. In particular, the box labeled *Model* is the model, the input labeled *Perceptual input* is visual (movie) input, and the output labeled *Linguistic output* is the set of output nodes we are familiar with, one for each spatial term being learned. However, this version of the model is also equipped with the wherewithal to have desires and to take physical action toward fulfilling those desires. Moreover, it may learn to achieve its goals in the physical world before learning to speak, and in this way can acquire a prelinguistic conception of space. How would this happen? In addition to perceptual input, the model accepts a set of desires, presumably generated by a separate, nonmodeled part of the organism. This desire input could be a simple bit vector, with individual bits allocated for such simple desires as "be in possession of object." The model also produces outputs indicating actions that the organism may take, given its apprehension of the world (its perceptual input) and its desires. These would be simple physical actions such as "pick up object" and "drop object." These actions will affect the physical environment, which will in turn give rise to new perceptual input; and the cycle continues. The idea is that the model will learn to act so as to fulfill its desires—to act so that its actions, when applied to the environment, result in the desired state of affairs. This will then give it a prelinguistic notion of space upon which linguistic acquisition can build. This idea is still in its infancy, but it is important to note that there are at least conceivable remedies to what is probably the model's most significant flaw.

Another advantage of the sort of mechanism outlined in the figure is that it would enable the modeler to examine the influence of language on nonlinguistic behavior. In general in this book we have been examining the manner in which experience of the world, as constrained by the nature of our perceptual apparatus, can constrain the nature of language. But we have also seen that in some cases language may affect nonlinguistic experience (Whorf 1956). The Guugu Yimithirr and rural Tamil speakers studied by Levinson (1992a) and Pederson (1995) demonstrated this. These languages use absolute rather than relative coordinates to express spatial relations (e.g., north and south rather than left and right), and this bias for absolute orientations extends into nonlinguistic domains as well. One possible interpretation of these results is that the absolute coordinates encoded by the language come to affect not only the way in which speakers linguistically express spatial relations, but also their very conception of space, as evidenced in their nonlinguistic spatial behavior. In the core model, the features of the visual environment that are noticed are certainly a function of the language being learned, and one might view this as a case of language affecting perception. The problem, however, is that the model is at bottom a linguistic one, and such a demonstration would simply show that different languages make different perceptual distinctions—which is something we already knew. What would make things more interesting is a demonstration that the language being learned affects not only the language-relevant aspects of the agent's behavior, but also nonlinguistic aspects. In the extended model, we can examine this issue, since the extended model has nonlinguistic as well as linguistic outputs. For example, if training the model on a particular language consistently resulted in the model's tending to reach for objects in a particular way, that would be an indication that the language affects the model's nonlinguistic conception of space, since reaching behavior is clearly not linguistic in character. This could also be taken as a prediction made by the model regarding that language. And somewhat more in the spirit of constrained connectionism, if the structures of this extended model could be shown to predict certain relationships between language and spatial conception, those could also be submitted for empirical falsification. This vision is of course exceedingly speculative, and quite simplistic. Nonetheless, the hope is that it helps to illustrate the general sorts of questions that can be addressed given a model extension of this nature.

7.4   Key Events

One direction for possible extension, examined by David Bailey at the University of California at Berkeley, involves the use of *key events* in the analysis of motion.

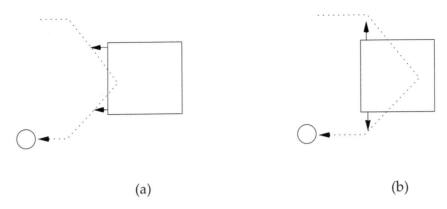

Figure 7.16
The role of key events and proximal orientation in English *through*

Under this scheme, the source-path-destination buffers in the current model would be replaced by a representation of a series of key frames in the movies, frames that carry the bulk of the movies' semantic content. For example, consider figure 7.16, which portrays two examples of a circle moving into and then out of a square. In this figure, (a) does not appear to be a very good example of English *through*, at least not to my eyes, whereas (b) does. In both cases, however, the circle starts and ends in the same position relative to the landmark, enters and exits the landmark en route, and follows a trajectory of the same shape. Why the discrepancy in the appropriateness of using *through* in these two cases, then? One thing that does differentiate these two scenes is the relation of the proximal orientation just prior to entering and just after leaving the landmark. These orientations are shown by the small arrows attached to the landmark in the figure. In (a) the proximal orientation right before entry and right after exit is essentially the same (i.e., entry and exit occur on the same side of the landmark), whereas in (b) they are diametrically opposed (i.e., on opposite sides of the landmark). Under this analysis, entry and exit from the landmark are key events. As such, they should be detected, and an explicit representation of the events stored, much the way the initial frame of the movie is saved now. This would allow the model to effect comparisons of the sort described above.

7.5   Distance

One obvious—and easily rectifiable—shortcoming of the model as it stands is that it does not take into account any representation of the *distance* between trajector and landmark, other than the nondirectional feature map representations. Moreover, these only detect relations in which the landmark and trajector are either touching or interpenetrating. Distance was deliberately left out of the model, for two complementary reasons. On the one hand, its inclusion would

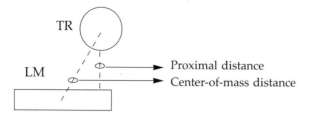

Figure 7.17
Proximal and center-of-mass distances

have necessitated significantly larger training sets and therefore significantly longer training sessions, a less convenient proposition all in all. For example, instances of *above* showing the trajector just above, at medium distance above, and far above the landmark would all be required, simply so that the model would learn to abstract away from distance altogether and focus on the vertical dimension when learning *above*. On the other hand, it is fairly straightforward to imagine how distance would be incorporated into the model, as we shall see. Thus, the theory behind the model has a clear notion of distance, even if the model itself does not. Let us consider just what that notion of distance is, and how it could be brought into the model as it stands.

There are two distance features that could serve to make up for this deficiency: the *proximal distance* and the *center-of-mass distance*, illustrated in figure 7.17. These are the lengths of the directed line segments whose orientations define the proximal and center-of-mass orientations, respectively. More specifically, the proximal distance is the length of the imaginary directed line segment connecting the landmark to the trajector where the two objects are closest, and the center-of-mass distance is the length of the imaginary directed line segment connecting the center of mass of the landmark to that of the trajector.

There is casual evidence suggesting that, just as proximal and center-of-mass orientations are both necessary features, so are both the proximal and center-of-mass distances. Consider, for example, figure 7.18. To my eyes at least, (a) is a good example of English *near*, (b) is not quite as good an example, and (c) is a good deal worse. What is interesting here is that in (a) and (b) the proximal distance is the same, so the fact that (a) seems a better example of *near* than (b) indicates that there is more to the concept than just the proximal distance. Analogously, in (b) and (c) the center-of-mass distance is the same, so the judgment difference for these two scenes cannot be due to that feature. The assumption is that these two distance features both play a role in judgments of this sort, much the way proximal and center-of-mass orientations both play a role in judgments of *above* and other directional terms.

These features can be shown to play a role in the semantics of spatial terms other than *near, far,* and other overtly distance-expressing terms. For example,

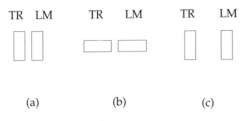

Figure 7.18
The role of distance features in English *near*

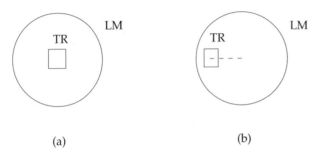

Figure 7.19
Good and poor examples of Russian *posredi* ("in the middle of")

consider figure 7.19, which illustrates a good and a poor example of the Russian preposition *posredi*. This preposition expresses the notion "in the middle of." It was chosen rather than its English counterpart because it is monolexemic, and the focus of our interest here is the semantics of single spatial terms. In (a), the good example, the center-of-mass distance between the circular landmark and the small square trajector is essentially zero, and is not shown. In (b), the poor example, it is shown as a dashed line. Thus, the center-of-mass distance is an excellent indicator of the degree to which the trajector is in the middle of—or *posredi*—the landmark.

However, there is more to even some very simple distance-related concepts than actual distance. For example, consider figure 7.20. This figure illustrates the effect of the *focus of attention* within a scene on judgments of *near* and *far*. If one were to ask whether circles A and B are *near* each other, the response would depend not only on the distance features outlined above, but also on whether or not both clusters of circles lay within the focus of attention, that is, whether or not both clusters were being considered. If only the leftmost cluster is being considered, A is not very *near* B; but if both are being considered, it is, since A is clearly much nearer to B than either is to C. (I am indebted to Helmut Schnelle for this example.) The point here is that terms such as *near* and *far* refer not to absolute distance, but to distance as compared to some implicit

Figure 7.20
The effect of attentional focus on English *near* and *far*

norm. Let us consider another concrete example, this one from the San Francisco Bay Area. When standing on the Berkeley pier, one can see San Francisco across the bay. Coit Tower is a tower on the other side of the bay, in San Francisco. Given this physical layout, we can say "Berkeley is *near* San Francisco," but not "The Berkeley pier is *near* Coit Tower," although the proximal distance is essentially the same in the two cases, and the center-of-mass distance is less in the case of the pier and Coit Tower (they are both right on the water, whereas the centers of mass of the cities are further inland). An explanation for this is that when considering distances between cities, a different norm is used than when considering distances between smaller entities such as piers and towers. Similarly, in the case of the circles in figure 7.20, a different norm for distance is used when considering just the leftmost cluster than when considering both clusters, presumably because the size of the focus of attention itself is larger in the latter case.

7.6 Convex Hulls

Another useful extension to the model would be to incorporate explicit representations of the *convex hulls* of objects. (The convex hull of an object is the smallest convex region containing that object. It can be thought of informally as the shape that would result if one were to put a rubber band around the object.) This is of particular importance since, as we shall see, it allows us to account for spatial relations among nonconvex objects. A major limitation of the work described in this book is that the analysis has proceeded on the assumption that the objects to be dealt with are convex. Since there is some evidence that convex objects have a perceptually privileged status (Hoffman and Richards 1985), they provide a sensible foundation for analysis; at the same time they clearly do not tell the whole story. In this section we shall see how including convex hulls in the model may help on this point, and some others as well.

Consider, for example, figure 7.21. Here we see three scenes in which the convex hull of the landmark (or of the co-landmarks, in (b) and (c)) appears to play a central role in the way the spatial relations are verbalized. Of these three, (a) is the most urgent example, since it potentially falsifies the model presented in this

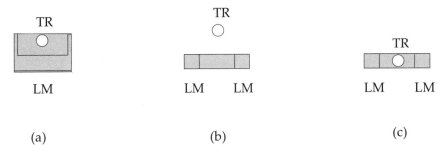

Figure 7.21
Using the convex hull of the landmark(s)

book. This scene shows a nonconvex U-shaped landmark, and a trajector located in the cup of the U, such that the proximal and center-of-mass orientations from the landmark to the trajector are both aligned with upright vertical. These are exactly the conditions under which we would expect the model to pronounce the scene a strong example of *above*, but this trajector is located such that one would almost certainly not describe it as *above* the landmark. How can the convex hull, shown in gray, help us here? It is possible that what we should really extract from the image are the proximal and center-of-mass orientations *from the convex hull* of the landmark to the trajector, rather than from the landmark itself to the trajector. In addition, when making *above* judgments, we should perhaps check to see whether the trajector falls within the landmark's convex hull, and if it does, rule the scene out as an example of *above*. All the examples we have considered so far concern convex objects only, for which the object and its convex hull are coextensive, so the distinction between the two has not been critical yet. It clearly is critical once we broaden our scope to encompass nonconvex objects as well.

This way of handling nonconvex objects receives support from an unexpected quarter: the determination of a trajector's location relative to two or more landmarks. Consider scene (b), for example. Here we see two small square landmarks and a circular trajector above them. This seems an excellent instance of the English sentence "The circle is *above* the squares," even though it is not a particularly good instance of the circle being *above* either the left or the right square taken alone. The idea here is that if we take the phrase "the squares" in the above sentence to actually refer to the convex hull of the two squares, the problem vanishes; for if we focus on the proximal and center-of-mass orientations from the convex hull of the two landmarks to the trajector, we find that these orientations align perfectly with upright vertical. This makes the example consistent with the view of *above* that we have been taking. Scene (c) also shows that the convex hull can be a useful construct when accounting for spatial relations involving two landmarks. The scene shows two square landmarks again, and a small circular trajector *between* them. The convex hull of the landmarks

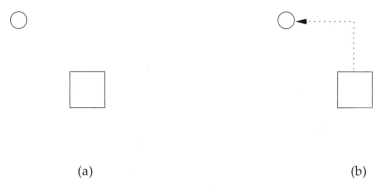

Figure 7.22
Implicit paths: The circle is above and to the left of the square

provides a simple means of characterizing the region between two objects, or the region in which a trajector could be said to be *among* a number of landmark objects: the degree to which a trajector lies within the convex hull, but not within the landmarks themselves, is an indication of the degree to which it is *between* the landmarks. It is of some interest that the convex hull, which was proposed to account for spatial relations involving nonconvex objects, has these other uses as well. This multiple use of the construct suggests that it may be playing a significant role in spatial semantics.

7.7   Implicit Paths

There are a number of phenomena that are not covered by any of the extensions we have discussed so far and that seem to call for the introduction of *implicit paths*. Figure 7.22(a) depicts a situation that is well described by the sentence "The circle is *above and to the left of* the square." However, the location of the circle is at best a weak example of each of *above the square* and *to the left of the square*. One explanation that seems credible is that the phrase *above and to the left of* in fact describes an implicit path directing the listener how to get to the trajector (from the landmark). This is shown in (b).

Implicit paths also help to make sense of a number of English prepositions. For example, consider the use of the preposition *across* in "Kim is *across* the table (from me)." Here, although Kim is probably not in fact physically lying across the table, the preposition is used because the implicit search path that would take me from where I am to where Kim is passes across the table. This phenomenon is referred to as *endpoint focus* (Brugman 1981; Lakoff 1987), since the trajector is located at the endpoint of an implicit search path.

Another example that seems to involve an implicit search path, although not through endpoint focus, is "His office is *along* the corridor," or alternatively "His office is *along* here somewhere." In these uses of *along*, the only thing that is actually *along* the landmark (the corridor in this case) is the imagined search path that will take the listener from where he or she is to the trajector.

This is similar to Talmy's concept of *fictive motion* (Leonard Talmy, personal communication). Talmy notes that sentences such as "Those rods *go through* the ceiling," in which a verb of motion and a preposition are used to describe the static relationship of an elongated trajector relative to some landmark, can be explained by positing a mental scanning along the length of the trajector on the part of the speaker. The verb of motion and the preposition then in fact refer to the relationship between the landmark and the moving focus of attention of the speaker along the trajector, not simply the trajector itself. The examples of implicit paths do not involve overt use of motion terms as the case of fictive motion does, but the two phenomena are similar in that in both cases there appears to be a conceptualization of motion underlying the description of a static scene.

Of the possible directions for extension outlined in this chapter, the notion of implicit paths is probably the least fleshed out. Clearly, implicit paths involve imputing to the scene a trajectory that is not actually there, and once this is done, the usages of particular words to describe situations appear to make more sense. However, the circumstances under which imputation of this sort takes place, the processes by which it happens, and the ramifications these would have for a modeling effort of the sort this book has concerned itself with have not yet been worked out.

In general, we have seen several existing extensions from the core model, and an indication of further possible extensions. These would address some of the many relevant issues not covered by the core model. As noted earlier on, the number of directions for possible extension, and the fact that some of the more linguistically interesting issues are addressed by the extensions rather than the central model itself, suggests that we view the modeling effort to date largely as preliminary spadework, rather than anything like a definitive and all-encompassing theory of spatial semantics.

Chapter 8

Discussion

If our descriptions of meaning are not anchored in something which is per se comprehensible—they will always be futile.
—A. Wierzbicka

A good scientist can draw an elephant with three parameters, and with four he can tie a knot in its tail.
—G. Miller, E. Galanter, and K. Pribram

The goals of this book have been to characterize the human semantic potential for spatial relations and to present the philosophy of constrained connectionism. As we saw at the outset, this double duty very naturally defines two broad frameworks within which one may evaluate the work. On the one hand, the model may be viewed primarily scientifically, as a model of the human semantic potential. In this case the primary evaluative criterion is the degree to which the model provides an explanatory account of semantic potential in the domain of spatial events and relations. If the model is linguistically unenlightening, if it does not tell us anything about language, it will fail to meet this criterion regardless of any other merits it may have. On the other hand, the model may be viewed methodologically, as a concrete instance of the modeling philosophy of constrained connectionism. In this case the criteria for evaluation are quite different. Rather than focus on the particular explanation, or preliminary steps toward explanation, offered by the model, this view judges the work on the basis of the wide applicability of those ideas inherent in the philosophy itself. Here, the burden is to show that constrained connectionism is not simply an appropriate choice for the task at hand, but rather an attractive approach to cognitive modeling more generally.

I have tried to situate this work within both frameworks throughout our exploration of these ideas. Thus, I have attempted to demonstrate both that the model under consideration does shed some light on the human capacity for linguistic expression of spatial relations and that the philosophy of constrained connectionism exhibits features that may be useful for cognitive modeling generally. I have also tried to highlight the interdependence of these two frameworks. The search for an adequate model of the human semantic potential propelled me into a part of network design space that I probably would not have considered otherwise, and in this sense the modeling methodology and its adoption are dependent on the actual scientific task at hand. There is a strong dependency relationship in the other direction as well. In particular, the model's characterization of semantic potential for spatial relations flows primarily from the structures selected and from the manner in which they are embedded in the network.

How successful has the book been in demonstrating these points? The reader will no doubt have already formed an opinion on this matter. This chapter is my chance to contribute to the process of evaluating the work, and situating it in its larger context, explicitly relating it to a cluster of issues on which it impinges. In my estimation, the degree to which the work succeeds varies considerably depending on the particular aspect of the work examined. From some standpoints, the model lives up to expectations; from others, it does not. Which cases are which? In this chapter we shall be sorting this out and, in the process, trying to answer two very broad but important questions: what does all of this tell us about language, and what does it tell us about modeling methodology?

8.1   Inquiry into Linguistic Universals

The primary scientific thrust of this work has been to characterize the human semantic potential, that capacity for meaning that is shared by all humans and is shaped through the process of language acquisition into the semantic system of the speaker's native language. The idea has been to determine what limits there are, if any, to this capacity. Can any word mean anything, or are there clearly specifiable constraints on the possible semantic contents of words? This core question has guided and informed all the work described here. The particular aspect of semantics under consideration has been the semantics of closed-class forms for spatial events and relations, and possible constraints on what such forms may come to mean. The approach taken toward a characterization of the semantic potential for these forms has been to ground the acquisition process in a perceptually based model, a model that incorporates structural ideas similar to those in the visual system. Given such an acquisition model, we can then determine what semantic contents are learnable by the model. The idea is that if a concept is unlearnable by the model, we can predict on that basis that it is unlearnable by humans as the semantics for a single closed-class form; and we therefore predict that this concept will never appear as the semantic content of a closed-class form in any human language. In this manner, through analyzing the model and determining what sorts of concepts will be learnable, we can arrive at a preliminary characterization of the human semantic potential for spatial terms.

As illustrated in figure 8.1, this mode of investigation into possible semantic universals bears a resemblance to two quite distinct research programs: on the

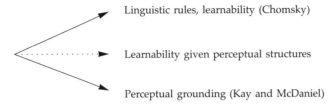

Linguistic rules, learnability (Chomsky)

Learnability given perceptual structures

Perceptual grounding (Kay and McDaniel)

Figure 8.1
Three approaches to the study of linguistic universals

one hand, the work of Chomsky (1965, 1980, 1986), and on the other hand, the work of Kay and McDaniel (1978). The notion of viewing the nature of language through the lens of language learnability, an approach I have adopted here, is associated primarily with Chomsky. On the other hand, learnability in this model is assessed with respect to universal structures that are perceptual rather than linguistic in character. Since the grounding of semantics in perception is strongly associated with Kay and McDaniel's work in color semantics and with cognitive linguistics more generally, their approach has significantly influenced the present effort as well. The mode of inquiry adopted for this modeling effort is therefore shown as a dotted arrow between the two arrows representing learnability, on the one hand, and perceptual grounding, on the other. Let us consider the model's relation to each of these.

Chomsky argues that the linguistic input received by language-learning children is so impoverished and error-ridden that children cannot possibly acquire competence in their native language unless guided in the acquisition process by a set of innate linguistic principles. He therefore posits the existence of a biological linguistic endowment that allows children to acquire language under these unfavorable circumstances. Chomsky's goal, then, is to characterize that innate endowment, that human syntactic potential, so to speak, that can adapt itself to the syntactic structure of whichever human language it encounters in the world. For instance, the concept of a sentence might be an element of that innate endowment (McNeill 1970), as might the principle of mutual exclusivity. The search for universals can be seen as part and parcel of this endeavor, for a characterization of the innate endowment would tell us not only how children are able to acquire existing human languages, but also what constrains the structure of that endowment places on possibly learnable languages. In other words, the same potential for language that makes learning possible will also place limitations on the sorts of languages that can be learned, and these limitations will then translate directly into predicted universals; for if we state that a linguistic form or structure is unlearnable by the human language acquisition device, we are indirectly stating that it will not appear in any human language. This general notion of using language learnability as a window on the nature of language itself also appears in the work of Pinker (1984, 1989).

My search for a characterization of the human semantic potential has clearly borrowed the basic format of its argumentation from Chomsky. Like Chomsky's program, this work stresses the role of language *learnability* in our theorizing about the nature of language itself. That is, both programs try to say something about language by specifying constraints on language acquisition, the idea being that these constraints will tell us what sorts of languages can and cannot be learned. To exemplify this point, the intermediate sequentiality prediction states that no language will encode path-internal sequentiality in a closed-class form. This is predicted precisely because that semantic content would not be learnable by the model. This inability on the model's part, this constraint on the set of semantic contents it can learn, therefore translates into a predicted semantic universal. After all, the model is a model of the human capacity for closed-class spatial term acquisition—if it cannot learn a certain semantic content, it is implicitly predicting that that concept is not learnable by humans as the semantic content for a single closed-class form.

In addition, both programs view innate or universally acquired structure as the basis for knowledge of language. At this point, however, they diverge in a significant way. Although Chomsky focuses on the acquisition of syntax, and the innate endowment he posits is therefore linguistic in character, my approach emphasizes spatial semantics, and—critically—the structures are correspondingly primarily perceptual rather than linguistic. Thus, there is talk here of an innate predisposition for semantics, and of resulting constraints on what is and is not learnable, but there is little emphasis on peculiarly linguistic innate predispositions. Rather, the work emphasizes the reliance of linguistic semantic content on nonlinguistic perceptual structure. This emphasis then leads to a consonance in spirit with the philosophy of cognitive linguistics, which emphasizes the interrelatedness of linguistic and nonlinguistic phenomena. In all fairness, the mutual exclusivity heuristic that was used in learning without explicit negative evidence could be viewed as a purely linguistic element of the human semantic potential, but it is clearly in the minority. Most of the rest of the model's structure derives at least some motivation from perceptual rather than linguistic sources, and this is what lends the model its cognitive linguistic character.

Chomsky's, then, is one branch of research directed at language universals, and the current work clearly bears some relation to it. It also bears a relation to the second branch, namely, the work of Kay and McDaniel, which we reviewed in chapter 2. In fact, my work's point of connection with that of Kay and McDaniel is precisely its point of departure from that of Chomsky; for the core of Kay and McDaniel's argument is that semantic universals can be traced to universal human perceptual structures. In their case, as we saw, empirically observed universals in the semantics of color terms (Berlin and Kay 1969) are explained in terms of the neurophysiology of the human visual system. Berlin and Kay's empirical work demonstrates that although languages have widely differing color systems, although they do carve up the color spectrum in different ways, they also exhibit commonalities. In particular, all languages seem to exhibit the same color foci—those points on the color spectrum that are chosen by native speakers as the best examples of particular colors. Berlin and Kay argue that there are 11 such foci, which structure the color lexicon of every human language. Kay and McDaniel provide an explanation for these empirical findings by linking these color foci to specific, well-known structures in the visual system. Although this linkage has been called into question (Hood and Finkelstein 1983; Teller 1991), the work remains as an impressive first step toward a perceptually based explanation for semantic universals. This book can be viewed as an attempt to begin doing for space what Kay and McDaniel have done for color. In fact, it may be instructive to compare this work directly with that of Kay and McDaniel, to determine to what extent this goal has been met.

The primary shortcoming on this score is that the current work does not ground semantics directly in identifiable neural structures, as did Kay and McDaniel's work on color. Instead, the approach taken here has been to build a computational model whose structures bear some resemblance to known structures in the brain, but to stop well short of attempting any structure-to-structure mapping between the model and the brain. Thus, although semantics is grounded in perception here, it is grounded in perceptual mechanisms that are motivated by, rather than functionally identical to, known neural structures. This is a very real distinction, and it constitutes a weakness of the model as it stands. In this sense, the spatial model is less firmly grounded in perception than is the color model.

The longer-term goal, however, is to provide a thorough perceptual grounding of spatial semantics, and if possible to tie it solidly to the neural substrate. The approach has taken and will continue to take the form of postulating innate perceptual structures so as to enable learning by exposure to experience, and then searching for predicted universals.

The idea of an endowment for spatial semantics is not a new one, and it is interesting to compare it in its current form with some of its earlier incarnations. The work of H. Clark (1973b) is an early and notable example. Clark begins by considering the Chomskyan argument that the child's success in language acquisition given the poverty of the linguistic input implies an innate linguistic endowment. He then suggests that for the domain of spatial semantics, that endowment may be simply the child's prelinguistic conception of space. Under this view, the child's prelinguistic experience in manipulating the environment results in a conception of space, and spatial language then simply names these preexisting spatial concepts. There is a good deal of evidence indicating that the acquisition order of spatial terms is affected by nonlinguistic spatial conceptual development (E. Clark 1973, 1980; Johnston and Slobin 1979; Huttenlocher, Smiley, and Ratner 1983; Johnston 1984, 1985, 1988; Mandler 1992; Smiley and Huttenlocher 1994), although it is not clear that this happens precisely as Clark suggests. The most intriguing aspects of all of this are the implications for semantic and conceptual variation. This view implies that whatever the range of crosslinguistic variation in spatial semantic structure, that variation does not in any way correspond to a conceptual difference across languages. There is a universal shared human conception of space, derived from prelinguistic experience, and although different languages may pick up on different aspects of that shared conception, no language can ever encode something that is conceptually alien to speakers of other languages. If we are to take the data from Mixtec and Guugu Yimithirr seriously, this conclusion seems counterintuitive. The Mixtec concept "located in, at, or on the head region of" and the absolute coordinate system of Guugu Yimithirr both seem profoundly novel from an Anglophone point of view. Indeed, one of Levinson's (1992a) central points regarding Guugu Yimithirr is that it affects the very conception of space held by its speakers. More evidence against the conclusion comes from Choi and Bowerman (1992). Examining longitudinal data from English-speaking and Korean-speaking children, they conclude that the semantic patterns carried by the child's native language influence the meanings the child associates with words from a very early age. In other words, children appear to create semantic representations appropriate to their linguistic input, rather than simply map words onto preexisting concepts. A similar argument is made by Bavin (1990) on the basis of data from Warlpiri, an Australian language. In any event, whatever its strengths and weaknesses may be, Clark's stance is at one extreme on the spectrum of possible views regarding semantic universals in the domain of space: here, there definitely are semantic universals, and they are given to us by our prelinguistic knowledge of space. The adoption of this view would lead one to conclude that a characterization of the child's prelinguistic conception of space would also be a characterization of the human semantic potential for space, since language simply names preexisting spatial concepts.

At the other extreme is the work of Gopnik (1984), who argues that there cannot be semantic universals because children's concepts change in profound, radical ways. She observes that simple spatial terms such as *down, in,* and *on,* which have straightforward locative meanings in adult language, actually mean something quite different to children. In child language, these terms indicate the child's intention to move external objects in particular ways, rather than simply static location. She argues that these concepts are not even built out of elements present in adult language. In contrast to Clark, then, Gopnik views the child's conception of space not so much as a solid basis upon which to build a semantic system, but more as a landscape of shifting sands whose profound changeability makes any talk of semantic universals pointless. It is important to notice that this works as an argument against a fixed lingua mentalis (Fodor 1975; Wierzbicka 1980), but not necessarily as an argument against universals per se. Consider, for example, a model that predicts the existence of universals on the basis of the learnability or unlearnability of particular semantic contents—such as the model we have been examining. Such a model could of course also exhibit the sort of semantic variation throughout development that Gopnik highlights, and yet as we have seen, it can also predict semantic universals. One way to view this is that Gopnik's work provides interesting behavioral data that such a model would have to match, but it does not really provide an in-principle argument, as suggested, against the possibility of semantic universals.

How does my model fit into this discussion? As we saw, one of its most serious shortcomings is that it gives no account of prelinguistic conceptual development and is therefore unfortunately not qualified to contribute fully to the ongoing debate regarding the degree to which conceptual development affects language acquisition, and language affects conceptual development. However, at least one point regarding the model's relationship to these issues is relevant here. It concerns Clark's notion of spatial terms simply coming to refer to preexisting spatial concepts. In the model, all learning is linguistically driven, and the process of acquiring a spatial term consists of much more than simply matching it to a single preexisting concept. Rather, this process involves combining evidence from a number of perceptual structures, those structures that have commanded our attention throughout this book. This is clearly a very different vision of the acquisition process than that proposed by Clark, and it is therefore definitely to the model's advantage that there is evidence against Clark's theory, evidence indicating that children seem to create semantic representations based on the semantic structure of the language being learned. Consider the situation had it been otherwise. If it appeared to be the case that there was nothing more to the semantic acquisition process than associating of words with fully formed and individuated concepts, the model would clearly be not only incomplete—as indeed it is—but also fundamentally wrong. In this case there would be no need to posit any form of linguistically driven training based on perception. This is so because under Clark's view, the extraction of perceptual primitives and their combination into this or that spatial notion are already complete by the time the child begins to speak, and these processes therefore require no linguistically driven training whatsoever.

We have seen Clark's work opposed to Gopnik's along the dimension of the possibility of semantic universals, the former indicating that there clearly are semantic universals, given by the child's prelinguistic conception of space, and the latter arguing that no such universals can exist. It will now also be helpful to contrast Clark's work with my own, along a different dimension: namely, the degree to which semantic acquisition is linguistically driven. Clearly, my model is at one extreme, in that the entire acquisition process is linguistically driven and involves the combination of evidence from disparate perceptual sources. Equally clearly, Clark's is at the other, in that on his account, acquisition amounts to the pairing of words with preexisting concepts. The important point here is that the truth almost certainly lies somewhere in between. We have seen that there is a significant amount of evidence implicating prior conceptual development in the order of acquisition of spatial terms, so my purely linguistically driven model cannot represent the whole truth. On the other hand, we have also seen evidence that the semantics of the language being learned does affect the acquisition process, so that the direct mapping model appears unrealistic, and we have even seen evidence suggesting that the language learned affects the resulting conception of space. The picture that eventually emerges, then, is one of prelinguistic conceptions of space providing an initial framework for—rather than replacing—linguistically driven semantic acquisition of the sort on which this book has focused.

The semantics of space is a subject that has attracted a wide range of theorizers and modelers, quite apart from those we have been discussing (Miller and Johnson-Laird 1976; Jackendoff 1983, 1990; Bajcsy et al. 1985; Herskovits 1986; Hays 1987; Cosic and Munro 1988; Harris 1989; Siskind 1990, 1991, 1992; Bartell and Cottrell 1991; Munro, Cosic, and Tabasko 1991; Nenov 1991; Plunkett et al. 1992; Landau and Jackendoff 1993). I shall not situate my own model with respect to each of these—perhaps to the reader's relief. Instead, in an attempt to focus on some of the critical conceptual issues underlying the field, I shall compare it with two major pieces of inquiry, the classic work of Miller and Johnson-Laird and the more recent work of Landau and Jackendoff.

Miller and Johnson-Laird (1976) devote part of their book *Language and Perception* to the linguistic expression of spatial relations, and they propose definitions for a set of English spatial prepositions. For example, by their definition for the central sense of *on*, trajector x is on landmark y if the following condition holds:

[ON:] INCL(x,REGION(SURF(y))) & SUPPORT(y, x).

Here, the predicate INCL(i, j) denotes inclusion of object i in object j; REGION(i) denotes the region immediately adjacent to i; SURF(i) denotes the surface of object i; and SUPPORT(i, j) denotes support of object j by object i. Therefore, this expression translates roughly into "x is on y if x is included in the region immediately adjacent to the surface of y and y supports x": this is the sense of *on* found in the sentence "The book is *on* the table."

Two points about this general way of doing things are relevant. First, since these formulations are expressed in predicate logic, no notion of graded response is possible here. There is no such thing as a fairly good *on* or *in* or *above*—a candidate instance either fits the criteria or it does not. This is of course not the case for human responses, and ideally one would like some way to capture the idea of evidence for a categorization converging from a number of different sources. When all sources agree, we have a prototypical instance of the term, and when they diverge, we have a less than prototypical one. Such is the case with the connectionist model we have been reviewing. A possible response to this objection is that these definitions are definitions of prototypes, and if the operations of logical conjunction and disjunction were to be replaced with something less discrete, graded responses could be obtained from a characterization fairly similar in form to those offered by Miller and Johnson-Laird. This is quite conceivable, and in any event the intention here is not so much to criticize previous research as it is to focus on large issues that pervade the field. The important point is that characterizations of spatial language based on predicate logic are inadequate, given the graded responses exhibited by humans. This is a simple point, but given the prevalence of predicate logic generally in semantic theorizing, it is worth mentioning.

The second issue is not so easily dismissed, and is in fact one addressed by the authors themselves: the definitions are somewhat ad hoc and incohesive. Another way to view this is that although the definitions provide characterizations of a number of English spatial terms, there is no indication of exactly what larger system this is a specific instance of. Are there any constraints on the ways in which predicates may be combined, or is anything allowed? Can we tell by examining these definitions what the limits are on semantic content for closed-class forms? We are of course coming back to the issue of the human semantic potential: the point here is that accurate definitions are not enough, or at least not for our purposes. If we are really interested in getting at the nature of the human semantic potential, we need to have some idea of not only how to characterize specific spatial terms, but also how to characterize the space of all possible spatial terms. In this light, then, the advantage of the current model is that it supplies a single architecture that learns the semantics for a range of different spatial terms, and whose design places clear (although only posited) constraints on what spatial terms are possible. It is of course unfair to fault Miller and Johnson-Laird for not doing something they did not have on their agenda to begin with—again, the idea here is primarily to point out the larger conceptual issues that the work brings up, rather than to nitpick.

It is also interesting to compare the current approach with the recent work of Landau and Jackendoff (1993). They analyze the English prepositional and nominal systems in terms of an underlying distinction in the visual system between neural structures that determine "what" an object is and others that determine "where" it is (Ungerleider and Mishkin 1982; Mishkin, Ungerleider, and Macko 1983). This what/where distinction has excited a fair amount of interest and has even attracted some connectionist modeling work in its own right, quite apart from any relation with semantics (Kosslyn et al. 1992). Landau and Jackendoff associate the "what" system with object-denoting nouns and the "where" system with locative prepositions. Clearly, their attempt to bring neural constraints to bear on semantic structure is kindred in spirit to the approach taken here, although in the case of my model, inspiration was drawn from biology, psychophysics, and linguistics for the benefit of what is at bottom a linguistic model, and no claim is made that the structural devices in this model correspond to particular neural structures. Rather, they are loosely motivated by their functional similarity to known structures, the idea being that this indicates that the computations being performed are of the same general nature as those performed in the brain. My approach, then, stops well short of a structure-to-structure mapping between the model and the brain, whereas Landau and Jackendoff's approach attempts to make such a connection.

One of the central predictions that flows from Landau and Jackendoff's analysis is that only minimal representations of object shape are available to the closed-class locative system; this is similar in spirit to the intermediate sequentiality prediction here in that both predictions posit a glossing over of perceptual detail in the closed-class system. The primitives extracted from the image by my model are similarly of a rather basic nature, and yet they seem to suffice for locative expressions in a range of languages. (This is also similar to the point made by Levinson (1992b) in his analysis of the Mexican language Tzeltal: he observes that the locative system uses only very gross geometric information, including such information as the major axis orientation of objects, but not more detailed information concerning the shape of subparts of an object.)

There are divergences, however. Although Landau and Jackendoff do refer to non-English structurings of space, the bulk of their analysis is based on English, whereas I have very deliberately taken a crosslinguistic approach. In addition, unlike theirs, my work is based on the analysis of an implemented computational model with a demonstrated ability to acquire the semantics of closed-class spatial terms from a range of languages. The larger question being raised here is the following: what is the appropriate manner in which to approach issues of semantic structure? Should one study a single language in depth, or should one take a more crosslinguistic approach? In fact, I see no reason to adopt one approach exclusively over the other; to my mind, the two complement each other and may provide an effective division of labor in the search for the underpinnings of human spatial semantics.

8.2 Falsifiability

Let us consider, one last time, the model's double footing: on the one hand, its appropriation of the Chomskyan notion of studying language learnability as a means to knowledge of language itself, and on the other hand, its application of this style of argumentation in a cognitive linguistics setting, in a domain emphasizing the interrelatedness of human linguistic and nonlinguistic capacities. We may view the language learnability argument and cognitive linguistics as the model's intellectual parents; and following this metaphor, we might wonder what has been passed down to the model from these parents. Interestingly enough, the same serious charge has been leveled at both parents: both have been accused of making statements that are unfalsifiable. Has the model inherited this rather undesirable trait? Let us consider the charges against the parents first, and then examine the model itself.

Comrie (1981) takes the Chomskyan paradigm to task on the grounds that it is not potentially disconfirmable. This comes up when Comrie compares Chomsky's approach to the study of linguistic universals with that of Greenberg (1963).

The Chomskyan paradigm tends to study a single language (English) in rather abstract terms and relies almost exclusively on innateness as an explanation for universals. In contrast, Greenberg's approach examines a wide range of languages rather concretely and offers a variety of explanations for universals. Comrie's chief objection to the Chomskyan paradigm concerns the use of innateness as an explanation for linguistic universals. This idea is, in Comrie's eyes, scientifically empty. It is simply a name given to the set of universals themselves—whatever we observe to be universal, we may posit as part of the human innate linguistic endowment. Thus, the innateness argument is a means of translating an empirically observed linguistic tendency into something that sounds like an explanation, but cannot be shown to be false.

Cognitive linguistics has sustained a similar attack, although on somewhat different grounds. While presenting his theory of conceptual semantics, Jackendoff (1990) compares it with semantic inquiry within cognitive linguistics. He acknowledges that the two approaches share a commitment to viewing semantics in terms of mental representations rather than truth conditions on actual situations in the world. However, he also highlights some points of difference, mentioning among them a commitment on his part to rigorous formalism, for the sake of rendering the theory as testable as possible. Citing this as a point of difference clearly amounts to an implication that cognitive linguistics is informal perhaps to the point of unfalsifiability. It is true that some work in cognitive linguistics assumes an informal character, but this is by no means true across the board; and even if it were, informality in and of itself need not translate into unfalsifiability. In any event, for our purposes here, it suffices to note that the charge has been leveled.

For us the real question is the following: has this modeling effort left itself open to the same accusation that was directed at its parents, namely, that of unfalsifiability? I shall argue that the answer is no. The model is falsifiable, and this falsifiability results from the clarity of analysis afforded by adopting constrained connectionism as a modeling philosophy. More specifically, falsifiability follows directly from the fact that the model makes concrete predictions, and this in turn follows from the practice of embedding independently motivated structures in the network architecture. This is of particular interest given that Comrie's objection to the Chomskyan innateness argument was that innateness is simply a convenient label to attach to empirically observed tendencies; for in the case of the current model, the innate endowment is not an essentially arbitrary and unconstrained set of linguistic rules, but a set of independently motivated perceptual structures. Their specificity and their independent motivation mean that it is not the case that any observed tendency can be viewed as resulting from them, for the structures have certain functional properties that give rise to some phenomena and do not give rise to others.

Let us consider this issue of falsifiability in more detail. Although it would be premature to claim on the basis of these preliminary results that the model

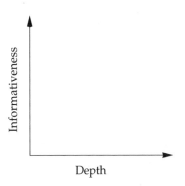

Figure 8.2
Two dimensions of possible failure

as currently constituted will be able to learn the spatial system of any human language, it can be taken as an initial model of the human capacity for closed-class expression of spatial relations. Given this, it will be useful for us to map out the space of possible ways in which this model might fail, when faced with a new linguistic spatial system that it cannot learn. Some forms of failure will be theoretically devastating to the endeavor as a whole, and others will not. Some will be helpful, and others will not.

Figure 8.2 presents two dimensions of possible failure: *depth* and *informativeness*. Along the dimension of depth, the two extremes are shallow and profound failure. Shallow failure occurs when it becomes clear that it is necessary to add some structure to the model, but that structure fits in perfectly with the basic principles that guided the model's design. For example, if it were found that there were too few units in some subpart of the model as it stands and that more of the same were needed, that shortage would be an example of shallow failure, since the solution does not involve leaving the basic paradigm. Profound failure occurs when it becomes evident that the fundamental approach to the model is wrong. For instance, if it were shown that tripartite trajectory representations or orientation-sensitive units were simply not appropriate at all, that demonstration would indicate profound failure. Profound failure can be viewed as a failure of the basic idea behind the model; shallow failure is merely the reflection of a minor implementational flaw that can easily be remedied.

The other dimension shown in the figure is that of informativeness. It is possible that the model may fail in ways that are either informative or uninformative, enlightening or unenlightening. If the model fails for a clearly specifiable reason, and if that then tells us something new about language, the model has failed informatively. (The idea of false models being useful as stepping-stones to more accurate theories is discussed in Wimsatt 1987.) On the other hand, if the model simply fails, and we are unable to analyze it so as to determine just why, there is nothing we can take away from this other than a sense of disappointment. This, then, is uninformative failure.

The current model is false, and this can be trivially demonstrated. Consider the languages Guugu Yimithirr and rural Tamil, which use absolute coordinates such as north and south rather than relative coordinates such as left and right. The model as it stands is not equipped with the reference orientations north and south and is therefore unable to learn these terms. This is an example of shallow failure since it would be both straightforward and within the spirit of the model as a whole to rectify the situation by adding orientation-sensitive nodes tuned to the four cardinal directions. It is also an example of moderately informative failure. It is clear what we would need to do to fix the model, and that sheds some light on the nature of spatial semantics: in particular, it highlights the fact that the human semantic potential includes absolute coordinates of this type. The objection could be raised that this is evident directly from the data, and indeed this is a point that Levinson (1992a) and Pederson (1995) emphasize in their empirical work. It is in this sense that the failure is only moderately interesting: although it does tell us something interesting about language, what it tells us is not really new.

We have also seen that the model is incomplete. Specifically, we have seen that it lacks an account of prelinguistic conceptual development and the influence that that development has on the process of semantic acquisition. This failure of the model is not as easily dismissed as is the lack of a few orientation-sensitive nodes, for it indicates that something critical is missing, something that will force us to leave the basic paradigm. In particular, as we saw earlier, it forces us to conceive of a model that not only observes its input and learns to classify it, but also learns to take nonlinguistic action on the basis of its perceptions and desires. Such a model would then acquire a prelinguistic conception of space upon which language-driven learning could build. The fact that we are compelled to think in terms so different from those informing the model indicates that this is an example of profound failure, not merely an implementational quibble.

Given all this, of what explanatory use is the model? How is one to view the model if it is openly acknowledged that it fails in a profound fashion? This is where we need to tread carefully. I believe there is insight to be derived from the model, but doing so properly requires that we keep the model's flaws saliently in mind.

The model's weak point is that it assumes that semantic acquisition is purely language-driven. This false assumption means that we cannot expect the model to be applicable in those cases in which acquisition is only trivially linguistically driven, that is, those situations in which a good case can be made that acquisition is simply a matter of matching words to preexisting concepts. We are justified in applying it, however, when acquisition is in fact linguistically driven in a more substantive manner. For example, if we are discussing the acquisition of the semantics of English *in*, the chances are excellent that prelinguistic learning will have given rise to the concept of inclusion and that acquisition will rely critically upon that preexisting concept; therefore, the predictions that flow from this model are probably not applicable to this word. On the other hand, if we are discussing the acquisition of a term like Mixtec *šini* ("head"), the predictions are applicable, for *šini* denotes location of the trajector above or on top of a vertically extended landmark. The significance of this is that the notion is fairly complex—one that draws on the combination of perceptual information from several sources, and therefore one that is probably not supplied by prelinguistic conceptual development. The crucial point, then, is that the model is a model of those aspects of the acquisition process that involve linguistically driven combination of perceptual information, and it will be applicable only in situations that are reasonably characterized in this manner. By shrinking the domain of the model's explanatory responsibility this way, we arrive at a suitable framework within which to consider the model generally, and its predictions more particularly. Thus, the work to date can still provide some insight, by pointing out general principles and constraints that inform the linguistically driven aspect of the human capacity for learning to categorize space.

8.3   The Nature of the Model

One question that may well have nagged at the reader as we made our way through the book is the following: exactly what sort of model is this? Is it an attempt to reduce spatial semantics to the neural level? If so, why not tie the work more tightly to neuroanatomical structures known to subserve spatial cognition? And if not, why the emphasis on neural structures at all? These are valid questions. It is indeed the case that the model does not make contact with some of the neuroanatomical work concerning the bases of much of spatial cognition. For example, the work of O'Keefe and colleagues (O'Keefe and Nadel 1978; O'Keefe and Speakman 1987; O'Keefe 1991) has long implicated the hippocampus in spatial cognition. In particular, there are so-called place-field cells in the rat hippocampus, which reach their maximum firing rate only when the animal is at a particular location relative to a set of landmarks. And a connectionist model of these results has already been realized (Zipser 1986), so modeling at this level is clearly possible. Another brain area thought to underlie spatial perception and cognition is the posterior parietal cortex (Andersen, Essick, and Siegel 1985; Stein 1991). Neurons in this area appear to respond to both eye position and the retinal location of a visual stimulus, combining these two sources of information so as to yield the location of the stimulus in head-centered, rather than eye-centered, coordinates. Again, there has been connectionist modeling of this area (Zipser and Andersen 1988; O'Reilly et al. 1990), meaning that such modeling is well within our reach today. If this is the case, why not base the model directly on these results, rather than on the structures outlined earlier? The primary reason is that although these results are clearly germane to the issue of spatial perception generally, they do not address that aspect of spatial perception with which I am most centrally concerned, namely, the articulation of spatial relations through language. If we take the function of posterior parietal cortex to be the translation of eye position and retinal location into head-centered location, following Zipser and Andersen, this function is interesting but not something of obvious import to the linguistic structuring of space. Similarly, if the function of the place-field cells of the hippocampus is to signal the animal's location in a particular part of its environment, this result may be significant once we extend our scope to consider deixis more seriously, but until then it is only intriguing and probably irrelevant; we have been focusing here on spatial relations between two objects external to the viewer, and neural representations of the viewer's position in space are not essential in these situations. Clearly, when a deictic center is brought into the picture, things change dramatically: the viewer's position in space is of paramount importance at that point. In sum, the primary reason these results concerning the neural underpinnings of spatial perception were not brought into play here is that they address issues somewhat different from those we have focused on.

To return to the main question: what is the nature of the model? If these neurophysiological results were left aside because of lack of relevance rather than lack of a desire to reduce semantics to the neural level, can we consider this a neural model? The answer is no, or at least not entirely. A reduction of semantics to the neural level would be immensely exciting, but it is unrealistic in the extreme to expect such a thing in the foreseeable future. Not enough is known about the neural bases of spatial cognition to bring about such a reduction—or at least not enough is known by me in the mid-1990s. Given this, I took the course of bringing constraints to bear from as many different levels of analysis as possible. Some of the structures in the model are neurally motivated, such as the orientation combination and map comparison mechanisms. Some are psychophysically motivated, such as the filling-in operation used for finding the interior of objects. Finally, some are linguistically or psycholinguistically motivated, such as the motion integration mechanism and the use of mutual exclusivity as a learning heuristic. I felt that given incomplete knowledge of the domain, the most prudent course was to apply any knowledge I might be able to find. The result is the heterogeneous architecture we have been analyzing, with different structures embodying constraints drawn from different levels of analysis. The ability to do this is where constrained connectionism comes into its own, for from the standpoint of the network, a structure is simply a structure, regardless of its inspiration. It is a device constraining the operation of the network in a particular way, corresponding to whatever insight the modeler wanted to bring to bear on the problem, from whatever sources.

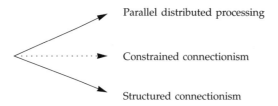

Parallel distributed processing

Constrained connectionism

Structured connectionism

Figure 8.3
Three approaches to connectionist modeling

8.4   What Have We Learned about Models?

Earlier, when we were reviewing modes of inquiry into linguistic universals, we considered two well-established methods of inquiry and then eventually chose a third method that combines aspects of the first two. When we turn our attention to connectionist modeling methodologies, a similar pattern emerges. This is illustrated in figure 8.3. Here, the two established philosophies are parallel distributed processing or PDP (Rumelhart, McClelland, and the PDP Research Group 1986; McClelland, Rumelhart, and the PDP Research Group 1986) and structured connectionism (Feldman, Fanty, and Goddard 1988). The middle road, the one actually taken, is constrained connectionism. As we have seen, PDP is characterized by the use of distributed representations, that is, representations in which an individual unit's role has no clear symbolic interpretation. This representational format exhibits a number of desirable features, among them graded responses, graceful degradation, and perhaps most important, the fact that they can be learned. Given a training set of input/output pairings, a multilayer perceptron can be trained to exhibit the behavior seen in the training set, and can in doing so produce distributed representations of the input in its hidden layers. This means that the modeler need not painstakingly specify in advance exactly what each connection strength will be. In contrast, units in structured connectionist models generally do have clearly identifiable symbolic interpretations, and connections are specified by the designer. These networks are composed of connection structures that are designed to reflect the modeler's knowledge of the domain, and it is from this fact that the methodology derives its name. Analyzing these structures and their effect on the model's overall behavior is usually a fairly straightforward matter—indeed, a significant part of the appeal of structured connectionism is that the resulting model is one that the modeler truly understands in detail. This approach is useful when addressing inherently structured domains such as language or vision, in which it is unrealistic to expect a single undifferentiated learning mechanism, such as a multilayer perceptron, to learn to exhibit complex behavior.

The path I have taken, constrained connectionism, is an attempt to apply the philosophy of structured connectionism to PDP. In particular, the idea is to embed complex structural devices, of the sort found in structured connectionism, in a PDP network, a multilayer perceptron. The network is then trained, such that distributed representations develop under the influence of the training algorithm, as is the case in standard PDP networks. To a degree, then, the operation of these networks is dictated by the training set and training algorithm. At the same time, though, it is constrained in clearly specifiable ways by the embedded structures. This approach to modeling has three advantages. First, constrained networks exhibit enhanced generalization from the training set to the test set, since the dimensionality of the search space is dramatically reduced. Second, if the built-in structures can be independently motivated, that provides a form of independent motivation for the model as a whole. But perhaps the most significant scientific advantage enjoyed by this design philosophy is the articulability of the structure-induced constraints mentioned above. The ability to state what a cognitive model can and cannot do translates into an ability to make clear, concrete predictions on the basis of the model: we predict that whatever is impossible for the model will never be empirically observed in the world. In sum, our understanding of the model and its implications need not be limited to whatever we can glean from empirical observation of its operation, but may rather be based on prior analysis of the structures and the constraints they embody.

Let us see if we can situate constrained connectionism and the issues it addresses within the context of current debates over the status of connectionism in cognitive theorizing (Broadbent 1985; Rumelhart and McClelland 1985; Smolensky 1988; Fodor and Pylyshyn 1988; McClelland 1988; Massaro 1988; McCloskey 1991; Seidenberg 1993). We have seen some of these points already, but it may be useful to review them now that we have looked at a concrete example of the philosophy of constrained connectionism. I shall try to illustrate some of the major points by relating this work to a few of its better-known neighbors in intellectual space, rather than attempting an exhaustive survey of all related work. This is the same approach that I took in the discussion of semantics and conceptual development above—in both cases, my hope is that the basic issues are fairly well represented in the limited sample.

Let us begin by reacquainting ourselves with the players. Massaro (1988) and McCloskey (1991) have both argued that the role of connectionist models in cognitive theory is problematic. Their criticisms are directed in particular at PDP models of the sort commonly trained under back-propagation, and it is to these criticisms that Seidenberg (1993) responds. Interestingly enough, all three provide compelling arguments for constrained connectionism.

Let us begin with Massaro, whose central criticism is that multilayer perceptrons with hidden units are too computationally powerful to be informative. To illustrate this point, he reports a set of computational experiments he conducted with a multilayer perceptron, in which the network successfully adapted itself to three different data sets implying three mutually exclusive psychological processes. He presents this as a demonstration that connectionist networks are too unconstrained, too general a mechanism to be falsifiable. In other words, their computational power undermines their explanatory power. After all, if a system can learn to exhibit a wide range of possible behaviors, what do we learn if it turns out that one of those possible behaviors happens to match human behavior? The central point here is that we should ask of a model not only that it match human behavior, but also that it fail to match behavior that a human would not produce. If the model is too general to do this, it cannot tell us much about the constraints that characterize specifically human behavior. The work of Cybenko (1989) helps to drive this point home. He provides a proof that a feedforward multilayer perceptron with a sufficient number of hidden units in a single hidden layer can approximate any continuous function whose arguments range from 0 to 1. Since we can always scale our data down to fit in the 0 to 1 range, this last restriction is not particularly severe. Now of course a network with many hidden units will be able to represent more functions than will a network with just a few, but it is unfortunately not clear exactly how the number of hidden units limits the set of representable functions. In any event, the importance of this proof here is that it substantiates Massaro's claim that multilayer perceptrons, as a class, are capable of representing so many functions that it is unclear what their success in representing any particular function should come to mean for us.

This line of argument reads almost as if it had been conceived with structured or constrained connectionism in mind: if the objection is that most networks are underconstrained, a constrained version of connectionism is as appropriate a response as one could imagine. If we can steer clear of overly general mechanisms, if we can deliberately limit our too-powerful models such that they are no longer capable of learning a wide range of functions, but rather can only learn a clearly demarcated subset of all possible functions, we are beginning to say something: namely, that whatever the human process is that is under study, it is consistent with the constraints that we built into the model. The important point here is that constrained or structured connectionism can pull us away from overly general and therefore ultimately unenlightening models. A decrease in computational power results in an increase in explanatory power.

McCloskey pursues a related argument and makes it concrete by tying it to the visual word recognition model of Seidenberg and McClelland (1989). He begins by asking us to pretend that we have a black box that performs this task perfectly: given an orthographic representation of a word, it classifies and pronounces the word as a human reader would, in the same amount of time a human would take. In other words, it provides a flawless simulation of human performance. Now, given such a simulation, are we justified in viewing it as an explanatory theory, or even as an element of such a theory? Clearly not, he argues; for we are unable to crack open the black box and explain *why* the system behaves as it does. There is no articulation of general principles underlying the visual word recognition process, and therefore there is no illumination of that process. Instead, there is an accurate but scientifically empty simulation. And its emptiness is a direct result of our inability to open the black box and analyze it. If we were able to open it, and could determine exactly why it works as it does, those insights could then be a part of a theory. The central point here is that simulation and theory are very different things: simulation is mechanical mimicry of some real-world process, whereas theory is an explanation of that process, a verbal description of exactly why the process appears as it does. The black box gives us the first, and by virtue of its opacity cannot give us the second. McCloskey then suggests that we replace the black box with a trained multilayer perceptron exhibiting the same performance (this is of course exactly the sort of network used by Seidenberg and McClelland). We have full access to the weights on the connections and activation functions used—in a word, the box is no longer black. Can this be taken as a theory? It would seem so, at least at first. After all, we have been given a full specification of a mechanism that exhibits humanlike behavior. McCloskey's view is that nonetheless such a network should not be taken as a theory. Why not? The central reason is that the model is not readily analyzable. We cannot reliably determine what in the model is theoretically significant and what is incidental. We cannot tell what knowledge is embodied in the network. In a sense, what has happened is that we have gone from too coarse a level of description to too fine a level. In the black box case, we knew nothing about the workings of the box apart from its input/output behavior; this is as coarse a level of description as possible. And now that we have access to all the weights, we are at too fine a level of description to extract anything that can amount to a verbalizable theory of visual word recognition. We can use cluster analysis to try to tease out some of the knowledge encoded in the weights, but this is simply a more sophisticated form of empirical observation of the network. It does not amount to analysis in the sense of determining the causal forces at work. McCloskey's point is that it does not really matter if the box is no longer black, as long as we cannot understand what we see inside it.

This also reads very much as if it had been written as an argument for structured or constrained connectionism, for as we have seen, analyzability is precisely what is gained by such an approach. When the black box is cracked open, we find structures that lend themselves to straightforward analysis, facilitating the process of extracting some form of articulable insight from the model. The predictions we reviewed above are the results of this. Credit and blame assignment is also relatively simple, in that it is known which structures lead to which constraints on the model's operation—if it is determined that one of the built-in constraints is inappropriate, we will know what to change in the model. In fact, McCloskey concedes that connectionist simulation could be taken as theory if the modeler constructed the simulation by hand, such that it was clear exactly what knowledge was being built into the model. This is of course what is done in both structured and constrained connectionism. It is interesting in this regard to compare McCloskey's pessimism regarding the role of connectionist models with the early optimism of Feldman and Ballard (1982). As it happens, the latter two authors were for the most part considering highly structured and therefore easily analyzable models, and this makes their optimism understandable—such models are not vulnerable to the charges leveled by McCloskey. The real point in all of this, then, is that structured or constrained connectionist modeling can help to bridge the chasm between model and theory.

Seidenberg, arguing from the PDP perspective, has responded to these objections, focusing in particular on those of McCloskey. It may seem unlikely that a defense of a purely PDP approach to modeling would inadvertently provide a strong case for constrained connectionism, but this is exactly what happens. Seidenberg's response to these objections in fact brings up an issue of central importance to constrained connectionism, the issue of independent motivation. He begins by acknowledging that McCloskey's arguments seem to have some force, but then points out that whether PDP networks can be seen as contributing directly to theory depends on one's notion of what constitutes a theory. Following Chomsky (1965), he distinguishes between descriptive and explanatory theories. Descriptive theories are those that allow the theorist to capture significant generalizations on the basis of the data observed, and to generate falsifiable predictions. Explanatory theories do this as well, but in addition they yield a deeper sort of understanding: they are more illuminating in that they show how the phenomenon under study flows from independently motivated principles. Thus, in the case of explanatory theories we are not simply trying to come up with a set of principles that neatly summarizes the data; rather, we are trying to show how the data result from something else whose existence we had already acknowledged. Seidenberg's stance is that PDP connectionism provides exactly this sort of explanatory theory, since there is a set of independently motivated principles underlying it: the neurally motivated principles of connectionism. The long-term promise, of course, is that these will evolve into a close match with neurophysiology, yielding more fully fleshed out explanatory theories, theories in which cognitive function is grounded in neural principles. This is an attractive prospect, of course, but in this case we can have our cake and eat it too. What Seidenberg has done is shift the focus of the discussion away from analyzability and toward independent motivation, but in fact independent motivation need not come at the expense of straightforward analyzability. Although comparatively unstructured PDP networks provide one path to neurally motivated and hence explanatory theories, they are by no means the only such path. Independent motivation for embedded structures is one of the primary advantages of the constrained connectionist approach as well, and as we have seen, analyzability is another.

In sum, then, each of these three authors has presented arguments that may be retreaded in the service of constrained connectionism. This is no coincidence. The idea of constrained connectionism did not spring from an intellectual vacuum—I view it as a very natural extension of trends already current in the field. As we saw earlier, the idea of building structure into connectionist learning models is not new. And taking this one step further, to a cognitive modeling philosophy emphasizing the articulability, motivation, and enhanced generalization offered by such structures, is a natural move.

8.5   A Final Word

I began this book by indicating that I wanted to characterize the human semantic potential in the domain of spatial terms. Taking on a topic of this size has a fairly obvious downside: the chances of attaining a complete characterization are poor. This is balanced by two considerations, however. First, there is of course such a thing as partial success; that is, there is always the possibility that even a flawed and incomplete model can shed some light. Second, the potential pay-off is substantial. A characterization of the human semantic potential would tell us not just a few curious facts about language, but something genuinely interesting about ourselves, about the nature of humans as linguistic animals. I do not pretend to have reached this goal, but I like to think I have started down the path toward it. If I have succeeded in nothing else, I hope to have at least conveyed some of the excitement that surrounds the search for such a characterization.

I also hope to have presented a reasonable case for constrained connectionism, for adaptive networks whose structure embodies specific hypotheses regarding the domain being modeled. This methodology and its ramifications have been every bit as absorbing for me as the semantic search out of which they grew. One of my main hopes for this work is that it will help to demonstrate the utility of this approach to connectionist modeling and will thereby encourage others to think in these terms. Although the specific model we have examined concerns a fairly tightly circumscribed corner of linguistic inquiry, the methodological principles involved are generally applicable and could potentially be useful to modelers working in unrelated domains.

The results of this work as a whole are preliminary and are perhaps best viewed as suggestive. However, if they can serve as a stepping-stone to more complete models of semantic acquisition, or to better modeling methods, they will have served their purpose.

Appendix

Some minor technical details have been relegated to this appendix, in the interest of preserving the readability of the main text. These details concern the extraction of perceptual primitives from the input image, and learning in the map comparison structures.

Perceptual Primitives

Center of Mass

We have seen how trajector and landmark outlines are filled in. Once this is done, we can easily compute the centers of mass for these objects. This is necessary in order to find the center-of-mass orientation for the scene.

For a given object, let n be the area of the object. This is easily determined by counting the activated pixels in a filled-in copy of the object. In addition, let Obj be the set of points making up the object, and $\vec{p} = (x, y)$ be an arbitrary point in the image. Then the center of mass of the object is given by $(\bar{x}, \bar{y})$, where

$$\bar{x} = (\frac{1}{n}) \sum_{\vec{p} \in Obj} x; \quad \bar{y} = (\frac{1}{n}) \sum_{\vec{p} \in Obj} y.$$

Major Axis Orientation

The major axis orientation of the landmark appears to be useful as a reference orientation. There exists a standard computer vision method for determining the major axis orientation of an object. This method, which is the one used here, amounts to finding the orientation of that line for which the integral of the square of the distance to points in the object is a minimum (i.e., the orientation of minimum dispersion). The integral used is

$$E = \iint_I r^2 b(x, y) \, dx \, dy,$$

where r is the perpendicular distance from the point (x, y) to the line sought after, I is the image, and $b(x, y)$ is the *characteristic function* of the object (i.e., 1 if (x, y) is part of the object and 0 otherwise). The orientation of the line that minimizes this integral is the major axis orientation of the object. There exists a straightforward formula that yields this orientation of minimum dispersion; details may be found in Ballard and Brown 1982 or Horn 1986.

Proximal and Center-of-Mass Orientations

Determining the proximal orientation is currently done in the simplest possible manner. For each pair of points $[\vec{l}, \vec{t}]$, where $\vec{l}$ is a point on the boundary of the landmark and $\vec{t}$ is a point on the boundary of the trajector, we find the distance between the two points and pick that pair of points $[\vec{l}_m, \vec{t}_m]$ for which the distance is minimum. The proximal orientation is then the orientation of the directed line segment connecting $\vec{l}_m$ to $\vec{t}_m$.

The center-of-mass orientation is also simple to compute; this is done in an analogous manner once the centers of mass of the two objects have been determined, as described above.

Learning in Map Comparison Structures

As we have seen, the model is trained under a variant of back-propagation, and this becomes problematic in the map comparison structure. Recall from section 5.3 that this structure contains feature maps and that each feature map is headed by a head node. The head node receives input from each node in the map below it and takes either the maximum or the average of the activation of nodes in the feature map. We shall be training the weights *below* the feature map under back-propagation, so we shall have to propagate error through the head nodes.

However, one cannot back-propagate error through a head node that takes the maximum of all its inputs, since the maximum function is nondifferentiable. (There do exist differentiable functions that are similar in functionality to the maximum, such as the *softmax* function discussed by Bridle (1990). The maximum was used here because it is simpler than softmax, and because the required deviation from straightforward back-propagation is both minor and effective.) Therefore, the approach taken here is to view the head node taking the maximum essentially as a "virtual" node of the type found in the map below. More precisely, such a head node of a feature map is treated as if it were itself that node i in the map below that had the maximum response. Clearly, since its output is the maximum of all outputs in the feature map below, it will behave like node i during the forward pass. We arrange to have it behave like node i during the backward pass as well. Essentially, the feature map structure as a whole, head node a included, will behave as if it were node i.

If m is the head node of a feature map and takes the maximum of its inputs, then during the backward pass of back-propagation, the value $\delta_m = -\frac{\partial E}{\partial net_m}$ is computed for head node m as if m were that unit i in the map below that had the maximum response during the forward pass, that is, as if m were a unit whose activation function was of the form shown in equation (5.2), located at position i in the map. This value is then propagated down to feature map node i itself, such that $\delta_i = \delta_m$, enabling us to determine the weight updates for the incoming weights of node i. Node i then updates the weights on its incoming links. Since all nodes in the feature map are constrained to have the same incoming weight vectors, the weight vectors for all other feature maps are now set to be identical to that for node i. It is in this sense that m, and indeed the feature map structure as a whole, is treated as if it were that feature map node i with the maximum response.

Things are a good deal more straightforward in the case of head nodes that take the average of their inputs, since the average is a differentiable function. We need only determine the derivative of this function and then use back-propagation as we would on any other node in the system.

References

Ahmad, Subutai. 1991. Efficient visual search: A connectionist solution. In *Proceedings of the 13th Annual Conference of the Cognitive Science Society*. Hillsdale, N.J.: Lawrence Erlbaum.

Ahmad, Subutai, and Stephen Omohundro. 1990. A connectionist system for extracting the locations of point clusters. Technical Report TR-90-011, International Computer Science Institute, Berkeley, Calif.

Andersen, R., G. Essick, and R. Siegel. 1985. Encoding of spatial location by posterior parietal neurons. *Science* 230, 443–455.

Anderson, James, Andras Pellionisz, and Edward Rosenfeld, eds. 1990. *Neurocomputing 2: Directions for research*. Cambridge, Mass.: MIT Press.

Anderson, James, and Edward Rosenfeld, eds. 1988. *Neurocomputing: Foundations of research*. Cambridge, Mass.: MIT Press.

Bajcsy, Ruzena, Aravind Joshi, Eric Krotkov, and Amy Zwarico. 1985. LandScan: A natural language and computer vision system for analyzing aerial images. In *Proceedings of the 9th International Joint Conference on Artificial Intelligence*. Los Altos, Calif.: Morgan Kaufmann.

Ballard, Dana. 1987a. Cortical connections and parallel processing: Structure and function. In *Vision, brain, and cooperative computation*, ed. by Michael A. Arbib and Allen R. Hanson. Cambridge, Mass.: MIT Press.

———. 1987b. Parameter nets. In *Readings in computer vision: Issues, problems, principles, and paradigms*, ed. by Martin A. Fischler and Oscar Firschein. Los Altos, Calif.: Morgan Kaufmann.

Ballard, Dana, and Christopher Brown. 1982. *Computer vision*. Englewood Cliffs, N.J.: Prentice-Hall.

Bartell, Brian, and Garrison Cottrell. 1991. A model of symbol grounding in a temporal environment. In *The AAAI Spring Symposium Workshop on Connectionist Natural Language Processing*. Stanford University.

Barto, A., and P. Anandan. 1985. Pattern recognizing stochastic learning automata. *IEEE Transactions on Systems, Man, and Cybernetics* 15, 360–375.

Bavin, Edith. 1990. Locative terms and Warlpiri acquisition. *Journal of Child Language* 17, 43–66.

Behrend, Douglas. 1989. Default values in verb frames: Cognitive biases for learning verb meanings. In *Proceedings of the 11th Annual Conference of the Cognitive Science Society*. Hillsdale, N.J.: Lawrence Erlbaum.

———. 1990. The development of verb concepts: Children's use of verbs to label familiar and novel events. *Child Development* 61, 681–696.

Berlin, Brent, and Paul Kay. 1969. *Basic color terms: Their universality and evolution*. Berkeley: University of California Press.

Bolinger, Dwight. 1965. The atomization of meaning. *Language* 41, 555–573.

———. 1971. *The phrasal verb in English*. Cambridge, Mass.: Harvard University Press.

Bowerman, Melissa. 1983. How do children avoid constructing an overly general grammar in the absence of feedback about what is not a sentence? In *Papers and Reports on Child Language Development* 22. Stanford Linguistics Association, Stanford University.

——. 1989. Learning a semantic system: What role do cognitive predispositions play? In *The teachability of language*, ed. by Mabel Rice and Richard L. Schiefelbusch. Baltimore, Md.: Paul H. Brookes.

Braine, M. 1971. On two types of models of the internalization of grammars. In *The ontogenesis of grammar*, ed. by Dan Slobin. New York: Academic Press.

Bridle, John. 1990. Training stochastic model recognition algorithms as networks can lead to maximum mutual information estimation of parameters. *Advances in Neural Information Processing Systems* 2, 211–217.

Broadbent, Donald. 1985. A question of levels: Comment on McClelland and Rumelhart. *Journal of Experimental Psychology: General* 114, 189–192.

Brugman, Claudia. 1981. Story of *over*. M.A. thesis, University of California, Berkeley. Available from the Indiana University Linguistics Club.

——. 1983. The use of body-part terms as locatives in Chalcatongo Mixtec. In *Report No. 4 of the Survey of California and Other Indian Languages*. University of California, Berkeley.

Bushnell, M. Catherine, Michael E. Goldberg, and David Lee Robinson. 1981. Behavioral enhancement of visual responses in monkey cerebral cortex. I, Modulation in posterior parietal cortex related to selective visual attention. *Journal of Neurophysiology* 46, 755–772.

Casad, Eugene. 1982. Cora locationals and structured imagery. Ph.D. dissertation, University of California, San Diego.

Casad, Eugene, and Ronald Langacker. 1985. "Inside" and "outside" in Cora grammar. *International Journal of American Linguistics* 51, 247–281.

Choi, Soonja, and Melissa Bowerman. 1992. Learning to express motion events in English and Korean: The influence of language-specific lexicalization patterns. In *Lexical and conceptual semantics*, ed. by Beth Levin and Steven Pinker. Cambridge, Mass.: Blackwell.

Chomsky, Noam. 1965. *Aspects of the theory of syntax*. Cambridge, Mass.: MIT Press.

——. 1980. *Rules and representations*. New York: Columbia University Press.

——. 1986. *Knowledge of language: Its nature, origin, and use*. New York: Praeger.

Chou, Paul, and Rajeev Raman. 1987. On relaxation algorithms based on Markov random fields. Technical Report 212, Department of Computer Science, University of Rochester.

Clark, Eve. 1973. Non-linguistic strategies and the acquisition of word meanings. *Cognition* 2, 161–182.

——. 1977. Strategies and the mapping problem in first language acquisition. In *Language learning and thought*, ed. by John Macnamara. New York: Academic Press.

——. 1980. Here's the *top*: Nonlinguistic strategies in the acquisition of orientational terms. *Child Development* 51, 329–338.

——. 1987. The principle of contrast: A constraint on language acquisition. In *Mechanisms of language acquisition*, ed. by Brian MacWhinney. Hillsdale, N.J.: Lawrence Erlbaum.

Clark, Herbert. 1973. Space, time, semantics, and the child. In *Cognitive development and the acquisition of language*, ed. by Timothy Moore. New York: Academic Press.

Cleeremans, Axel. 1993. *Mechanisms of implicit learning: Connectionist models of sequence processing*. Cambridge, Mass.: MIT Press.

Comrie, Bernard. 1981. *Language universals and linguistic typology*. Chicago: University of Chicago Press.

Cooper, Paul. 1989. Parallel object recognition from structure. Technical Report 301, Department of Computer Science, University of Rochester.

Cosic, Cynthia, and Paul Munro. 1988. Learning to represent and understand locative prepositional phrases. In *Proceedings of the 10th Annual Conference of the Cognitive Science Society*. Hillsdale, N.J.: Lawrence Erlbaum.

Cottrell, Garrison. 1985. A connectionist approach to word sense disambiguation. Ph.D. dissertation, University of Rochester.

Cross, G. R., and A. K. Jain. 1983. Markov random field texture models. *IEEE PAMI* 5, 25–39.

Crowder, Robert. 1976. *Principles of learning and memory*. Hillsdale, N.J.: Lawrence Erlbaum.

Cybenko, George. 1989. Approximations by superpositions of a sigmoidal function. *Mathematics of Control, Signals, and Systems* 2, 303–314. Also available as Report 856, Center for Supercomputing Research and Development, University of Illinois at Urbana-Champaign.

Denker, J., D. Schwartz, B. Wittner, S. Solla, R. Howard, L. Jackel, and J. Hopfield. 1987. Large automatic learning, rule extraction and generalization. *Complex Systems* 1, 877–922.

Denny, J. Peter. 1982. Semantics of the Inuktitut (Eskimo) spatial deictics. *International Journal of American Linguistics* 48, 359–384.

Denny, J. Peter, and Luke Issaluk. 1976. Semantically organized tables of Inuktitut locatives. Technical Report 352, Department of Psychology, University of Western Ontario.

Elman, Jeff. 1988. Finding structure in time. Technical Report 8801, Center for Research in Language, University of California, San Diego.

Essen, David Van, and John Maunsell. 1983. Hierarchical organization and functional streams in the visual cortex. *Trends in Neurosciences* 6, 370–375.

Fahlman, Scott. 1988. An empirical study of learning speed in back-propagation networks. Technical Report CMU-CS-88-162, Department of Computer Science, Carnegie Mellon University.

——. 1991. The recurrent cascade-correlation architecture. Technical Report CMU-CS-91-100, Department of Computer Science, Carnegie Mellon University.

Fanty, Mark. 1988. Learning in structured connectionist networks. Technical Report 252, Department of Computer Science, University of Rochester.

Farah, Martha, and James McClelland. 1991. A computational model of semantic memory impairment: Modality specificity and emergent category specificity. *Journal of Experimental Psychology: General* 120, 339–357.

Feldman, Jerome. 1989. Neural representation of conceptual knowledge. In *Neural connections, mental computation*, ed. by Lynn Nadel, Lynn A. Cooper, Peter Culicover, and R. Michael Harnish. Cambridge, Mass.: MIT Press.

Feldman, Jerome, and Dana Ballard. 1982. Connectionist models and their properties. *Cognitive Science* 6, 205–254.

Feldman, Jerome, Mark Fanty, and Nigel Goddard. 1988. Computing with structured neural networks. *IEEE Computer* 21, 91–104.

Fodor, Jerry. 1975. *The language of thought*. New York: Crowell.

Fodor, Jerry, and Zenon Pylyshyn. 1988. Connectionism and cognitive architecture: A critical analysis. *Cognition* 28, 3–71.

Forrester, Neil, and Kim Plunkett. 1994. Learning the Arabic plural: The case for minority default mappings in connectionist networks. In *Proceedings of the 16th Annual Conference of the Cognitive Science Society*. Hillsdale, N.J.: Lawrence Erlbaum.

Freyd, Jennifer, Teresa Pantzer, and Jeannette Cheng. 1988. Representing statics as forces in equilibrium. *Journal of Experimental Psychology: General* 117, 395–407.

Geman, Stuart, and Donald Geman. 1984. Stochastic relaxation, Gibbs distributions, and the Bayesian restoration of images. *IEEE PAMI* 6, 721–741.

Georgopoulos, Apostolos P., Andrew B. Schwartz, and Ronald E. Kettner. 1986. Neuronal population coding of movement direction. *Science* 233, 1416–1419.

Goddard, Nigel. 1992. The perception of articulated motion: Recognizing moving light displays. Technical Report 405, Department of Computer Science, University of Rochester.

Gopnik, Alison. 1984. Conceptual and semantic change in scientists and children: Why there are no semantic universals. In *Explanations for language universals*, ed. by Brian Butterworth, Bernard Comrie, and Östen Dahl. Berlin: Mouton.

Greenberg, Joseph H. 1963. *Universals of language*. Cambridge, Mass.: MIT Press.

Guyon, I., P. Albrecht, Y. LeCun, J. Denker, and W. Hubbard. 1991. Design of a neural network character recognizer for a touch terminal. *Pattern Recognition* 24, 105–119.

Harris, Catherine L. 1989. A connectionist approach to the story of "over." In *Proceedings of the Fifteenth Annual Meeting of the Berkeley Linguistics Society*. Berkeley Linguistics Society, University of California, Berkeley.

Hays, Ellen M. 1987. A computational treatment of locative relations in natural language. Technical Report MS-CIS-87-31, Department of Computer and Information Science, University of Pennsylvania.

Hebb, D. 1949. *The organization of behavior*. New York: Wiley.

Heider, Eleanor R. 1972a. Probabilities, sampling, and ethnographic method: The case of Dani colour names. *Man* 7, 448–466.

———. 1972b. Universals in color naming and memory. *Journal of Experimental Psychology* 93, 10–20.

Henn, Volker, and Bernard Cohen. 1976. Coding of information about rapid eye movements in the pontine reticular formation of alert monkeys. *Brain Research* 108, 307–325.

Herskovits, Annette. 1986. *Language and spatial cognition: An interdisciplinary study of the prepositions in English*. Cambridge: Cambridge University Press.

Hertz, John, Anders Krogh, and Richard G. Palmer. 1991. *Introduction to the theory of neural computation*. Redwood City, Calif.: Addison-Wesley.

Hill, Clifford A. 1978. Linguistic representation of spatial and temporal orientation. In *Proceedings of the Fourth Annual Meeting of the Berkeley Linguistics Society*. Berkeley Linguistics Society, University of California, Berkeley.

Hinton, Geoffrey. 1990. Connectionist learning procedures. In *Machine learning: Paradigms and methods*, ed. by Jaime Carbonell. Cambridge, Mass.: MIT Press.

Hirsch, Joy, and Eric Mjolsness. 1992. A center-of-mass computation describes the precision of random dot displacement discrimination. *Vision Research* 32, 335–346.

Hoffman, Donald, and Whitman Richards. 1985. Parts of recognition. In *Visual cognition*, ed. by Steven Pinker. Cambridge, Mass.: MIT Press.

Hood, Donald, and Marcia Finkelstein. 1983. A case for the revision of textbook models of color vision: The detection of appearance of small brief lights. In *Colour vision: Physiology and psychophysics*, ed. by J. D. Mollon and L. T. Sharpe. London: Academic Press.

Hopfield, J. J. 1982. Neural networks and physical systems with emergent collective computational abilities. *Proceedings of the National Academy of Sciences of the USA* 79, 2554–2558.

———. 1984. Neurons with graded responses have collective computational properties like those of two-state neurons. *Proceedings of the National Academy of Sciences of the USA* 81, 3088–3092.

Horn, Berthold Klaus Paul. 1986. *Robot vision*. Cambridge, Mass.: MIT Press.

Hubel, D., and T. Wiesel. 1959. Receptive fields of single neurones in the cat's visual cortex. *Journal of Physiology* 148, 574–591.

———. 1962. Receptive fields, binocular interaction and functional architecture in the cat's visual cortex. *Journal of Physiology* 160, 106–154.

———. 1977. Functional architecture of macaque monkey visual cortex. *Proceedings of the Royal Society of London, series B* 198, 1–59.

Hummel, John, and Irving Biederman. 1990. Dynamic binding in a neural network for shape recognition. Technical Report 90-5, Department of Psychology, University of Minnesota.

Huttenlocher, Janellen, Larry Hedges, and Susan Duncan. 1991. Categories and particulars: Prototype effects in estimating spatial location. *Psychological Review* 98, 352–376.

Huttenlocher, Janellen, Patricia Smiley, and Hilary Ratner. 1983. What do word meanings reveal about conceptual development? In *Concept development and the development of word meaning*, ed. by Thomas Bernhard Seiler and W. Wannenmacher. Berlin: Springer-Verlag.

Jackendoff, Ray. 1983. *Semantics and cognition*. Cambridge, Mass.: MIT Press.

———. 1990. *Semantic structures*. Cambridge, Mass.: MIT Press.

Jacobs, Robert, Michael Jordan, and Andrew Barto. 1990. Task decomposition through competition in a modular connectionist architecture: The what and where vision tasks. Technical Report COINS 90-27, Department of Computer and Information Science, University of Massachusetts, Amherst.

Jain, A., A. Waibel, and D. Touretzky. 1992. PARSEC: A structured connectionist parsing system for spoken language. In *IEEE International Conference on Acoustics, Speech, and Signal Processing*.

Janda, Laura, 1984. A semantic analysis of the Russian verbal prefixes *za-, pere-, do-,* and *ot-.* Ph.D. dissertation, University of California, Los Angeles.

Johnston, Judith. 1984. Acquisition of locative meanings: *behind* and *in front of.* *Journal of Child Language* 11, 407–422.

———. 1985. Cognitive prerequisites: The evidence from children learning English. In *The cross-linguistic study of language acquisition.* Vol. 2, *Theoretical issues,* ed. by Dan Slobin. Hillsdale, N.J.: Lawrence Erlbaum.

———. 1988. Children's verbal representation of spatial location. In *Spatial cognition: Brain bases and development,* ed. by Joan Stiles-Davis, Mark Kritchevsky, and Ursula Bellugi. Hillsdale, N.J.: Lawrence Erlbaum.

Johnston, Judith, and Dan Slobin. 1979. The development of locative expressions in English, Italian, Serbo-Croatian and Turkish. *Journal of Child Language* 6, 529–545.

Jordan, Michael. 1986. Attractor dynamics and parallelism in a connectionist sequential machine. In *Proceedings of the 8th Annual Conference of the Cognitive Science Society.* Hillsdale, N.J.: Lawrence Erlbaum.

Jurafsky, Dan. 1993. Universals in the semantics of the diminutive. In *Proceedings of the Nineteenth Annual Meeting of the Berkeley Linguistics Society.* Berkeley Linguistics Society, University of California, Berkeley.

Kalaska, J., R. Caminiti, and A. Georgopoulos. 1983. Cortical mechanisms related to the direction of two-dimensional arm movements: Relations in parietal area 5 and comparison with motor cortex. *Experimental Brain Research* 51, 247–260.

Kanizsa, Gaetano. 1979. *Organization in vision: Essays on gestalt perception.* New York: Praeger.

Kay, Paul, Brent Berlin, and William Merrifield. 1991. Biocultural implications of systems of color naming. *Journal of Linguistic Anthropology* 1, 12–25.

Kay, Paul, and Chad K. McDaniel. 1978. The linguistic significance of the meanings of basic color terms. *Language* 54, 610–646.

Keeler, James, David Rumelhart, and Wee-Kheng Leow. 1991. Integrated segmentation and recognition of hand-printed numerals. Technical Report ACT-NN-010-91, Microelectronics and Computer Technology Corporation.

Kim, John J., Gary F. Marcus, Steven Pinker, Michelle Hollander, and Marie Coppola. 1994. Sensitivity of children's inflection to grammatical structure. *Journal of Child Language* 21, 173–209.

Kolers, Paul A. 1972a. *Aspects of motion perception.* New York: Pergamon Press.

———. 1972b. The illusion of movement. In *Perception: Mechanisms and models. Readings from* Scientific American. San Francisco: W. H. Freeman.

Kosslyn, Stephen M., Christopher F. Chabris, Chad J. Marsolek, and Oliver Koenig. 1992. Categorical versus coordinate spatial relations: Computational analyses and computer simulations. *Journal of Experimental Psychology: Human Perception and Performance* 18, 562–577.

Kruglyak, Leonid. 1990. How to solve the *n* bit encoder problem with just two hidden units. *Neural Computation* 2, 399–401.

Kuffler, S. 1953. Discharge patterns and functional organization of mammalian retina. *Journal of Neurophysiology* 16, 37–68.

Lakoff, George. 1987. *Women, fire, and dangerous things: What categories reveal about the mind.* Chicago: University of Chicago Press.

Lakoff, George, and Mark Johnson. 1980. *Metaphors we live by.* Chicago: University of Chicago Press.

Landau, Barbara, and Ray Jackendoff. 1993. "What" and "where" in spatial language and spatial cognition. *Behavioral and Brain Sciences* 16, 217–265.

Langacker, Ronald. 1987. *Foundations of cognitive grammar I: Theoretical prerequisites.* Stanford, Calif.: Stanford University Press.

LeCun, Y. 1989. Generalization and network design strategies. Technical Report CRG-TR-89-4, Connectionist Research Group, University of Toronto.

LeCun, Y., B. Boser, J. S. Denker, D. Henderson, R. E. Howard, W. Hubbard, and L. D. Jackel. 1990. Handwritten digit recognition with a back-propagation network. *Advances in Neural Information Processing Systems* 2, 396–404.

Lehky, Sidney, and Terrence Sejnowski. 1988. Network model of shape-from-shading: Neural function arises from both receptive and projective fields. *Nature* 333, 452–454.

Levinson, Stephen C. 1992a. Language and cognition: The cognitive consequences of spatial description in Guugu Yimithirr. Working Paper 13, Cognitive Anthropology Research Group, Max-Planck Institute for Psycholinguistics.

————. 1992b. Vision, shape, and linguistic description: Tzeltal body-part terminology and object description. Working Paper 12, Cognitive Anthropology Research Group, Max-Planck Institute for Psycholinguistics.

Lindner, Sue. 1982. What goes up doesn't necessarily come down: The ins and outs of opposites. In *Papers from the Eighteenth Regional Meeting, Chicago Linguistic Society*. Chicago Linguistic Society, University of Chicago.

MacWhinney, Brian. 1989. Competition and lexical categorization. In *Linguistic categorization*, ed. by Roberta Corrigan, Fred R. Eckman, and Michael Noonan. Amsterdam: John Benjamins.

Mandler, Jean. 1992. How to build a baby. II, Conceptual primitives. *Psychological Review* 99, 587–604.

Marchman, Virginia. 1993. Constraints on plasticity in a connectionist model of the English past tense. *Journal of Cognitive Neuroscience* 5, 215–234.

Markman, Ellen M. 1987. How children constrain the possible meanings of words. In *Concepts and conceptual development: Ecological and intellectual factors in categorization*, ed. by Ulric Neisser. Cambridge: Cambridge University Press.

Maskara, Arun, and Andrew Noetzel. 1992. Forced simple recurrent neural networks and grammatical inference. In *Proceedings of the 14th Annual Conference of the Cognitive Science Society*. Hillsdale, N.J.: Lawrence Erlbaum.

Massaro, Dominic. 1988. Some criticisms of connectionist models of human performance. *Journal of Memory and Language* 27, 213–234.

Matsumoto, Yo. 1994. Subjective change expressions in Japanese and their cognitive and linguistic bases. In *Mental space, grammar, and discourse*, ed. by Eve Sweetser and Gilles Fauconnier. Chicago: University of Chicago Press.

McClelland, James. 1988. Connectionist models and psychological evidence. *Journal of Memory and Language* 27, 107–123.

McClelland, James, David Rumelhart, and the PDP Research Group. 1986. *Parallel distributed processing: Explorations in the microstructure of cognition*. Vol. 2, *Psychological and biological models*. Cambridge, Mass.: MIT Press.

McCloskey, Michael. 1991. Networks and theories: The place of connectionism in cognitive science. *Psychological Science* 2, 387–395.

McCulloch, W. S., and W. Pitts. 1943. A logical calculus of the ideas immanent in nervous activity. *Bulletin of Mathematical Biophysics* 5, 115–137.

McNeill, David. 1970. *The acquisition of language: The study of developmental psycholinguistics*. New York: Harper and Row.

Merzenich, M., and J. Kaas. 1982. Reorganization of mammalian somatosensory cortex following peripheral nerve injury. *Trends in Neurosciences* 5, 434–436.

Métin, Christine, and Douglas Frost. 1989. Visual responses of neurons in somatosensory cortex of hamsters with experimentally induced retinal projections to somatosensory thalamus. *Proceedings of the National Academy of Sciences of the USA, Neurobiology* 86, 357–361.

Miikkulainen, Risto. 1991. Parsing embedded clauses with simple recurrent networks. In *The AAAI Spring Symposium Workshop on Connectionist Natural Language Processing*. Stanford University.

————. 1993. *Subsymbolic natural language processing: An integrated model of scripts, lexicon, and memory*. Cambridge, Mass.: MIT Press.

Miller, George A. 1956. The magical number seven, plus or minus two. *Psychological Review* 63, 81–97.

Miller, George A., Eugene Galanter, and Karl H. Pribram. 1960. *Plans and the structure of behavior.* New York: Holt, Rinehart and Winston.

Miller, George A., and P. N. Johnson-Laird. 1976. *Language and perception.* Cambridge, Mass.: Harvard University Press.

Minsky, Marvin, and Seymour Papert. 1969. *Perceptrons.* Cambridge, Mass.: MIT Press.

Mishkin, M., L. G. Ungerleider, and K. A. Macko. 1983. Object vision and spatial vision: Two cortical pathways. *Trends in Neurosciences* 6, 414–417.

Mitchell, Tom M. 1980. The need for biases in learning generalizations. Technical Report CBM-TR-117, Computer Science Department, Rutgers University.

Moran, J., and R. Desimone. 1985. Selective attention gates visual processing in the extrastriate cortex. *Science* 229, 782–784.

Morgan, N., and H. Bourlard. 1989. Generalization and parameter estimation in feedforward nets: Some experiments. Technical Report TR-89-017, International Computer Science Institute, Berkeley, Calif.

Mozer, Michael. 1988. A focused back-propagation algorithm for temporal pattern recognition. Technical Report CRG-TR-88-3, Connectionist Research Group, University of Toronto.

Mozer, Michael, Richard Zemel, and Marlene Behrmann. 1991. Learning to segment images using dynamic feature binding. Technical Report CU-CS-540-91, Department of Computer Science, University of Colorado at Boulder.

Munro, Paul, Cynthia Cosic, and Mary Tabasko. 1991. A network for encoding, decoding and translating locative prepositions. *Connection Science* 3, 225–240.

Nenov, Valeriy. 1991. Perceptually grounded language acquisition: A neural/procedural hybrid model. Ph.D. dissertation, University of California, Los Angeles.

Nenov, Valeriy, and Michael Dyer. 1988. DETE: Connectionist/symbolic model of visual and verbal association. Technical Report UCLA-AI-88-6, Computer Science Department, University of California, Los Angeles.

Nowlan, Steven J. 1990. Competing experts: An experimental investigation of associative mixture models. Technical Report CRG-TR-90-5, Connectionist Research Group, University of Toronto.

O'Keefe, John. 1991. The hippocampal cognitive map and navigational strategies. In *Brain and space,* ed. by Jacques Paillard. Oxford: Oxford University Press.

O'Keefe, John, and Lynn Nadel. 1978. *The hippocampus as a cognitive map.* Oxford: Clarendon.

O'Keefe, John, and A. Speakman. 1987. Single unit activity in the rat hippocampus during a spatial memory task. *Experimental Brain Research* 68, 1–27.

Olson, Thomas. 1989. An architectural model of visual motion understanding. Technical Report 305, Department of Computer Science, University of Rochester.

O'Reilly, R., S. Kosslyn, C. Marsolek, and C. Chabris. 1990. Receptive field characteristics that allow parietal lobe neurons to encode spatial properties of visual input: A computational analysis. *Journal of Cognitive Neuroscience* 2, 141–155.

Osterholtz, L., C. Augustine, A. McNair, I. Rogina, H. Saito, T. Sloboda, J. Tebelskis, and A. Waibel. 1992. Testing generality in JANUS: A multi-lingual speech translation system. In *IEEE International Conference on Acoustics, Speech, and Signal Processing.*

Patarnello, S., and P. Carnevali. 1987. Learning networks of neurons with Boolean logic. *Europhysics Letters* 4, 503–508.

Pearlmutter, Barak A. 1990. Dynamic recurrent neural networks. Technical Report CMU-CS-90-196, Department of Computer Science, Carnegie Mellon University.

Pederson, Eric. 1994. Language as context, language as means: Spatial cognition and habitual language use. Working Paper 26, Cognitive Anthropology Research Group, Max-Planck Institute for Psycholinguistics.

———. 1995. Language as context, language as means: Spatial cognition and habitual language use. *Cognitive Linguistics* 6, 33–62.

Piaget, Jean, and Bärbel Inhelder. 1967. *The child's conception of space.* New York: Norton.

Pinker, Steven. 1984. *Language learnability and language development*. Cambridge, Mass.: Harvard University Press.

———. 1989. *Learnability and cognition: The acquisition of argument structure*. Cambridge, Mass.: MIT Press.

Pinker, Steven, and Alan Prince. 1988. On language and connectionism: Analysis of a parallel distributed processing model of language acquisition. *Cognition* 28, 73–193.

Plunkett, Kim, and Virginia Marchman. 1988. U-shaped learning and frequency effects in a multi-layered perceptron: Implications for child language acquisition. *Cognition* 28, 73–193.

Plunkett, Kim, Chris Sinha, Martin Moller, and Ole Strandsby. 1992. Symbol grounding or the emergence of symbols? Vocabulary growth in children and a connectionist net. *Connection Science* 4, 293–312.

Poggio, T., and S. Edelman. 1990. A network that learns to recognize three-dimensional objects. *Nature* 343, 263–266.

Pollack, Jordan. 1988. Recursive auto-associative memory: Devising compositional distributed representations. In *Proceedings of the 10th Annual Conference of the Cognitive Science Society*. Hillsdale, N.J.: Lawrence Erlbaum.

———. 1990a. Language acquisition via strange automata. In *Proceedings of the 12th Annual Conference of the Cognitive Science Society*. Hillsdale, N.J.: Lawrence Erlbaum.

———. 1990b. Recursive distributed representations. *Artificial Intelligence* 46, 77–105.

Ramachandran, Vilayanur S. 1992. Blind spots. *Scientific American* 266, 86–91.

Ramachandran, Vilayanur S., and Richard L. Gregory. 1991. Perceptual filling in of artificially induced scotomas in human vision. *Nature* 350, 699–702.

Regier, Terry. 1991. Line labeling and junction labeling: A coupled system for image interpretation. In *Proceedings of the 12th International Joint Conference on Artificial Intelligence*. San Mateo, Calif.: Morgan Kaufmann.

———. 1994. A preliminary study of the semantics of reduplication. Technical Report TR-94-019, International Computer Science Institute, Berkeley, Calif.

Renals, Steve, Nelson Morgan, and Herve Bourlard. 1991. Probability estimation by feed-forward networks in continuous speech recognition. Technical Report TR-91-030, International Computer Science Institute, Berkeley, Calif.

Rosch, Eleanor. 1973. On the internal structure of perceptual and semantic categories. In *Cognitive development and the acquisition of language*, ed. by Timothy E. Moore. New York: Academic Press.

———. 1977. Human categorization. In *Studies in cross-cultural psychology*, Vol. 1, ed. by Neil Warren. London: Academic Press.

———. 1978. Principles of categorization. In *Cognition and categorization*, ed. by Eleanor Rosch and Barabara B. Lloyd. Hillsdale, N.J.: Lawrence Erlbaum.

Rosenblatt, Frank. 1962. *Principles of neurodynamics*. Washington, D.C.: Spartan.

Rumelhart, David, Geoffrey Hinton, and Ronald Williams. 1986. Learning internal representations by error propagation. In *Parallel distributed processing: Explorations in the microstructure of cognition*. Vol. 1, *Foundations*, by David Rumelhart, James McClelland, and the PDP Research Group. Cambridge, Mass.: MIT Press.

Rumelhart, David, and James McClelland. 1985. Levels indeed! A response to Broadbent. *Journal of Experimental Psychology: General* 114, 193–197.

———. 1986. On learning the past tenses of English verbs. In *Parallel distributed processing: Explorations in the microstructure of cognition*. Vol. 2, *Psychological and biological models*, by James McClelland, David Rumelhart, and the PDP Research Group. Cambridge, Mass.: MIT Press.

Rumelhart, David, James McClelland, and the PDP Research Group. 1986. *Parallel distributed processing: Explorations in the microstructure of cognition*. Vol. 1, *Foundations*. Cambridge, Mass.: MIT Press.

Seidenberg, Mark. 1993. Connectionist models and cognitive theory. *Psychological Science* 4, 228–235.

Seidenberg, Mark, and James McClelland. 1989. A distributed developmental model of word recognition and naming. *Psychological Review* 96, 523–568.

Sejnowski, Terrence J., and Geoffrey H. Hinton. 1987. Separating figure from ground with a Boltzmann machine. In *Vision, brain, and cooperative computation*, ed. by Michael A. Arbib and Allen R. Hanson. Cambridge, Mass.: MIT Press.

Servan-Schreiber, David, Axel Cleeremans, and James McClelland. 1988. Encoding sequential structure in simple recurrent networks. Technical Report CMU-CS-88-183, Department of Computer Science, Carnegie Mellon University.

Shastri, Lokendra. 1988. *Semantic networks: An evidential formalization and its connectionist realization.* Los Altos, Calif.: Morgan Kaufmann.

Shastri, Lokendra, and Venkat Ajjanagadde. 1993. From simple associations to systematic reasoning: A connectionist representation of rules, variables and dynamic bindings using temporal synchrony. *Behavioral and Brain Sciences* 16, 417–494.

Shepard, Roger N. 1989. Internal representation of universal regularities: A challenge for connectionism. In *Neural connections, mental computation*, ed. by Lynn Nadel, Lynn A. Cooper, Peter Culicover, and R. Michael Harnish. Cambridge, Mass.: MIT Press.

Siegelman, Hava, and Eduardo Sontag. 1991. Neural nets are universal computing devices. Technical Report SYCON-91-08, Center for Systems and Control, Rutgers University.

Siskind, Jeffrey. 1990. Acquiring core meanings of words, represented as Jackendoff-style conceptual structures, from correlated streams of linguistic and non-linguistic input. In *Proceedings of the 28th Annual Meeting of the Association for Computational Linguistics.*

———. 1991. Naive physics, event perception, lexical semantics and language acquisition. In *The AAAI Spring Symposium Workshop on Machine Learning of Natural Language and Ontology.* Stanford University.

———. 1992. Naive physics, event perception, lexical semantics and language acquisition. Ph.D. dissertation, MIT.

Slobin, Dan. 1985. Crosslinguistic evidence for the language-making capacity. In *The crosslinguistic study of language acquisition.* Vol. 2, *Theoretical issues*, ed. by Dan Slobin. Hillsdale, N.J.: Lawrence Erlbaum.

Smiley, Patricia, and Janellen Huttenlocher. 1994. Conceptual development and the child's early words for events, objects and persons. In *Beyond names for things: Young children's acquisition of verbs*, ed. by Michael Tomasello and William Edward Merriman. Hillsdale, N.J.: Lawrence Erlbaum.

Smolensky, Paul. 1988. On the proper treatment of connectionism. *Behavioral and Brain Sciences* 11, 1–74.

Stein, John F. 1991. Space and the parietal association areas. In *Brain and space*, ed. by Jacques Paillard. Oxford: Oxford University Press.

Stolcke, Andreas. 1990. Learning feature-based semantics with simple recurrent networks. Technical Report TR-90-015, International Computer Science Institute, Berkeley, Calif.

Suzuki, I., S. J. B. Timerick, and V. J. Wilson. 1985. Body position with respect to the head or body position in space is coded by lumbar interneurons. *Journal of Neurophysiology* 54, 123–133.

Talmy, Leonard. 1983. How language structures space. In *Spatial orientation: Theory, research, and application*, ed. by Herbert Pick and Linda Acredolo. New York: Plenum Press. Also available as Technical Report 4, Institute of Cognitive Studies, University of California, Berkeley.

Taube, A. M., I. W. Litvinova, A. D. Miller, and R. C. Daglish. 1987. *Russian-English dictionary.* Moscow: Russky Yazyk Publishers.

Teller, Davida. 1991. Simpler arguments might work better. *Philosophical Psychology* 4, 51–60.

Tomasello, Michael. 1987. Learning to use prepositions: A case study. *Journal of Child Language* 14, 79–98.

Traugott, Elizabeth Closs. 1978. On the expression of spatio-temporal relations in language. In *Universals of human language.* Vol. 3, *Word structure*, ed. by Joseph H. Greenberg. Stanford, Calif.: Stanford University Press.

Treisman, Anne, and Stephen Gormican. 1988. Feature analysis in early vision: Evidence from search asymmetries. *Psychological Review* 95, 15–48.

Ullman, Shimon. 1984. Visual routines. *Cognition* 18, 97–159.

Ungerleider, L. G., and M. Mishkin. 1982. Two cortical visual systems. In *Analysis of visual behavior*, ed. by David G. Ingle, Melvyn A. Goodale, and Richard J. W. Mansfield. Cambridge, Mass.: MIT Press.

Vandeloise, Claude. 1991. *Spatial prepositions: A case study from French*. Chicago: University of Chicago Press.

von der Heydt, R., E. Peterhans, and G. Baumgartner. 1984. Illusory contours and cortical neuron responses. *Science* 224, 1260–1262.

Waibel, A. 1989. Modular construction of time-delay neural networks for speech recognition. *Neural Computation* 1, 39–46.

Waibel, A., T. Hanazawa, G. Hinton, K. Shikano, and K. Lang. 1987. Phoneme recognition using time-delay neural networks. Technical Report TR-1-0006, ATR Interpreting Telephony Research Laboratories, Japan.

Waibel, A., A. Jain, A. McNair, H. Saito, A. Hauptmann, and J. Tebelskis. 1991. JANUS: A speech-to-speech translation system using connectionist and symbolic processing strategies. In *IEEE International Conference on Acoustics, Speech, and Signal Processing*.

Waltz, David, and Jordan Pollack. 1985. Massively parallel parsing: A strongly interactive model of natural language interpretation. *Cognitive Science* 9, 51–74.

Watrous, Raymond L. 1990. Phoneme discrimination using connectionist networks. *Journal of the Acoustical Society of America* 87, 1753–1772.

Weber, Susan Hollbach. 1989a. Figurative adjective-noun interpretation in a structured connectionist network. In *Proceedings of the 11th Annual Conference of the Cognitive Science Society*. Hillsdale, N.J.: Lawrence Erlbaum.

———. 1989b. A structured connectionist approach to direct inferences and figurative adjective-noun combinations. Ph.D. dissertation, University of Rochester. Also Technical Report 289, Department of Computer Science, University of Rochester.

Weigend, Andreas, Bernardo Huberman, and David Rumelhart. 1990. Predicting the future: A connectionist approach. Technical Report Stanford-PDP-90-01, PDP Research Group, Stanford University.

Werbos, Paul J. 1974. Beyond regression: New tools for prediction and analysis in the behavioral sciences. Ph.D. dissertation, Harvard University.

Whorf, Benjamin Lee, and John B. Carroll, ed. 1956. *Language, thought, and reality*. Cambridge, Mass.: MIT Press.

Wierzbicka, Anna. 1980. *Lingua mentalis: The semantics of natural language*. Sydney: Academic Press.

Williams, Ronald, and David Zipser. 1989. A learning algorithm for continually running fully recurrent neural networks. *Neural Computation* 1, 270–280.

Wimsatt, William C. 1987. False models as means to truer theories. In *Neutral models in biology*, ed. by Matthew H. Nitecki and Antoni Hoffman. London: Oxford University Press.

Woodward, Amanda, and Ellen Markman. 1991. Constraints on learning as default assumptions: Comments on Merriman and Bowman's "The mutual exclusivity bias in children's word learning." *Developmental Review* 11, 137–163.

Zadeh, Lotfi A. 1965. Fuzzy sets. *Information and Control* 8, 338–353.

———. 1971. Quantitative fuzzy semantics. *Information Sciences* 3, 159–176.

Zipser, David. 1986. Biologically plausible models of place recognition and goal location. In *Parallel distributed processing: Explorations in the microstructure of cognition*. Vol. 2, *Psychological and biological models*, by James McClelland, David Rumelhart, and the PDP Research Group. Cambridge, Mass.: MIT Press.

Zipser, David, and Richard Andersen. 1988. A back-propagation programmed network that simulates response properties of a subset of posterior parietal neurons. *Nature* 331, 679–684.

Zlatev, Jordan. 1992. A study of perceptually grounded polysemy in a spatial microdomain. Technical Report TR-92-048, International Computer Science Institute, Berkeley, Calif.

Index